The Pain Mothers Must Never Expose

Confronting the Silences of Maternal Life

Edited by Michelann Parr

DEMETER

The Pain Mothers Must Never Expose
Confronting the Silences of Maternal Life
Edited by Michelann Parr

Demeter Press
PO Box 197
Coe Hill, Ontario
Canada
K0L 1P0
Tel: 289-383-0134
Email: info@demeterpress.org
Website: www.demeterpress.org

Demeter Press logo based on the sculpture "Demeter" by Maria-Luise Bodirsky
www.keramik-atelier.bodirsky.de

Printed and Bound in Canada

Cover design: Michelann Parr
Typesetting: Michelle Pirovich
Proof reading: Jena Woodhouse

Library and Archives Canada Cataloguing in Publication
Title: The pain mothers must never expose: Confronting the silences on maternal life / Edited by Michelann Parr.
Names: Parr, Michelann, 1964- editor.
Description: Includes bibliographical references.
Identifiers: Canadiana 20240412427 | ISBN 9781772585025 (softcover)
Subjects: LCSH: Motherhood—Psychological aspects. | LCSH: Mothers—Psychology. Classification: LCC HQ759.P35 2024 | DDC 306.874/3—dc23

Funded by the Government of Canada

Canadä

The publisher gratefully acknowledges the support of the Government of Canada

A Disclosure, an Apology, and a Dedication

I recognize that there are many voices notably absent from this collection. Despite a broad call, missing are the experiences of mothers who have lost their children through war/violence, addictions, or crime; those who have surrendered their children to fostering, adoption, or kincare in the hope of a better life; those who mother children not their own and navigate the complexities of their chosen family; and those who want or hope to have children but face struggles with fertility. It is possible that this call, even within its breadth, felt too normative and perhaps even inaccessible. It is also possible that some pain is relatively fresh and new, not yet fully uncovered or ready to show itself to the world. Yet it is possible that what is contained within this collection are the types of pain that have gained acceptance in society, which suggests that the work of the matricentric feminist collective is taking root. As I have heard on multiple occasions and in many different ways, the only stories that help are the true ones. It is within this spirit that we offer this collection.

To those whose voices are not captured in this collection, I offer a sincere apology and an open invitation. Like these companions, your pain is real and worthy of exploration. It is to you that I dedicate this collection with the hope that you find strength and hope in the chapters that follow and recognize this as just the beginning.

Acknowledgements

I express a deep sense of gratitude to Andrea O'Reilly and Demeter Press for creating a space for women and mothers to write about motherhood and the multitude of social and emotional intersections experienced through mothering in all its forms. In an era of disconnection, alienation, and isolation, it makes sense to return to our experience of mothering as a starting point to redefine pain as a site of compassion, empathy, and inspiration.

As the editor, I am deeply indebted to Jacqueline Rose's work for inspiration, for the numerous quotes that frame the introduction, and of course, for the title of this collection:

"What the pain of mothers must never expose is a viciously unjust world in a complete mess" (12).

I am indebted to my fellow companions who accepted the call to expose the pain of mothers in its myriad of forms. I have come to understand that not all pain is negative and that not all that we encounter is entirely personal. When we make space for stories of all kinds, we can understand that pain, such as our experience of motherhood, is a function of time and place. The more we share, the more we know. When we know differently, we can do differently if only to reframe and publicly call out our pain—no longer leaving it held in a secret room, no longer leaving mothers to suffer in silence. In this collection, we collectively acknowledge that where there is motherhood, there is "love, pain, and the whole damn thing" (Sky, *Love*).

Finally, as I always do, I express gratitude to my children for their encouragement and support in writing my way through the pain and towards the light. I am thankful for the opportunities they offer daily to know and grow myself through my experience of motherhood. I am still learning not to take things so seriously and to find grace in the ordinary miracles of motherhood (Sky, *Ordinary*).

Works Cited

Rose, Jacqueline. *Mothers: An Essay on Love and Cruelty*. Farrar, Straus, and Giroux, 2018.

Sky, Amy. *Love and Pain and the Whole Damn Thing*. Ordinary Miracles, 1998.

Sky, Amy. *Ordinary Miracles*. Ordinary Miracles, 1998.

Contents

What do we want from each other
after we have told our stories
do we want
to be healed   do we want
mossy quiet stealing over our scars
do we want
the all-powerful unfrightening sister
who will make the pain go away
the past not be so
—Audre Lorde (*Our Dead*)

Introduction

Michelann Parr

Why, if not that mothers remain our favourite sacrificial objects,
as dispensable as they are indispensable to life? Why, if not
that mothers continue to be the container for all our plaints,
and to bear the brunt of an unjust world?

—Jacqueline Rose 63

Although there has been a proliferation of research articles, books, websites, blogs, popular culture books, and even movies about motherhood, few have named and confronted the pain of mothers head-on. While deeply exploring the ordinary pains and silences of my motherhood (Parr, *Silences*), I encountered Jacqueline Rose's *Mothers: An Essay on Cruelty and Love*. Written in 2018, long after seminal writers such as Adrienne Rich, Sara Ruddick, Audre Lorde, and Tillie Olsen had taken up the cause of motherhood and silence, Rose warns: "Unless we recognise what we are asking mothers to perform in the world—and for the world—we will continue to tear both the world and mothers to pieces" (2).

Despite multiple waves of feminism (hooks), women's ways of knowing (Belenky et al.), and a burgeoning wave of matricentric feminism (O'Reilly), mothers continue to be silenced (Olsen). They are often forced to go underground with their pain (Solnit) and accept it without quibble or reservation: "What the pain of mothers must never expose is a viciously unjust world in a complete mess" (Rose 12). The agony of mothers "to deflect from our awareness of human responsibility for the world has a long history" (Rose 12) and has become a burden often found in the shadows, borderlands, and liminal spaces of mothering.

Over the years, I have discovered that anxiety, fear, pain, and suffering often emerge when we hold ourselves up to the mirror of expectations and comparison, which are taken for granted in patriarchal motherhood. We judge ourselves and others, often dismissing the need to make peace with our pain and suffering and accept that all mothers fail (Rose). Instead, we get caught unknowingly in our spiral of silence (Noelle-Neuman): "We tuck away the hurt, pain, and evil of our daily existence [storing] it all in a box hidden deep within ourselves. Like Pandora, we keep this box stuffed to the brim with things unspoken, locked, and hidden out of plain sight, embodying the myth that suggests that to do differently would put mothers' very identity in jeopardy" (Parr 59).

Knowing that I was not alone, I gathered companions for my journey and listened deeply to the stories they had to tell. I walked alongside as their pain and grief wandered outside the frame of the requisite pathos, keeping these questions nearby:

> What are mothers being asked to carry, what forms of failure and injustice are they made accountable for, above all, in the modern Western world? What are the fears we lay on mothers, both as accusation and demand (the one following the other)? Why do we expect mothers to subdue the very fears we ourselves have laid at their doors?" (Rose 37)

In this collection, we—contributors and companions—begin to reject the narrative suggesting that pain must never be exposed. We come to understand the pain of motherhood as an intersectional and complex practice (Crenshaw). We take up the challenge of unravelling our stories regardless of how difficult and how painful; we resist the urge to defend and judge ourselves as we think others might; and we suspend judgment of other mothers. We reach for a life-sustaining and hopeful shift in consciousness (Macy and Johnstone; Wolfelt), leaning in and listening to what pain has to offer. We bridge our differences and transform our pain and silence into action (Lorde, *Sister Outsider*). We embrace Carolyn Ellis's advice: "Writing difficult stories is a gift to self, a reflexive attempt to construct meaning in our lives and heal or grow from the pain" (26). Story motivates us and gives us something to reach for: "When we find a good story and fully give ourselves to it, that story can act throughout us, breathing new life into everything we do. When we move in a direction that touches our heart, we add to the momentum of deeper purpose that makes us feel more alive" (Macy and Johnstone 33).

We recognize that at the heart of matricentric feminist (O'Reilly) and MotherScholar (Spradley et al.) work are mothers who have, at one time or another, carried their pain and suffering, remained silent, and are now willing to assume a hopeful stance—not only to expose their pain but ultimately to discover who they are, who we are, and to make the world a better place for future generations. We take an active stance, recognizing that it serves no purpose, and is not sustainable, to deny, shut away, and neglect our own pain and that of mothers around the world. Instead, we must explore what pain has to teach us and "find a way to break our silences and expose our pain in honest and authentic ways that preserve our maternal integrity; are morally and ethically responsible; and don't present as a lifelong list of complaints and resentments" (Parr 60).

Through our writing, we discover that pain, grief, fears, failure, and injustice are not concepts in our minds, and we settle into "a deeper sense of purpose or connectedness with a greater life that is not dependent on explanations or anything conceptual any longer ... a kind of re-birth" (Tolle). And when we let go of holding on to our pain and suffering as a way of being, when we connect with sorrow, when we connect with joy, and when we drop our resentment and complaint, we begin to open our hearts to the suffering and the pain that is not just our own but is the suffering and pain of all beings. We realize that all this is not just our life but life itself (Chödrön). We come to appreciate that we can only know joy because we have known sadness, pain, and suffering; they do not exist without each other.

A Companioning Stance

> We must venture into the darkest core of our misjudgment—of her and of ourselves—simply walk in, with one another, behind one another, while the crash of collapsing walls sounds in our ears.
>
> —Jacqueline Rose 71

Throughout this project, I have come to understand the uniqueness of pain and suffering, the contrasting emotions, and the individual styles of expressing pain (Strada). Each pain-filled yet hopeful experience I encountered led me to explore further the edges of my pain, and I came to understand that we cannot resolve grief and pain; instead, we can reconcile, surrender, heal, become whole again, integrate pain and grief into ourselves, and learn to continue our changed lives with fullness and meaning (Wolfelt). As this collection's editor, I leaned into the stories, listened deeply, and supported each individual's unique and personal experience to write through their pain and suffering without a preconceived notion of how that process should present or develop (Strada). I carefully prompted, probed, and offered feedback, adopting Alan Wolfelt's stance of companioning alongside the more traditional editing:

- Honour the spirit; it is not about focussing on the intellect.

- Be compassionately curious; it is not about expertise.

- Learn from others; it is not about teaching them.

- Walk alongside; it is not about leading.

- Be still; it is not about frantic movement forward.

- Discover the gifts of sacred silence; it is not about filling every moment with words.

- Listen with the heart; it is not about analyzing with the head.

- Bear witness to the struggles of others; it is not about judging or directing these struggles.

- Be present to another person's pain; it is not about taking away the pain.

- Respect disorder and confusion; it is not about imposing order and logic.

- Go to the wilderness of the soul with another human being; it is not about thinking you are responsible for finding the way out.

I am grateful for the trust gifted to me throughout the gathering of this collection and for the kinship I found with these mothers. I appreciate the willingness of my companions to honour their spirits, be still with their pain, and move beyond what was comfortable to expose the less visible pain and suffering that the world would like to deny.

Making Peace with Pain

> In many accounts of motherhood, there is often something
> missing or pushed aside: a mother's right to know her own mind.
>
> —Jacqueline Rose 110

As a psychology major, and the daughter of a Roman Catholic deacon who specialized in bereavement, I would be remiss not to mention Elisabeth Kübler-Ross's well-known stages of grieving—denial, anger, bargaining, depression, and acceptance—which are after all, fundamentally life lessons, responses, and reactions to loss (Kübler-Ross, Kessler, and Shriver): "Every one of us has had to give up something we loved. We've sacrificed cherished plans or dreams, felt grief and loss. Already, all of us have experienced impermanence, which is another form of dying" (Halifax 47). When we observe the changing nature of our everyday situations, we begin to find freedom from suffering. We accept this as our life search: "Consciously or not, we are all on a quest for answers, trying to learn the lessons of life. We grapple with fear and guilt. We search for meaning, love, and power. We try to understand fear, loss, and time. We seek to discover who we are and how we can become truly happy" (Kübler-Ross and Kessler).

Our children cause us the most exquisite suffering: "It is the suffering of ambivalence: the murderous alternation between bitter resentment and raw-edged nerves, and blissful gratification and tenderness" (Rich, *Of Woman Born* 21). In and through writing, we make peace with our pain in a way that not only moves us forward but reaches out into the world; here, we find that "only the willingness to share private and sometimes painful experience can enable women to create a collective description of the world which will be truly ours" (Rich, *Of Woman Born* 16).

The mothers in this collection—my companions—have embarked upon a quest for answers. Not shying away from the pain that is often denied, suppressed, or disenfranchised, we lower our protective armour and step into our pain. We really get to know it and learn to live with it. We open our hearts to the exquisite pain of what we feel we have lost, given up, were denied, or was taken from us. We "write with a painful consciousness of [our] own Western cultural perspective and that of most of the sources available to [us]: painful because it says so much about how female culture is fragmented by the male culture, boundaries, groupings in which women live" (Rich, *Of Woman Born* 17). As Joan Halifax states, "Grief is like the mother I heard about who bathed her dead baby in her own breast milk. She teaches us tenderness and patience with our own sorrow and reminds us lovingly not to hold on too tightly. Impermanence is inescapable, we learn; no one and nothing escapes her touch" (194).

Our Exposition of Pain

> I have never met a single mother (myself included) who is not far more complex, critical, at odds with the set of clichés she is meant effortlessly to embody, than she is being encouraged —or rather instructed—to think.
> —Jacqueline Rose 18

The longer I sat with the storied chapters, the wider I read on pain, suffering, mourning, and unresolved grief. My guiding intention was to expose pain in a way that showed strength, self-acceptance, activism, healing, and hope. I was committed to showing how we—in an effort to heal ourselves, for ourselves, for our children, and for the world—draw pain closer instead of pushing it away:

> Instead of transcending the suffering of all creatures, we move toward the turbulence and doubt. We jump into it. We slide into it. We tiptoe into it. We move toward it however we can. We explore the reality and unpredictability of insecurity and pain, and we try not to push it away. If it takes years, if it takes lifetimes, we let it be as it is. At our own pace, without speed or aggression, we move down and down and down. With us move millions of others, our companions in awakening in fear. (Chödrön 92)

I struggled through many iterations of how best to organize individual contributions. My first attempt was a structure that moved from silence towards activism, inspiring readers to explore and reconsider the stories of our lives with the following possible headings: holding our mother tongues; bearing witness to pain; breaking free of maternal labour pains; resisting entanglements and separations; and hearing pain's wisdom. The second attempt offered what I envisioned as a life cycle of maternal pain: birthing pain, feeling pain, visualizing pain, reimagining pain, and transforming intergenerational pain. Still unsatisfied, I continued to search for a meaningful structure that would call sound out of the silences of motherhood and something from what has often been viewed as nothing (Griffin).

Staying with the search and peeling back layer upon layer of these storied contributions, I reached first for what I knew—Kübler-Ross; I found an instant kinship with Michael Doxtater's interpretation of her process. Although I found instant comfort in his "Triple D" process for healing—denial, disorientation, and discovery, I still sensed that more was needed to account for the complexity of pain and suffering experienced by mothers across time, place, and context. Denial merged with disenfranchisement, and destabilization found a home between disorientation and discovery, signalling the formal role of both feminism and matricentric feminism as disruptors to hegemonic institutions and structures.

Denial and disenfranchisement, disorientation, destabilization, and discovery felt like a hopeful structure that offered a way to move us through the pain of our initial introduction to motherhood, all towards accepting and discovering ourselves in and through motherhood. In "Part I: Denial and Disenfranchisement—Birthing and Naming Pain," we experience the birthplace of pain as the contributors identify and call out their pain. We see dissociation from pain, limited realization of what happened, insightful realization of what happened, and (de)personalization of traumatic events or loss (Doxtater). We experience how maternal knowledge is often denied, suppressed, and disenfranchised, forcing mothers to take their pain and suffering underground as a protective mechanism (Attig). We see mothers who did not need experts on their lives "but the opportunity and the validation to name and describe the truths of [their] lives, as they have known them" (Rich, *On Lies* 257).

In "Part II: Disorientation—Searching for Stable Ground," we are weighed down by the persistent distress that is accompanied by hard feelings, jealousy, misunderstanding, expectation, misdirected anger, shame, blame, frustration, bitterness, and guilt, which affect our ability to make sense of our pain and suffering (Doxtater). We rant, create artwork, stage dialogues, and craft autobiographical sketches that show how debilitating and disorienting unacknowledged and disenfranchised pain and grief can be. We also see how these authors begin to gesture towards hopeful futures.

Somewhere between disorientation and discovery, many mothers realize that being a mother may not be as good as we thought it would be; we come to understand motherhood as experience and institution (Rich, *Of Woman Born*) and begin to push back against the way things are. In "Part III: Destabilization—Reimagining Nonnormative Mothering," contributors resist the business-as-usual narrative and critically imagine nonnormative ways of mothering; we set aside hegemonic institutions and structures that no longer serve, inviting readers to imagine a different future for ourselves, our children, and for the world.

Finally, in "Part IV: Discovery—Transforming Intergenerational Pain," we seek to revise our lives by looking back, seeing with fresh eyes, and entering an old text from a new critical direction (Rich, *On Lies*). We begin to answer the question of "Who are you?" as we showcase our developing ability to cope with trauma by embracing impermanence and change, processing our suffering, seeking to understand self, letting go of how things should be, feeling pain and joy as fully as possible, and ultimately being kind to ourselves (Chödrön; Doxtater).

In this four-part exposition of pain, we hope for a different way, a better way, knowing that hope fundamentally matters (Maracle, Robb, and Carter). "Hope is an expression of a good that is yet to be. It is an expression of the present alive with a sense of the possible. It is a belief that healing can and will occur" (Wolfelt 4). Hope breathes life into our shadowy crevices and lends us strength to trudge through the muck and mud of pain, suffering, and grief. "Hope gives us a sense that there is a point to working things out, working things through. Hope does not only or always point toward the future, but carries us through when the terrain is difficult, when the path we follow makes it harder to proceed. Hope is behind us when we have to work for something to be possible" (Ahmed 2).

Part I: Denial and Disenfranchisement—Birthing and Naming Pain

> Above all, whenever any aspect of mothering is vaulted as the
> emblem of health, love, and devotion, you can be sure that a whole
> complex range of emotions, of what humans are capable of feeling,
> is being silenced or suppressed.
>
> —Jacqueline Rose 86

In Part I, companions dig deep into the experiences of motherhood that
cause mothers pain and suffering; we experience both the denial and
disenfranchisement of maternal pain and suffering. Not only do mothers
deny their pain, but many are also denied access by systems and structures
that refuse to honour their deep knowing and intuition, resulting in
trauma and immeasurable pain. Equally traumatic as denial, Thomas
Attig discusses how the disenfranchisement of grief "falls primarily upon
failure to respect suffering" (205). He continues: "It stresses both the
failure to empathize with the suffering of the bereaved (empathic failure)
and the ethical failure of denial of the right to suffer or to cope with it
(though it never explicitly identifies such failure as an ethical one) (205).

Collectively, Maya Bhave, Rachel O'Donnell, Teela Tomasetti, and
Libby Jeffrey offer their stories so that readers might develop empathy
and a respectful response to the denied and disenfranchised to liberate
mourners from

> discounting or dismissal of the significance of their losses or of the
> extent and depth of their suffering, discouragement of expressions
> of their hurt, oppressive interference in efforts to come to terms
> with brokenness and anguish, isolation, and inappropriate social
> sanction. Respect from others promotes mourners' self-respect
> and self-esteem as it welcomes and embraces them in caring
> community. (Attig 206)

Maya Bhave's short story "Unadorned Birth" is, at first glance, the
horrific story of a woman's pregnancy journey that ends in her first-born
son's stillbirth. Yet if we linger longer between the lines, we realize it is
about medical gaslighting, women's silenced voices, invisibilized per-
sonhoods, and the need to restructure the medical corporate system.

Some twenty-six years later, Bhave recognizes that this short story is about finding and using her voice—one in which multiple truths are spoken to be heard, acknowledged, and supported. For that, she is truly and deeply thankful.

"Replica" by Rachel O'Donnell is a prose poem in three parts. It begins with a scene that describes excitement surrounding a pregnancy, continues with the loss and pain of a missing child, and ends by describing the continual desire for the missing child, both real and imagined. The theme of the piece is the continual and timeless pain that mothers experience in seeing living children after a loss.

In "Becoming a Birth Trauma Specialst" by Teela Tomasetti, readers are asked to confront the idea of what it means to give birth. Tomasetti critiques the Hollywood version we are sold from a young age. Birth looks intense and dramatic for just a moment or two on screen, and then it is all over, as the camera pans in on a beautifully kept mother with pristine hair and makeup holding her perfect baby. The mother's face is glowing in the natural sunlight that pours in through the windows of the hospital room, and in this golden hour, family members watch nearby, smiling. In this chapter, Tomasetti counters the Hollywood version with the reality and lived experience of many mothers. One in three women describes their birth experience as traumatic, and most of these survivors struggle with the initial hours, days, weeks, and even months of bonding with their infant due to symptoms. Tomasetti offers an up-close look at the painful realities of birth trauma that are often silenced and hidden from a world that only wants to see happy Hollywood endings; she describes ways in which many mothers are expressing their pain and seeing comfort in the legitimation and collective bonding of others who understand and empathize.

"After Birth: After Raoul Fernandes's Poem 'After Lydia'" by Libby Jeffrey provides a bird's eye view into the myriad emotional responses to childbirth. The poem catches the slow-fast-slow sensation that the world is carrying on even while these intimate, life-altering, and granular moments unfold. For each subject in the poem, a new narrative into motherhood has begun. In form, the poem's line breaks mimic a heart rate monitor. This poem was written to celebrate the full expression of the postpartum experience. We hope that readers can relate to their emotional truth through the course of reading "After Birth."

Part II: Disorientation—Searching for Stable Ground

> Much about the experience of being a mother falls silently out
> of the public eye—since seeing oneself depends at least partly
> on being recognized by others—and out of the range of what
> many mothers can bear to know or think about themselves.
>
> —Jacqueline Rose 126

In Part II, companions encounter ambiguity, ambivalence, turbulence, and doubt. Motherhood is revealed as a space of reckoning and resistance—of being weighed down by expectations and assumptions we are often not yet aware of. These are the spaces of motherhood that we try to keep from the public eye, hiding our suffering and pain in the hope that it will never rear its ugly head. We are introduced to the uncertain space of loss that often is produced by ableist assumptions and beliefs about the mother-child bond, what it means to mother within the context of (dis)ability, mental health challenges, illness, decisions made, and life experiences (both those sanctioned by general society and those not). Finally, we are privileged with creative pieces that dramatically show us the results of maternal labour and the sense making that happens as we explore different ways of expressing our pain.

Collectively, Leanne Charette, Debra Guckenheimer, Claire Haddon, Kate Antosik-Parsons, Alex Maeve Campbell and Terry Anne Campbell, and Mandy Fessenden Brauer courageously experiment with different forms of representing their experience of motherhood, particularly its more painful moments and times that defy both separation and entanglement. In this part, we find poetry, scholarly and personal writing, mixed media collage and photography, dialogue, and autobiographical writing.

Leanne Charette's collection of poems—"Lines," "Your First Smile," and "Separation Anxiety"—was written from the perspective of a disabled mother. The poems touch on the experience of lost identity within motherhood and loss of joy in the parenting experience because of mental illness and societal ableism. Strongly held ideas of what constitutes an unfit mother are couched in ableist concepts of disability and mental illness. Many disabled mothers begin their parenting journeys needing to fight these assumptions, in some cases needing to advocate for the simple right to raise their children, and in subtler forms, finding themselves judged or doubted by those closest to them in their ability to parent. These barriers can further exacerbate mental health struggles for new mothers, sowing doubt in their abilities, and damaging the mother-child bond. These poems were written in the hope that these barriers in the path of motherhood would be broken down for future generations.

So much of the experience of being a mom is inaccessible. In her rant-like chapter "Confronting Ableism as a Disabled Mom," Debra Guckenheimer shares the pain and harm caused to disabled moms and their children by lack of access. She argues that granting moms like herself access would take so little effort, but instead they face intense ableism hurled at them by well-intentioned people. In this piece, Guckenheimer presents disability justice as a framework to rethink motherhood and community. She shares her experience attempting to attend a family camp for adopted children of colour and the intense ableism she encountered that alienated her from participation and engagement. She shows how her story fits within the ableism that is thrown at disabled moms every day and how being a white parent of children of colour in communities complicates the experience of ableism. As a hopeful gesture, she shares strategies for combatting ableism, explaining it to children, and finding creative ways to work around barriers.

"I Am a Mother. I Am an Artist" is a collection of works by Claire Haddon that explore her roles as an artist and a mother. "[Bracket Life]" is a prose poem developed from the day-to-day experience of being an artist-mother; these are the struggles that are not normally included in an application or publication. The poem demonstrates the self-editing we do as mothers, writers, and artists. "Outcomes" is a series of images documenting time spent in artistic practice, setting up a paradoxical relationship between the positive language of success (as an artist) and images of failure (as a mother). Here, visual space is given to the direct results or "Unintended Outcomes" of artistic practice. Finally, "Curriculum Vitae (Course of Life)" shows Haddon's attempt to frame her accomplishments as an authentic reflection of her life's experience and unveil the narrative we use to present ourselves. Little space and language have been offered for the gargantuan task of motherhood when laid alongside the traditional CV format and its expectation of productivity.

Kate Antosik-Parsons presents and explores her performative visual images in "*Motherlines* and *Maternal Entanglements*: Unravelling and Embracing the Multiplicity of Abortion, Embodiment, and the Maternal."

Grounding her artmaking in her embodied experiences of abortion, motherhood, and the fertile body, she discusses how she has navigated these seemingly contradictory experiences through visual art. In "Motherlines," she poses questions about her fertile body and relationship to her children. In "Maternal Entanglements," she considers the slippage between her identity as a woman who chose abortion and a mother. Antosik-Parsons's work unravels and renders visible the complexities of entanglements, subverting celebratory or essentialist ideas about motherhood, and embracing the layered, multiple, intersecting, and at times messy, versions of the maternal.

In "Pandemic and Pandemonium: Emerging from Emergency," Alex Maeve Campbell and Terry Anne Campbell stage a conversation in poetry, prose, and image, moving between daughter to mother and back again. It is set in the context of medical emergencies experienced individually and jointly. The large world context is a global pandemic; the small world context is comprised of events involving a daughter, Alex, and a mother, Terry. These authors provoke and probe the pain of the serious health problems they have encountered with the hope of transforming those emergencies into ongoing states of healing, health, and power. The common threads that braid together their near encounters with death include their voyages into the land of pain and their shared love of "The Love Song of J. Alfred Prufrock," by T.S. Eliot, to which they respond by feeling thinkingly and thinking feelingly. They discover the pressures of daughtering and mothering, especially from places of pain; the performances inherent in daughterhood and motherhood; and finally, the power that can be plumbed when we go deep enough.

"Lingering Regrets Revisited" by Mandy Fessenden Brauer captures the thoughts of an octogenarian who has lived internationally, working as a child psychologist helping children cope with war and other hardships. Three marriages and two children later, Brauer writes poignantly about her role as a mother where guilt and mistakes still haunt her: Being so depressed at times, even with ideas of suicide, raising children in California during the tumultuous sixties seemed like an overwhelming task. Looking back, Brauer focuses on how her own needs often took precedence, and she reveals through gut-wrenching poetry her resentment, pain, and guilt which has, along with writing about the vitally important role mothering plays throughout life, ultimately led to a semblance of self-forgiveness. Brauer hopes her words will help others appreciate the difficulties inherent in being a mother and forgive themselves for the little and not so little mistakes.

Part III: Destabilization: Reimagining Nonnormative Mothering

> Given voice, space, and time, motherhood can, and should,
> be one of the central means through which a historical moment
> reckons with itself.
>
> —Jacqueline Rose 17

In Part III, companions grapple with the pain and suffering caused by normative mothering: "Motherhood (even just the idea of it) is destabilizing. Unrelenting. Disconcerting. But whichever way we approach it, society makes us feel like we need to make it palatable, understandable" (Denford). Increasingly dissatisfied with the way things are, and in an attempt to make sense of experience, we demonstrate a willingness to problematize and unsettle maternal pain caused by patriarchal forces, societal expectations, and judgment of self and others.

Collectively, Gertrude Lyons, Júlia Campos Clímaco, and Andrea O'Reilly forge a way forward by turning their disorientation into action in a way that destabilizes hegemonic institutions and structures that no longer serve, ultimately showing how pain's wisdom can be used to (re)imagine pain and suffering as strength not weakness. They offer us hope in what can be achieved if we work together and channel our pain into action and activism. We are offered subtle and not-so-subtle ways to normalize the pain associated with motherhood and change the narrative typically associated with motherhood to become one less idealistic and more grounded in reality.

American culture has strayed far from a healthy relationship with pain. Women need to know options exist to normalize the pain experienced during conception, pregnancy, birth, and motherhood. In "Pain's Wisdom: From Normative to Relational Mothering," Gertrude Lyons discusses what is possible when we reframe pain and foster an inclusive relationship with the strong physical and emotional sensations we have been programmed to fear. The framing of pain as a limiting experience is one of many myths associated with motherhood that merge into what can be called the "mother code"—a set of assumptions and automatic reactions to the world around us meant to keep mothers from claiming the centrality of our role in society, which is instead dominated by patriarchy and technocracy. When women see the choices available to them to express their pain, they can rewrite their mother codes and end the oppression that silences them from their wisdom and locks them into a motherhood role that denies them the full developmental experience as a mother.

In "Dragon Mothers: Possibilities and Experiences of Mothers of Children with Incurable Diseases" written by Júlia Campos Clímaco, we encounter the experiences of two women who raised children with Tay-Sachs, a rare neurodegenerative disease leading to early childhood death. In their quest to redefine their mothering practices, these mothers found inspiration and empathy in a group of women who shared a similar path and who self-identified as "dragon mothers." This nonnormative form of mothering presented moral dilemmas that prompted them to experiment and expand the horizons of their lives. By reimagining their relationship with time and daily routines, they discovered novel ways of existing in the world. They became driven by and dedicated to care for themselves and their children.

This collection aims to expose mothers' pain, transform silence into action, and destabilize hegemonic institutions and structures. In its considerations of how normative motherhood is both reified and resisted in two climate-change novels, the chapter "Imagining Motherhood in a Post-apocalyptic World: Reifying and Resisting Normative Motherhood in the Climate-Change Novels *Clean Air* by Sarah Blake and *The New Wilderness* by Diane Cook" by Andrea O'Reilly articulates the pain that hegemonic institution of normative motherhood inflicts on mothers and considers how this institution may be destabilized through empowered mothering. More specifically, the chapter argues that whereas *Clean Air* presents normative motherhood as both natural and inevitable in a post-apocalyptic world, *The New Wilderness* imagines a mother outlaw who escapes from the normative motherhood of the destroyed old world to achieve maternal authenticity and agency in empowered mothering. Thus, the novels are read as cautionary narratives about climate change and as necessary interventions in how new worlds are being imagined for mothers.

Part IV: Discovery—Transforming Intergenerational Pain and Suffering

Such love is an offspring of guilt. There is agony lurking at its core.
A mother ... is most likely to go in search of it only so far as she feels
she has already failed.

—Jacqueline Rose 100

In Part IV, we come to understand that "Motherhood isn't just one thing, it's a collection of *every*thing and a vast nothingness all at once, and it could never be diluted or explained. It just *is*" (Denford). Accompanied by faith, trust, and authenticity, companions embark on a journey to answer the question: "Who are you?" As we emerge confidently into this m/otherworld (McDermott), we discover who we are and learn to love ourselves and make sense of our unique experiences.

This coming to know is not taken lightly. Michelann Parr, Hannah Frostad, Susan Picard, Drisana McDaniel, and Pamela Vickerson move in and out of past, present, and future. They come to understand why they make the decisions they do, how intergenerational connections have shaped them, and what type of legacy they would like to leave for future generations. Seeds of empathy for self and others are grown. These companions accept their role in transforming intergenerational pain and suffering not only in writing but in life and not only for the present but for generations.

In "Letting Go: An Exercise in Writing through the Pain," Michelann Parr recognizes the incredible gift afforded to her as a white, able-bodied, and cisgender female. She dedicates her chapter to mothers who continue to struggle against a maternal ideal, who find themselves oppressed under persistent patriarchy, who are historically muted, who are missing or lost, and whose pain is silenced with stories left untold. This personal journey of learning to let go was anything but linear. By researching truth and fantasy, exploring birthright, accepting days where survival was the goal, and moving through the phases of denial, betrayal, fate, and discernment, she finds moments of surrender and hope and ultimately, her homeplace. She comes to appreciate the immense responsibility of today's matricentric feminist collective and that we cannot heal the world until we first heal ourselves.

Hannah Frostad's poem, "If You Are a Mother," explores the emotional truths of her journey through motherhood. As a witness to spaces typecasting mothers as "supporting roles," Frostad challenges these labels. She shares her honest, vulnerable, and sometimes taboo thoughts that are too often met with scripted clichés. This poem advocates for mothers, challenges the status quo, and creates space for honest conversations.

In "Songs for My Daughters," Susan Picard shows how her songs bridge intergenerational bonds and how strength and resilience develop through maternal bonds. She recalls the time her mother told her that the most terrifying time in her life was when Picard, the youngest of five daughters, was in a difficult relationship with a schizophrenic man. To this admission, Picard replied, "But you lived through bombs dropping all around you during WWII." Her mother responded, "Yes." Picard recalls feeling such shame at causing her mother so much pain, yet in her eyes, she saw nothing but love. Many years later, she recalls some of the difficult times she and her daughters have been through. The biggest fear, and source of Picard's pain, is that she might not be enough for her daughters as they struggle with their challenges. And so, she writes them love songs, to sing in her heart as they wander this treacherous territory of life, often as what appears to be adversaries.

"Quiet as Kept" sees Drisana McDaniel embark on a multifaceted exploration of her role within her family lineage, as she aims to break intergenerational patterns and heal historical wounds by focussing on her offspring's wellbeing. Rooted in interconnected consciousness, McDaniel acknowledges her profound impact on future generations. Simultaneously, the narrative delves into enduring mother-daughter connections that transcend life and death and highlights the challenges of uncovering a motherline history marked by silences, forgetfulness, and trauma, emphasizing how detachment from this lineage leads to isolation and self-estrangement. McDaniel underscores memory's malleability in shaping self-conception and the evolving nature of personal narratives that mirror shifting perspectives. Ultimately, the chapter explores the empowerment of African American women through interventions designed to embrace their unique knowledge, foster interconnected love, and nurture psychospiritual strengths. McDaniel highlights the transformative potential of her healing journey in shaping a brighter future and liberating future generations from suffering's chains.

Pamela Vickerson's creative work "One Momma" is an outlet for grief. Her art practice involves studying and sorting past and present losses to examine ideas of absence and presence, the every day and the sacred, and her role as mother-witness. Her poem attempts to hold onto those narratives that tether one mother to a loved one and the related sacred spaces, which are no longer physically accessible. It is also a response to the pain caused by being continually labelled, silenced, and compared as privileged as though that diminishes or denies one's capacity to suffer or the need to have a voice. There is a restlessness, as more representation will always fail to relieve or remediate loss, but the strong desire to try persists. For Vickerson, seeking restorative effects for the heart and mind through the creative expression of grief becomes a gentle reentry point into community after the isolating experience of loss; it is an opportunity to hear others' stories.

Throughout this collection, we get to know pain and become familiar with it; we "look it right in the eye—not as a way to solve problems, but as a complete undoing of old ways of seeing, hearing, smelling, tasting, and thinking" (Chödrön 2). We keep ourselves in the midst of pain, finding a moment in time that captivates our attention: "When we stop there and don't act out, don't repress, don't blame it on anyone else, and also don't blame it on ourselves, then we meet with an open-ended question that has no conceptual answer. We also encounter our heart" (Chödrön 3).

Reading and Responding to Pain

> Mothers, we might say, are the original subversives, never—
> as feminism has long insisted—what they seem, or are meant to be.
> —Jacqueline Rose 18

And so, readers, you are now part of this story. As I did, I encourage you to adopt a companioning stance as you explore the dilemmas and mysteries posed by these mothers. In the ambiguities and uncertainties of these pieces, you are invited to suspend judgment, make your own meaning, and understand the nature of pain as a socially mediated construct that requires voice, time, and space to peel back its multiple layers to ultimately uncover, in its own time, the wisdom of what pain has to offer.

As you accept this challenge, "Remember that it is your own sense of urgency, your own memories, needs, questions, and hopes, your own painfully gathered knowledge of daughterhood and motherhood, which you must above all trust" (Rich, *On Lies* 259).

Acknowledge the pain that these mothers are exposing and compassionately send energy out into the world by developing empathy for mothers whose experiences might be similar. Take note of the thoughts and feelings that surface and recognize that some of our common responses do little more than disenfranchise the pain, alienate the mother, and shut down necessary communication.

I wish for you to find as much hope and strength in these journeys as I did. Let these courageous mothers be your companions as well. They can show you that you can survive the flood of pain and suffering, and that there is a reason to work through it. Reflect on your losses, fears, pains, and grief, remain open to your vulnerability, and accept tears as a sign that you are revising old wounds and developing empathy for self and others (Chödrön).

> Let this be a time, then, for hearing and speaking together, for breaking silences, not only within yourselves but among all our selves. What we all, collectively, have lived, as the daughters of women, as the mothers of children, is a tale far greater than any three or four of us can encompass: a tale only beginning to be told.
>
> —Adrienne Rich, *On Lies* 260

Works Cited

Ahmed, Sara. *Living a Feminist Life*. Duke University Press, 2017.

Belenky, Mary Field, et al. *Women's Ways of Knowing: The Development of Self, Voice, and Mind*. Basic Books, 1986.

Chödrön, Pema. *When Things Fall Apart: Heart Advice for Difficult Times*. Shambhala, 2016.

Crenshaw, Kimberlé. "She Coined the Term 'Intersectionality' Over 30 Years Ago. Here's What It Means to Her Today." Interview by Katy Steinetz, *Time*, 20 Feb. 2020, https://time.com/5786710/kimberle-crenshaw-intersectionality/. Accessed 8 May 2024.

Denford, Tetyana. *Conversations with Motherhood.* Kindle ed., Independently Published, 2021.

Doxtater, Michael. "Everyone Gets To Be Healed : Pedagogy of Healing." Presentation for *"Culture and Community Mental Health Rounds"* Aboriginal Mental Health Research Team, Institute of Community and Family Psychiatry. McGill University, Montreal QC, 2006.

Ellis, Carolyn. "Telling Secrets, Revealing Lives." *Qualitative Inquiry,* vol. 13, no. 1, January 2007, pp. 3–29.

Griffith, Susan. *Out of Sound. Silence. Out of Nothing. Something—A Writer's Guide.* Counterpoint, 2023.

Halifax, Joan. *Being with Dying: Cultivating Compassions and Fearlessness in the Presence of Death.* Shambhala Publications Inc., 2008.

hooks, bell. *Feminism Is for Everybody.* 2nd ed. Routledge, 2012.

Kübler-Ross, Elisabeth, David Kessler, and Maria Shriver. *On Grief and Grieving: Finding the Meaning of Grief Through the Five Stages of Loss.* Kindle ed., Scribner, 2014.

Kübler-Ross, Elisabeth, and Kessler, David. *Life Lessons: Two Experts on Death and Dying Teach Us About the Mysteries of Life and Living.* Kindle ed., Scribner, 2012.

Lorde, Audre. *Our Dead Behind Us.* Norton, 1986.

Lorde, Audre. *Sister Outsider.* 1984. Crossing Press, 2007.

Macy, Joanna, and Chris Johnstone. *Active Hope: How to Face the Mess We're in without Going Crazy.* New World Library, 2012.

Maracle, Lee, Coumpa Bobb, and Tania Carter. *Hope Matters.* Book*hug Press, 2019.

McDermott, Mairi. "Stories (of) Carrying Forth M/otherworlds From Our Matricentric Carrier Bags." *Mothering Outside the Lines: Tales of Boundary-Busting Mamas.* Edited by Michelann Parr and BettyAnn Martin. Demeter Press, 2023, pp. 7–13.

O'Reilly, Andrea. *Matricentric Feminism: Theory, Activism, Practice, The Second Edition.* Demeter, 2021.

Parr, Michelann. "Breaking The Silences of Motherhood: Rabbit Holes, False Starts, (Un)Finished Fragments, and Hopeful Connections. *Mothering Outside the Lines: Tales of Boundary-Busting Mamas.* Edited by Michelann Parr and BettyAnn Martin. Demeter Press, 2023, pp. 39–67.

Parr, Michelann, and BettyAnn Martin. *Mothering Outside the Lines: Tales of Boundary-Busting Mamas.* Demeter Press, 2023.

Rich, Adrienne. *Of Woman Born: Motherhood as Experience and Institution.* Norton, 1986/1995.

Rich, Adrienne. *On Lies, Secrets, and Silence: Selected Prose.* Norton, 1979.

Rose, Jacqueline. *Mothers: An Essay on Love and Cruelty.* Farrar, Straus and Giroux, 2018.

Ruddick, Sara. *Maternal Thinking: Toward a Politics of Peace.* Beacon Press, 1989.

Spradley, Elizabeth, et al. "Proving Our Maternal and Scholarly Worth: A Collaborative Autoethnographic Textual and Visual Storying of MotherScholar Identity Work during the COVID-19 Pandemic. *Journal of the Motherhood Initiative*, vol. 11, no. 2, 2020, pp. 189–209.

Solnit, Rebecca. *The Mother of All Questions.* HaymarketBooks, 2017.

Strada, E. Alessandra. *Grief and Bereavement in Palliative Care.* Oxford University Press, 2013.

Tolle, Eckhart. "On the Dark Night of the Soul." *Eckhart Tolle,* 2018, https://eckharttolle.com/eckhart-on-the-dark-night-of-the-soul/. Accessed 8 May 2024.

Wolfelt, Alan D. *Understanding Your Grief: Ten Essential Touchstones for Finding Hope and Healing Your Heart.* Companion, 2003.

Part I

Denial and Disenfranchisement
—Birthing and Naming Pain

1.

Unadorned Birth

Maya Bhave

It was the ducks I remember. They were all marching in a straight line, adorned with pink bowties with white polka dots. Pink? Bow ties? Yup. They were lined up precisely, akin to little girls wearing new Easter outfits in early spring, and I liked that.

The ducks appealed to my OCD. They were neat, tidy, and, honestly, well dressed. My eyes darted back and forth, watching them intently, much like the intensity of perusing those double pictures in puzzle magazines where you have to spot the ten differences. Were the ducks all the same, or was one slightly different? I was determined to find the outlier.

In the background, I could hear someone softly sniffling and another person bellowing. What a strange assortments of sounds.

Couldn't they see I was busy? Busy trying to make sense of the ducks and the holiday.

It was St. Patrick's Day, March 17, 1997.

Just three days before my due date—the first day of spring.

I heard my husband say, "She's in shock. She's in shock. Say something, Maya, please." The woman added, "He's gone, Maya. He's gone. I'm so sorry, but he's gone."

My eyes quickly flitted from the pleasant row of ducks near the ceiling to the rest of the room—a cold, sterile space decorated in blue and grey tones. I eyed an empty grey chair in the far corner while a whitish ultrasound machine still whirring from my recent fetal scan sat about two feet away from me, hiding the mottled grey tile floor. Four eyes were intently staring at me, just waiting for a response. My forehead furrowed, as I finally processed what Dr. K was saying: "He's gone, Maya, I'm so, so sorry." Tears welled up in her eyes.

It was at that moment that the ducks waddled right out of view.

The next breath was different. It wasn't simple or earthly. My screams took me above the building to a place I'd never been. "I told them. I told them," I bellowed, as Dr. K rushed to slam the examination room door shut—keeping my screams from patients waiting innocently and naively in the OB/GYN office waiting room. There were no tears yet, just yelling, which turned into a strange wailing and became increasingly louder and louder. I began to focus on the present conversation: "I told them something was wrong. I was there Saturday, and I spoke with her on Sunday."

Just forty-eight hours earlier, huddled in our tiny bed on the third floor of our brownstone, after about a day of nonprogressive labour pains, my waters had broken, soaking our old and threadbare green sheets. The bedframe had once held my husband's collegiate waterbed. I had adamantly said I wouldn't sleep on the water mattress, given I wanted nothing to do with his past fraternity days and nocturnal activities. We had splurged on a new mattress, which made me feel like an adult. I saw it as a grown-up, respectable purchase, and now I was going to cement my adulthood by becoming a mother.

On Saturday morning, the nurses on the phone at the maternity hospital told me to grab my bag and head down immediately. We dressed and drove down Lake Shore Drive but not before looking at each other and animatedly proclaiming, "We're gonna have a baby!!"

I waddled into the familiar OB/GYN hospital.

This time was different though. I walked slowly, my massive belly hindering my movements. I noticed for the first time that the walls were decorated with muted watercolour-framed prints, landscapes, and sea images. I wondered if there was a massive website—like *hospital images.com*—where hospitals bought soothing prints in bulk to calm new mothers.

Yet as I looked closer, more carefully and intently, I noticed the walls beneath had cracks and settling lines. It was clear that although the art images were serene, the underlying infrastructure was decaying, tired, and flawed.

The building was quite old, but I didn't care, I was there to have my first baby—our son, Andrew.

We were ushered into a large delivery room with unique oval windows revealing slivers of the large lake in the distance. Maple cupboards were flanking one wall, and there was a small matching rectangular coffee table and a roomy bathroom that made the room appear like a sparse Vrbo room sans kitchenette. It wasn't what I imagined a hospital room would look like.

Nurses arrived and quickly threw open the cupboards, revealing secret cubbies housing unfamiliar machines, large silver dials, tangles and tangles of clear plastic tubing, and fully stocked drawers of plastic medical pads, blankets and linens.

It was then I realized that this place was not as it first appeared.

It was a place that was surreptitiously masked.

Shortly after changing into a gown, a medical resident breezed in, telling me she was going to do a "fern test" to make sure my water had broken. I, of course, knew what had happened, but she wanted to be sure. It was right at this moment that I began to question myself.

Why weren't we all talking about this pending baby's arrival?

I thought there would be an army of staff to meet me and chat about my delivery, but thus far, I only had interactions with two nurses and one resident.

The resident finished her test, shook her head, and said "Well, your waters didn't break. They are intact, and you're not even fully dilated."

Immediately, I felt depleted, not just because I felt the delivery was near but because I knew something was wrong with how this narrative was progressing.

I knew my waters had broken.

I knew I was in labour.

I just wasn't textbook, and quite honestly, I never had been.

I told her, I tried, I did ... but somehow my voice, my knowledge, meant nothing.

She rebutted with how I couldn't possibly know because my sheets were green, and how, in all likelihood, I had just urinated on the bed.

She suggested that I couldn't possibly know any better, given that I was a first-time mother.

Moreover, she told me I was overreacting and needed to calm down; she encouraged me to "Just be patient, as it would all happen soon enough."

Repeating that I needed to go home, particularly since insurance wouldn't cover my unnecessary stay, the resident turned to me and said, "You'll be fine. You're a first-time mother. Everyone gets nervous. And maybe we will see you soon. We've been wrong before."

My elation for the day plummeted.

I went home feeling stupid.

Stupid that they had told me I didn't know enough about labour.

Stupid that they had me questioning my certainty of my waters breaking.

And stupid for thinking I was actually going to have a baby on March 15.

As I slowly walked to the bank of elevators, I briefly remembered but quickly dismissed the Ides of March.

The next day, I continued to have labour that wouldn't progress.

I felt increasingly uncomfortable and painful.

I called the maternity hospital hotline.

An attending I had never met called me back. "Just relax," she said, as the sounds of March Madness basketball—at her end—overwhelmed our conversation.

"Why don't you go for a walk or see a movie?" she asked me.

Relax I thought? I could barely move, I was so uncomfortable.

I continued to try and rest in our tiny apartment. That night at exactly 6:00 p.m., my son shuddered so violently that I mentioned it to my husband. It was a strange occurrence.

My son never moved again.

But I had been convinced.

Convinced that the medical professionals knew what they were doing and seeing.

Convinced that their vision was more complete than mine, even as my feminist intuition told me otherwise.

I slept fitfully. Monday morning after my husband left for work at the same hospital, I realized something was seriously wrong.

I had pain running down my legs, and I felt unsteady on my feet.

I called the hotline again and was told to go to a suburban clinic, twice as far away as the hospital, since my attending wasn't in her hospital office that day.

My husband came home and drove me to the satellite office.

That was when I spied those ducks adorning the walls.

It was just the ducks, the ultrasound machine, and me.

Me... screaming that I had been right and that I had known what was happening to my body.

After my screams subsided, Dr. K told me I couldn't have a C-section, and that I would have to go through labour to deliver my dead son.

I didn't believe her on either account.

Why not give me a C-section? What was the logic in making me go through labour?

And, why, at this point, would I believe her declaration that my son was actually dead?

At this very moment, something shifted.

I decided that this time they were not right.

They couldn't be.

They had been wrong on Saturday and Sunday, so today, on Monday, I was going to ignore their words.

And so for the next ten hours, I believed they were mistaken.

I believed that my son really wasn't dead.

That was impossible...

I believed that my son had tucked himself away safely—in essence hiding from them—and that's why we couldn't hear his heartbeat.

Decades later, I realize this was my way to protect my heart, a heart that I came to find out wouldn't ever beat the same again after March 17, 1997.

Yet again, I was ushered into a maple Vrbo room, similar to the one I had visited on Saturday. This time, though, many more people came in and out.

Dozens of techs, nurses, residents, and attending physicians breezed in and out, their ID badges swaying as they moved swiftly by my bed, studying the monitors and paper printouts on the floor.

They conversed in hushed tones about fluid, baby size, dilation, and sepsis.

It turns out I was quite ill at this point, but I didn't really know it.

They asked me about food, and drink.

I was perplexed: Why would I care about any of that?

I just wanted to deliver my baby boy.

I didn't for one second believe that he was dead.

How do you go from spending countless hours researching the best crib only to have no one to place in it?

It simply didn't add up.

I was ready.

I had worked feverishly for months buying just the right nonblue baby outfits—onesies, cute Baby Gap outfits, teeny socks, and hats.

I knew he wasn't going to be dressed in those horrid stereotypical light blue boy colours but rather soothing neutrals: beiges and whites.

Andrew and his world were going to be classy, bright and pristine.

Exhausted in my waiting, I looked up at the clock, the hands moving ever so slowly in this new delivery room, and that's when I realized there was one thing missing: the ducks.

Where were the ducks?

There were no sweetly adorned ducks to study or focus my vision on.

In fact, nothing was adorning these walls. They were ugly, vacant, and barren.

At about 9:00 p.m., Dr. K told me it was time to start pushing.

I tried, I really did, but I was so tir...

My thoughts were scattered and pushing felt like an unfair request.

I didn't feel like I could push or bare down anymore.

I had spent the day watching people look at me with their sad eyes, and I had listened as my husband called my parents in tears.

I was bone weary, drained, and weak.

"I can't push anymore," I said quietly. "I just can't. I'm done."

Dr. K's eyes grew wider as she responded, "Okay. I'll bring him out with forceps."

After some poking and prodding, Andrew Anant Bhave was delivered at 10:06 p.m. just as the Chicago bars were bursting with St. Patrick's Day revelry.

"G," the nurse who had stayed on long past her shift ended, tried to hand me Andrew, who was still bloody and appeared to be sleeping very peacefully.

I didn't want to hold him. I thought I just couldn't.

After coaxing, the nurse wrapped him up and placed him in my weary arms.

He was so sweet. As I studied the lines of his face, I noted he looked exactly like me. He had my chin, lips, and high cheekbones.

As an adoptee, this moment was like reaching the apex of Everest. I could see myself for the very first time. I was in awe. My first relative.

He didn't murmur, cry, or wiggle. His little lips didn't quiver, and he never opened his eyes.

He was in fact dead.

It was then that the tears came.

They streamed down my face, all the while dripping onto his white and blue hospital blanket.

And then they came in huge, ugly sobs.

Loud, messy, and deep.

I finally realized they had been wrong on the weekend but right on Monday.

I had been right on the weekend and wrong today.

How could one's validity and legitimacy shift so quickly?

In the weeks, months, and years later, I would decipher the concept of medical gaslighting, the privileging of medical science over women's wisdom, and the need for female patient voices to be more carefully listened to and responded to.

They gave me an hour with Andrew.

And then they wheeled me to a general surgery floor, telling me they "didn't want me to hear the cries of newborns."

We turned towards the elevator, and the nurse took me through the delivery waiting room. An empty blue-grey sectional couch had been pushed askew, revealing plastic cups scattered on the floor. I eyed an empty champagne bottle on its side on a table littered with magazines.

Oh, how I wanted this: the celebration, excitement, and happiness of birth.

In my visions, I was wearing my finest pink outfit to celebrate the newness of life alongside the arrival of spring.

In my reality, I had nothing but bare walls, an ugly hospital gown covering my brown and jaded body, and a stony, silent wheelchair ride.

When I got up to the surgical floor, without a baby in my arms, I was faced with a new reality.

A kind but slightly nervous nurse said, "I heard what happened. I'm so sorry. Try to get some sleep" and then rushed out, hoping to avoid a lengthy conversation.

As I lay, stuck on my side, and propped onto pillows, I peered over my now vacant belly and looked up at the ceiling.

This room had no ducks, no pink bowties, and little to bring me joy or interest. It was then—in that moment—that I realized the ducks from the morning had all been the same. *I* was the outlier.

The room suddenly grew dark, and I was overwhelmingly silent.

2.

Replica

Rachel O'Donnell

Everything Is Full

First, we descend to our basement with small windows that let in light. Even though it is cold, it is never grey. Space heaters and hot showers warm us by day, and at night we have each other. A home-made quilt. Stacks of books on night tables. A French press with loose-leaf tea.

Second, two desks back-to-back. Books opened on their spines. Stacks of papers to grade on the tiled floor. A small lamp on the desk.

Third, the love that surrounds us is satisfying and blissful, but when I discover it, I am alone. The news erupts over Skype. We must move away from the dusty pipes and the furnace with the open flame. The nausea strikes at night, but during the day, there is pure joy in the waiting.

Fourth, movement within, touching, glowing, and kicking. The mystery grows, and hair, eyes, and gender remain unknown.

Fifth, a lamp. A plan. A space heater. A huge ball to sit on. A name. A large black tub with warm water.

Sixth, a death. A heartbeat that was there and then was not. If only there could be a backward direction to the miserable forward. If only there were a way out.

Everything Is Empty

First, a quiet bedroom with a closed door.

Second, a girl. We know now what we have lost, and we want her back. A report that reads of a long slender body. Dark hair, bruising, red lips, incomprehensible numbers.

Third, silence. Unbearable silence. And sometimes self-hatred, desperation, and life before us like a cave without enough oxygen or an exit.

Fourth, a long scar with loose skin overhanging. We can no longer see below it without a mirror.

Fifth, the stopped bleeding and a void that has gone, an everyday loneliness. The geese fly overhead. New growth, cell upon cell, frogs swimming with tails flapping. Sea anemones are water-dwelling animals named for a terrestrial flower. Hiccups. Hands under ribs.

Sixth, the waiting. Again.

Everything Is Bare Life

First, at last, a birth where there is life. Small hands so wet they are wrinkled at the ends and feet, two crimson feet.

Second, eating and drinking are joyous again. Spring flowers. Outdoor baths. A wheeled carriage with a cup holder.

Third, a train trip. A waterfall. A street performer. An afternoon nap. A painting in one colour.

Fourth, a school with a pink tower. Skipping. Words for everything.

Fifth, a girl comes to a birthday party. The teacher laughs when I say he has invited her and tells me the glorious girl child does not know how to misbehave. She is a nymph with red hair against the snow as she walks up the stairs and removes her hat in slow motion. Her freckles are so bright they may burst, or perhaps she exists in high definition, I cannot decide. She sees the helium balloons against the ceiling and chases them, their strings hanging down into a plastic clip with a knot. She spoons red sauce onto a tiny circular pizza, pinches shredded cheese between her fingers, and rinses her hands under running water. She looks up at me and asks to use the bathroom. She does not need help. I say there will be a story, and she sits cross-legged and waits like she is expecting a gift. During the game, I ask, "Who wants to go next?" She says "Me!" and raises her arm straight to the sky. I do not want to blindfold her; the tails are attached to sharp pins, and she could stick herself. No, I want to take her quickly in my arms, remove her clothes, smell her hair, hold her against my breast, and offer her milk. Listen to her cry for just a moment and inexplicably stop it. There, there. I will take a warm wet rag and smooth it to wipe away her yellow stain. Clean and warm, her bare body asleep against my bare chest.

Sixth, six years. Every child is our child. The missing one. Balloons and birthdays and school buses. There, there.

Artist's Statement

How did this prose poem come about? A child was lost, and a new child was born. The spring after the living child finally arrived, I felt almost giddy walking him around the neighbourhood in his stroller. Finally, I had a baby to show off, my tiny baby with a fist in his mouth.

When he was two, I was nervous about enrolling him in preschool as we had not yet spent much time apart. Yet he did so well at school and was only there in the mornings. Each day, I picked him up at noon, gave him lunch and a nap, and kept working—writing a dissertation I thought would never get done, wondering where my life was headed after two back-to-back pregnancies and two maternity leaves, all the while travelling from one town to the next to teach and keep my benefits. During one of these long bus trips, I thought about my child, this second child, now in kindergarten, now with another younger sibling, and his birthday party. His sixth seemed significant, as he moved from early childhood to an age after which he would no longer need me as much. We had come so far since the loss of our first child, yet everything seemed to remain the same. We were haunted by that loss, even though we had a healthy six-year-old. Would our missing child have been like one of his preschool friends? Would she have been beautiful, red-headed and freckled? I imagined this kindergarten friend as the child we had lost. And so this prose poem came about on a long bus trip. It describes the way we treated that first pregnancy, a major life event with a move to a new house, all the planning that comes with a first pregnancy that was then taken away from us and the intense grief that came after. We had little time to grieve because just a few months later, I was pregnant again, nervous about the pregnancy and another potential loss, terrified that my stress was impacting the baby, unable to work sufficiently because I was so distracted

47

by the baby's every movement, worried about the impact of two closely spaced pregnancies and what that would mean for this child. Our living child was perfect, but in the moments I watched his friend at his birthday party, I yearned for both of my children, wishing I could comfort her or be comforted by her and wishing for a return to a life where I had not lost a child.

During the time of most intense grief, I remembered all the details of the pregnancy. This is where the objects came from, each detail perhaps a sign of the death to come that would bring us so much misery. The things that were there and then were not. I remember where I purchased things for the baby, how I told my husband about the pregnancy, and how we planned to change everything about our lives to welcome the coming child.

So this is "Replica," a prose poem in three parts. It begins with a scene describing the excitement surrounding a pregnancy, continues with the loss and pain of the missing child, and ends by describing the continual longing for my missing child. The major theme of the piece is the continual and timeless pain that grieving mothers experience in seeing living children, both their own and others. This pain surfaces at the most surprising times, even amid joyful moments with other children, no matter what.

My wish is that you give this prose poem to a mother who has lost a child and say this: I also remember your child.

3

Becoming a Birth Trauma Specialist

Teela Tomassetti

I remember the first time that I saw a birth. I was around ten years old and watching television with my mom. At the time, *A Baby's Story* was big on TLC. Each episode would follow a couple of pregnant women on their journey into motherhood. I remember sitting next to my mom that first time, not knowing what was to come, as I watched this woman sitting, in what looked to be, a small hot tub. As the woman on TV began to make sounds I had never heard before, and as she gripped her belly, I reached for my mother's hand. As the scene unfolded, the sounds intensified, and a nearby woman encouraged her and reminded her of her strength. And then, the sound came.

The sound of a baby's first cry.

I remember sitting there, feeling the tears in my eyes while I watched this mother begin to cry as she held this new life in her arms for the first time. I looked at my mom and exclaimed, "I want that one day Mom," and she chuckled.

That was it—the moment that I was hooked. I not only wanted a baby of my own but also dreamed of a home waterbirth, too.

I wanted that.

A beautiful birth.

The Hollywood Version

We have this idea of what giving birth is like. We are sold this Hollywood version of birth from a young age. It looks intense and dramatic for a moment or two, and then it's all over. We see a beautifully kept mother with perfect hair and make-up sitting up and holding her perfect baby. Her face is glowing in natural sunlight, which pours in through the windows of the hospital room or the room at home where she decided to give birth. Mother and child bask in their golden hour while family members smile nearby. As the scene ends, those watching sigh with relief knowing that the world feels perfect at that moment. The audience is given the notion that what they are witnessing is an ending versus a beginning, a pleasantry versus a trauma, and for many, it is.

But for some, it is not.

I think that this is where the silencing begins—with unfair and unrealistic expectations of mothers that start long before what ends in birth as the mother ensures that the days, weeks, months, and moments leading up to the actual birth go a specific way and that the events of the birth itself unfold in a way of absolute perfection. No other options are open to us as we grow into the age when we consider our motherhood initiation. We are typically offered the ideal, what must be attained, the experience that grants us the privilege of saying we did it the right way.

Perfectionism and idealism are both forms of silencing, which are created by a society that surrounds mothers with the joy of childbirth.

It doesn't take long until mothers are in the thick of it, and then they realize that perfectionism does not exist in parenting.

On the contrary, it's messy.

Yet the messages persist long before mothers become aware of their own.

Plot Twist: Birth Trauma Interrupts the Happily-Ever-After Narrative

"Birth is not always beautiful," I say often.

The reality for many does not paint a perfect picture.

For some, the scene unfolds chaotically, with confusion and fear. There may be a fight to save the life of the mother, the baby, or both.

For some, it unfolds with racism, abuse, and neglect.

For others, sacred and quiet moments of deep connection become interrupted and replaced with fear, uncertainty, and loss.

For many, it is about what didn't happen during the birth that leaves the biggest hole. Close to 45 per cent of women describe their birth story as traumatic (Gough and Giannouli). This translates to staggering numbers of mothers who give birth each year around the world without adequate tools, resources, or support. That this statistic goes unnoticed is an obvious indication of the silence surrounding the perinatal world. Every part of birth trauma is silenced. It is not sexy, and it is not glamorous or relatable unless you have been through it, and even there, it is often the experience that is only discussed behind locked doors with knowing others.

Birth trauma is not as sensationalized as postpartum psychosis, which often makes the news and paints maternal mental health in the most disturbing, scary, and unflattering way. Birth trauma is associated with a dislike of the birthing experience, which it may very well be, but it is so much more than that.

Birth trauma, for many, is in the eye of the beholder (Beck). There are so many ways in which birth trauma can be viewed and understood; mothers should be the ones to identify and name trauma, not someone else. I don't mean to suggest that trauma is a choice; no one chooses to be traumatized by what should be a beautiful day. What is trauma for one may not be trauma for another. Hormones and their impact on the body and nervous system decide for mothers what symptoms present, such as dissociation nightmares, flashbacks, guilt, shame, sex and intimacy issues, struggles to bond with or feed the baby, and more.

You Have to Love Your Baby and Birth Experience

Those who mother must never expose the struggle to bond with their baby, the frustration they experience at yet another sleepless night, and the devastation of a baby who doesn't feed well. Many birth trauma survivors struggle with the initial hours, days, weeks, and even months of bonding with their infant because of a nervous system running rampant with trauma, yet we hear little of these struggles. This effect of birth trauma is silenced and hidden. Much like the perfect childbirth we are conditioned to yearn for, so too are we convinced that every mother looks down at her baby for the first time and experiences love at first sight. We continue to offer mothers a set of unrealistic expectations and pressures, and we demand they carry them as their own. But how is the woman who just had an emergency Caesarean section and is unable to hold her new baby for the first few hours of their life meant to see themselves? Or the new parent who did not get to see their baby as it was whisked off to the neonatal intensive care unit, which becomes home for the first weeks or months of their life? What about the mother who suffered midwifery or obstetric violence during birth and has slipped into a world of dissociation to manage her fear and flashbacks? And then there is the mother who has to learn how to parent from nurses and doctors in the room, who has to ask to hold their child, and whose rights are all but ignored. How do we deal with their struggles? Mostly by telling them that they shouldn't or don't exist.

For many, the issues around immediate bonding are directly linked to birth trauma. These are not conscious choices made by mothers but choices that resulted from birth trauma that set an uncertain foundation; many birth trauma survivors doubt themselves early on, which creates emotional distance between them and the little one that they had longed for. For some, the bond is also interrupted by the intense fear that results from complications during pregnancy or being told their baby may not survive. Without even realizing it, some mothers form a protective shield around their hearts to prepare for the possibility that they may lose the thing they had spent so long dreaming of. All their plans begin to fall apart, and they begin to doubt their capabilities as a mother.

And then amid all this trauma, breastfeeding is often pushed as the best and most natural way to bond with your baby. Without breastfeeding, how will that little one know you exist and that you are their mother? The Hollywood version touts breastfeeding as the gold standard for how one feeds their baby; this is the image of motherhood we fall prey to. Yet breastfeeding for many survivors cannot be a reality. After my excessive postpartum hemorrhage—when I lost over half of the blood in my body and required blood transfusion, iron, IVs, and more to sustain my life—the last thing my body thought of doing was making milk for my daughter. It is common for those who had a traumatic birth to have breastfeeding difficulties, so it is of utmost importance to support mothers in these situations (Turkmen et al.). Without these supports, mothers may internalize this failure; messages of "breast is best" keep their struggles silent and make them feel shame, guilt, and fear if they do not bond with their baby. Imagine having a community of mothers or care staff available to assure these mothers struggling with bonding after birth trauma that it does not make them a bad mother but a mother in pain.

I recall feeling so alone in my struggles. I felt like I was letting my daughter down. I truly internalized that I had failed at giving birth, and now I was failing at providing her with food. My body was letting her down; my body was letting me down. I spent a great deal of time hiding, not sharing the cost of not being able to care for my daughter and how that was impacting my self-worth. My experience left me wondering: What happens when we create space for mothers to express their struggles and to share their cloaks of shame and guilt? As mothers learn they are not alone, they are more likely to step out of the shadows that silence creates and into a world where bonding after birth trauma is possible.

The Silencing Begins

My birth trauma unfolded in my very own home at the hands of midwives whom I trusted to support me as I entered the great unknown. I had chosen midwives because I wanted a "mothering feel" from the birth providers who would help me. I felt this would ease the sense of loss I felt without my mother who had passed away ten years before I became a mother myself. I have discovered a specific kind of silencing around those who choose their birth providers and are later met with mistreatment. It is a silence coated in blame and self-blame, and the idea that they made their bed, and now they should lie in it. I have come to discover that discussions about midwifery violence have gone underground and unnoticed. Instead, the prevailing notion is that midwives are safer, better, warmer, and more compassionate than one's typical OBGYN. I know from firsthand experience that unprofessional providers exist in every profession, and giving birth is no exception. The survivors who have messaged me willingly share their stories of midwifery violence. They speak about the isolation they feel because of their experiences, and that they do not believe their conversations of abuse, neglect, and mistreatment from a midwife are believed or treated as seriously as those at the hands of other providers. So, they do not share; they internalize and question what they did wrong to receive the mistreatment they did. If I have learned anything from running an Instagram that listens to and raises the voices of thousands of survivors it is that every single story is unique and that anything is possible when it comes to the mistreatment that women speak to.

As a mother, a professional, and now a scholar, I will never forget the first time that I read a research article by Rachel Reed, Rachael Sharman, and Christian Inglis stating that for 66 per cent of birth trauma survivors, the root of their birth trauma is the mistreatment they received from providers (3). Not only did this statistic make me feel like the silence around my own experience was being broken, but it also set a fire deep in my belly to change and challenge it. Systems silence birthers, people silence birthers, and other mothers silence birthers every single day; it is why we don't see enough conversations about birth trauma and mistreatment and how preventable it is.

Birth trauma connected to providers is highest among women of colour, who are often met with stereotypes, abuse, disrespect, and discrimination (Altman et al.). Black women are four times more likely to die giving birth than white women (MacDorman et al.). The layer of oppression and silencing that takes place when the birther is a person of colour often denies mothers their voices in the moment and in being able to ask for support after it takes place. Women of colour are silenced due to racism and cannot share their experiences, creating a sense of isolation and loneliness.

The Weaponization of Gratitude

One of the many ways that birth trauma survivors are silenced is through the use of a gratitude mindset. Gratitude is one of the only emotions new mothers are allowed and encouraged to express. Regardless of what happened, mothers should be grateful for their birth experience because it gave them their baby. That means it was all worth it. Anything less is a sure sign that they must not love their baby. Gratitude is weaponized in motherhood and used to silence the more difficult and negative emotions that are strong after trauma: anger, bitterness, resentment, and grieving the loss of what was intended. They are all valid, and one is not any better than the other. Every emotion has a story and a place and deserves a seat at the table. Yet we are encouraged not to be angry. Once again, the silencing begins, and mothers don their cloak of guilt and shame, hiding from the more difficult and untold parts of being a mother.

In the work that I do as a birth trauma psychologist, I often challenge the gratitude mindset in my space. Mothers enter the space and reassure me that they are so grateful for their baby and are wracked with the guilt and shame of feeling anything but pure bliss and joy. I challenge the false assumption that we can only feel one way towards the birth experience and the baby. I break the silencing by explaining the dangers of false dichotomies and how we live in a society that silences us through black-and-white, or all-or-nothing, thinking. I openly state that motherhood is swimming in shades of grey, where we can hold both negative and positive feelings; we do not need to dismiss or replace one but must allow both to coexist.

As mothers, we can experience both gratitude and grief. It is impossible to know one without the other. I came to terms with this quickly when I began my Instagram page; I was fearful that people would think I hated my baby because I gave voice to the other side. I imagined people reading and asking, "How can she talk about birth trauma and actually love her baby?" I feared that the people in my day-to-day life would lead the questioning.

I still wonder how my daughter will feel when she grows older and stumbles upon my page. I opt to leave it, wanting her to know that she has never been the cause of my trauma but the very reason to heal it. I need her to know that I would do it all again, that I love her with a love I have never known, and that the trauma surrounding her birth has been so incredibly difficult. I was so fearful to expose just how much pain I was in and that those around me would ignore the obvious magic between my daughter and me and begin only to see the pain and that they would instead dismiss the magic, replace it with pain, and associate it with a hidden dislike for motherhood. After a few months of her being with me, that fear dissipated because it was clear to her, me, and anyone else who saw us that we shared a deep love and bond. I no longer needed anyone else's approval of our relationship.

It is important to know that just because birth trauma survivors acknowledge the heavy emotions associated with birth trauma does not mean they hate being a mother. What it means is that they hate being a traumatized mother. They were forced to learn how to carry love and hate, joy and pain. Even as I write this, I find myself becoming defensive. It is truly exhausting to hold space for this understanding. It is a weight so great that many will not speak to it and instead retreat into their shame instead of rejecting the preconception that unequivocal gratitude must be a requirement of motherhood.

The Silencing of Toxic Positivity

Birth trauma is often minimized with two seemingly inconsequential words: "at least." This phrase requires trauma survivors to always look on the bright side: "At least, you survived; "At least, she is healthy"; At least... This type of toxic positivity can break an individual and put instant metaphorical tape over the survivor's mouth. It asks the one suffering to keep a positive mindset, regardless of the events. Toxic positivity often ignores the event's details and the short- and long-term impacts. It substitutes empathy for the survivor for dismissing any emotions not connected to joy, happiness, and celebration. It asks the survivor to focus on the bright side instead of being immersed in a world of darkness as a result of unanticipated birth trauma.

I remember the first time I was told "It could have been worse"—another toxic positivity phrase. I was lying in my hospital bed after surviving a hemorrhage, and a nurse looked at me and said those words: "It could have been worse."

I looked up and imagined saying: "Really? Yes, I agree. I am very aware of the fact that it could have led to my death, to me leaving my brand-new baby and my partner behind." I remember looking at her and wishing so badly that I could say "And it could have been better." That nurse's words stuck with me, and today, looking back, I realize that in the first few months after my birth trauma, I downplayed all that I had faced and continued to face; it could have been worse. Toxic positivity creates a state of confusion in the survivor and unrest; they begin to question whether how they are feeling is acceptable and permitted. My experience could have been better.

The Anniversary, AKA the Birthday

Many mothers must never expose the pain surrounding the birthday of their little one, especially when birth trauma is part of the story. In the birth trauma community, the birthday is known as the anniversary of the day the mothers' lives were forever changed—not just by the child's birth that they are madly in love with but by experiencing one of the worst days of their life. This is such a confusing state of existence: to be both excited and emotional that your little one is turning one (or another age) and to be debilitated with painful flashbacks. Mothers are not allowed to show this; they must be the birthday host and only express great joy on their child's birthday. They cannot leave even an ounce of space to grieve all that could have been. Again, they turn quiet and internalize, not wanting to take up space even though the emotions they experience may be intense.

Here is the thing about trauma: The body remembers even if we desperately do not want to (Kolk). The symptoms appearing at the time of the anniversary are not intentional, and survivors do not intentionally call forward memories from that time. The body brings them forward. Trauma survivors are often overlooked or dismissed as they struggle with the dichotomy of what that day means. Cheryl Tatano Beck argues there is a "failure to rescue" the mother on birthdays. I would argue that it is not just a failing to go unacknowledged and undiscussed on a day of great celebration. To stand there in love and pain is utterly exhausting and demands a great deal of effort and energy. My little one's birthday and the day of my first birth trauma anniversary were happy. But the day before, I was not: I sat sobbing in my living room as my body ached with the memories of it all. I felt like I couldn't move. I experienced flashbacks of how fast things went after my water broke when I got back from a long walk. Watching the video we took just moments after my water broke unsettles me in an unexplainable way. We both look so happy, so excited to give birth at home and meet our daughter. The day before her birthday, I was reminded of it all, reliving it. It made sense for this to surface the day before her birthday because the day before she was born was when my home became such an unsafe place due to the midwifery violence that would forever change me. The anniversary date and the attached symptoms, memories, and feelings do not necessarily happen the day of, nor are they predictable. They can show up the days and weeks leading up to and afterwards. These intense emotions need to be normalized to create safe spaces for women to grieve and express the symptoms as they arise, making room for mothers to process them instead of trying to ignore them.

Secondary Silencing

I found the courage to report my midwife for the violence she inflicted on me. Today, it seems ironic, albeit healing and empowering, to run an Instagram page for over sixteen thousand survivors and to support them in finding their voice and offering a supportive space but not be able to share the full truth of my own. When mothers find the bravery to share their traumatic birth experience and demand that changes be made to systems and people be held accountable, they are often told to be quiet; they are told that it is for their own good, not to advance the report they have made. Increasingly, I find myself reflecting on how these practices help hide the imperfections of a less-than-perfect system.

It has been over a year since I first reported my midwife and over a year of limited communication with the association. I have asked them questions and for clarification about where they are in this process, yet they respond only intermittently. In these moments, they are quick to silence me; they remind me that these things take time and that they are doing their best.

I remember the day I got the phone call. It was the day they discovered my Instagram page and the following I had amassed. I was reminded that I could not speak about my own experience and could certainly not mention who my midwife was. I remember the outrage I felt; once again, I was being silenced by their fears of what this would do to their reputation. I remember reminding the woman with whom I spoke that I have every right to share my story. The feeling of defeat was heavy when I hung up the phone. We both knew that I did have a right to use my voice, but if I wanted this reporting process to be successful, I would need to be quiet. I would need to let things unfold as they were meant to and hope my voice would be heard.

Today as I write this, I feel that I am one of the lucky ones. Hundreds of women have messaged me over the last year to share that they have reached out to their respective associations in Canada, the United States, the United Kingdom, and other parts of the world. The majority of them share how they were immediately silenced, how their concerns of abuse and neglect were shut down, dismissed, and denied, and how the impact of silencing left further layers of trauma.

After trauma occurs and goes unnoticed, it often grows and so too does the shame, guilt, and self-blame, which often turn into self-silencing, as society supports those who perpetuate the status quo and try not to challenge its many imperfections. So many survivors never feel safe enough to take up the space required to begin the reporting process, so they do not report the abuse, neglect, violence, and mistreatment they received during their most vulnerable moments as they enter motherhood.

They deny their own experiences by taking cues from the reactions of others around them.

And then there are the trolls, and here, I am not talking about the scary-looking gnome that sits under the bridge that you must pay a toll to pass. I mean the faceless troll, who sits on the other side of your screen and decides that your story must be silenced. Oddly enough, I did not expect it. I thought that people would understand that not everyone's birth goes as planned and that for many, it ends in trauma.

I was quite naïve to it all. I remember the first message I received from a troll who wanted me to shut down my account. I opened up my direct messages, thinking it would be yet another individual sharing their story with me and instead was met with the words: "You fear-mongering bitch, who do you think you are that you would try and turn a beautiful thing like birth into this. You should be ashamed of yourself." My heart sank and then sped up; I could feel the tears threatening to spill over as I held my breath. I did not know what to do. So, I apologized as every good woman does and thanked them for their feedback. There I sat, thinking that maybe they were right—maybe I should not be running a page like this.

My intent was never to create unnecessary fear in others, but maybe I was wrong to provide this space. I received more messages over the weeks, which were the darkest ones of hosting my Instagram page. Now I know that for every negative message I get, there are hundreds more thanking me for providing a platform for mothers to share their stories. Many have said that the page saved their life, gave them the freedom to speak their truth, and made them feel less alone.

Secondary silencing is powerful; we are made to feel that our trauma and pain should not be shared, let alone mentioned, which further perpetuates the intense shame that is often carried after a traumatic birth. Secondary silencing creates a sense and indication of telling the survivor to go back into the pit of isolation they emerged from and stay there. Within isolation, trauma symptoms grow and become magnified. When the troll silencing showed up in public, I was concerned for the survivors reading it. Today, I have found a way to turn that form of silencing into an educational tool. I have begun to share those trolling messages on my page, in posts, and on my Instagram stories so that the conversation becomes bigger and deeper than the initial mean and threatening message. I take the threat of being silenced, and I blow it up. I stay on top of it and magnify why we should get even louder about it. I remind my followers that together we are much more powerful than messages that insist we shouldn't be.

Breaking the Silence Surrounding Birth Trauma

It only feels right to end with a question that I am often asked on invited podcasts: "What can be done about birth trauma. What can women do to prevent it?" I always give the same answer, which takes people by surprise. I truly believe that we need to stop looking to the survivor for those answers and instead need to look to the very systems and providers that perpetuate birth trauma. We need to stop looking to victims to solve issues not in their control. Having a conversation like this—that is, understanding the life cycle of trauma and how we can disrupt it—is how we support survivors. We create safe, educated, and compassionate spaces for mothers to speak their truth, to shout it at the top of their lungs if they can, and find a community. The silencing that takes place surrounding birth trauma needs to be broken to make way for prevention, and this can only happen by bearing witness to and acknowledging survivors' experiences. We need committed systems that stress that the birth could have gone better instead of it could have gone worse.

To every survivor I have ever met through the work that I do in my therapy room and online, know that I hear you, I support you, and I believe you. I stand next to you and will find every way that I can to amplify your voices. Your voices, they matter. You matter. We matter. There is an amazing community that stands with you and sees the incredible value and potential healing to be found by sharing your story.

Works Cited

Altman, Molly, et al. "Information and Power: Women of Color's Experiences Interacting with Health Care Providers in Pregnancy and Birth." *Social Science & Medicine*, vol. 238, no. 1, 2019, pp. 1–9.

Beck, Cheryl Tatano. "Birth Trauma: In the Eye of the Beholder." *Nursing Research*, vol. 53, no. 1, 2004, pp. 28–35.

Beck, Cheryl Tatano. "The Anniversary of Birth Trauma: Failure to Rescue." *Nursing Research*, vol. 55, no. 6, 2006, pp. 381–390.

Gough, Elizabeth, and Vaitsa Giannouli. "A Qualitative Study Exploring the Experience of Psychotherapists Working with Birth Trauma." *Health Psychology Research*, vol. 8, no. 3, 2021, p. 9178.

Kolk, Bessell van de. *The Body Keeps the Score: Brain, Mind, and Body in the Healing of Trauma*. Viking, 2014.

MacDorman, Marian, et al. "Racial and Ethnic Disparities in Maternal Mortality in the United States Using Enhanced Vital Records, 2016–2017." *American Journal of Public Health*, vol. 111, no. 1, 2021, pp. 1673–81.

Reed, Rachel, et al. "Women's Descriptions of Childbirth Trauma Relating to Care Provider Actions and Interactions." *BMC Pregnancy Childbirth*, vol. 17, no. 21, 2017, pp. 1–10.

Turkmen, Hulya, et al. "The Effect of Labor Comfort on Traumatic Childbirth Perception, Post-Traumatic Stress Disorder, and Breast-feeding." *Breastfeeding Medicine*, vol. 15, no. 12, 2020, pp. 779–88.

4.

After Birth:
After Raoul Fernandes's
Poem "After Lydia"

Libby Jeffrey

Sally buried her placenta under the oak tree she used to climb. Liz laid
in bed as semis and buses shook her house. Nadia took a picture
of her bleeding nipples hoping to never forget this pain. Robin drowned
out the phantom cries by ripping the beige mesh hospital panties
into a dozen shreds. Patty cursed like her life depended on it. (It did.)
Brigette watched the digital clock, wailing the minute it struck one
week since his birth. Monica baked and shopped and stopped sleeping
entirely. Maggie wondered where the nurse put her placenta.
Garbage bin? No one asked me. And then Jackie remembered the baby,
and she gasped.

Artist's Statement

After reading Raoul Fernandes's poem, "After Lydia," there was one thing I couldn't unsee. I needed to write a poem that mirrored the tiny moments, actions, and contexts in which women experience postpartum. At the time of writing, I was facilitating birth story writing sessions. Although each instance and persona in this poem was from my imagination, the raw tension of the first hours and weeks postpartum was often in my mind. To my delight, it did not require many drafts to feel "After Birth" was complete in its emotional truth.

Part II

Disorientation—Searching for Stable Ground

5.

Lines, Your First Smile, Separation Anxiety

Leanne Charette

Lines

The blank space
where the second line should be
remains stubbornly empty, as do I;
one tiny dash dividing me from motherhood
I turn the test this way and that
trying to see lines that aren't there.

Moons wax and wane while I remain
static;
searching the night for parallel lines,

until long-awaited daybreak,
when the second line burns like filament
after waiting so long in darkness.
But he squints at them, "Are you sure?"
So faint they're nearly swallowed up

by the blankness behind.

"Don't get your hopes up."

But dormant dreams sprout wings,

take flight.

Because of you.

Tiny curling and twisting lines

the cords that bind us

as you dance, silver-white against a velvet black curtain

two hearts flickering on the screen

smaller than a whisper

you are more,

more

than I expected.

Galaxies smaller than my thumb.

And I am more and more still

the striae spread,

reddish purple

with gilt silver edges

radiating from my navel

as your roots inextricably tangle with my soul,

redrawing the parameters of who I am.

They cut a line and tear you from me,

scissors sever our connection.

State the boundaries of where

I end

and you

begin.

You're placed in my arms,

lines and plastic tubes pulling, catching;

tiny fingers entwined in my hair.

The scarred earth aches, where your roots were torn.

The lines between creation and destruction,

asleep and awake,

me and you,

diminish.

If you ask me who I am,

I say your names.

I write my name on the line that says "Mother,"

the borders fade as the ink dries,

the boundaries of myself are redrawn.

What lies beyond falls away,

and I can't pick it up,

my heart, my hands, too full.

Spilled milk and sloppy kisses,

sticky hands stretched for mine

smudge the edges of myself.

Yet you are incandescent.

Tired colours fade in your brightness,

your hues more vivid than mine.

Threadbare, old dreams and grass stains washed away,

once bright, now dull,

folding myself neatly

tucked away on the back shelf,

stale and creased;

I try to trace the lines of who I am,
but they all lead straight to you.

And you,
binary stars,
illuminate even my darkest shadows,
as you centre me within your orbit.
And yet

My outline is nearly swallowed up
by the blankness behind.
I squint at it, trying to see lines that aren't there,
the ink bleeds and the lines blur.
I am small, boundless,
enlarged, reduced
deep ocean spread thin by the tides.

Notes on "Lines"

I remember being told, early in my mothering journey, that young babies lack a sense of self and can't tell where they end, and their mother begins. I found this was also true in reverse. As a young mother of twins, there was always a baby or two in need of a feeding, a diaper change, or a nap against my skin, and with so little time to think of my own needs, I felt myself begin to fade. When doctors would ask how I was doing, I'd automatically respond by telling them how my babies were doing, how often they fed, or how long they slept. I couldn't tell where I ended, and they began. I had tucked myself away on a back shelf, behind an ever-growing pile of onesies in need of washing, and I couldn't find myself again. What began with months of hoping, searching for those two lines on the pregnancy test that would declare me a mother, went on to become a search to uncover the blurred boundaries between myself and my desperately wanted, endlessly needy children.

"Lines" describes this search, voicing the often-unspoken tension between joy and grief, lost and found, in motherhood. Just as the tides lead to an endlessly shifting shoreline, so too is my identity as a mother and an individual being continually reshaped. I will continue discovering new aspects of myself throughout every phase of life and parenting.

Sometimes this rediscovery process looks like grief, as in this poem; at other times, it looks like joy.

Your First Smile

Your first smile

was at 5:00 a.m., bleary-eyed morning feeding

as first light pierced the curtains, smote my sleepless eyes,

this tiny daybreak spreading across your face.

The dawn made halos in my matted hair,

for I was your sun, your eyes shining as they

beheld me rising faithfully in the East.

But I was no luminary. A cold surface

always half in darkness

fit only to orbit you,

reflect your light.

Love eclipsed by terror,

I pressed your first smile to my chest,

my eyes seeing starvation in your plump wrists and rolling thighs

"Why won't you drink?"

Notes on "Your First Smile"

This poem was born of my experience with postpartum depression and anxiety, putting into words the shadow that was cast over the sweetest memories and milestones of my children's early lives. I remember meeting my son's first gummy smile with terror. Didn't he know he would waste away if he spent his time smiling instead of eating?

I pushed the smile I had once dreamt of treasuring into my breast, heedless of his dimpled cheeks and healthy, pudgy legs, desperate to feed him before he starved.

Only later did I mourn the loss of this first smile, and so many other firsts, to such fear and sorrow, wondering how I could be the light of my children's lives when I felt so dark inside.

In writing of and describing this darkness, I can shine light on these memories, reclaiming them from the shadows, and discover their hidden pinpricks of light, no matter how deeply they are buried.

Separation Anxiety

They pulled the first relatives I'd ever known from my belly;

my skin was home, my voice safety,

tiny screams subsiding at the beating of my heart.

This disabled body, these restive arms, a haven.

I rolled my wheelchair back and forth,

and they were still.

But when tiny backs arched and stiffened in my hold,

doctors, friends, and passersby with narrowed eyes

sang the refrain:

You just need to relax. They can smell your fear.

And I tried deep breathing whenever I reached for my babies,

the crash and roll of each breath

not quite overpowering

the sharp hiss of worry

from my tight-throated audience,

who never failed to whisper,

Don't drop the baby!

They took the first relatives I'd ever known from my arms

at the slightest whimper

because I just needed to relax.

Until my skin wasn't home,

and my wheels didn't soothe,

my children crying when abled arms

extended them towards me.

Almost as though

They could smell your fear.

Notes on "Separation Anxiety"

I met my first blood relatives the day I gave birth to them. A disabled adoptee, I was lying in an operating room awaiting the Caesarean section that would bring my twins into the world. I had already attracted quite a large audience, ready to watch the spectacle of my entrance into motherhood, and I was deeply aware, the way an object of stares always is, that I was being closely watched.

This scrutiny has continued throughout every phase of my parenting journey. From the very beginning, nurses shook their heads disapprovingly, whispering about my perceived clumsiness when feeding my babies. They asked repeatedly whether I would ever be alone with my children, only stopping this barrage of questioning when I was pushed to respond that I would not. I was familiar with the fact that many disabled parents face difficulty in having their right to parent respected, and I knew that far too many disabled parents lose custody of their children simply for having a disability, but this blatant ableism shocked me nonetheless.

Once home, these attitudes continued to erode my confidence and damage my bond with my children.

Family members would gasp each time I picked up my children, filling me with fear, then criticize me for being anxious.

Helpers would swoop in to remove a fussing baby from my arms until they could only be calmed by the motions of walking, the gentle rolling of my wheelchair no longer the soothing safe haven it had once been.

I felt I couldn't complain.

After all, I was so fortunate to have abundant help! Yet it was this help, steeped in ableist assumptions about my ability to parent, that robbed me of a deep bond with my children in the early weeks of motherhood.

As an adoptee, bearing the unconscious scars of separation from my birth mother, this was an unspeakable pain.

For many disabled parents, the right to raise their children is fully denied, with loss of custody documented to be as high as 80 per cent for parents who are intellectually disabled (National Council on Disability). Loss of the right to parent can also take many subtler forms. Those who can raise their children at home often face a lifetime of scrutiny resulting from the pervasive and patently false idea that disabled people cannot, or should not, parent.

These attitudes cause harm to parents and children. My postpartum depression and anxiety, fuelled by pervasive judgments, were largely untreated. I was terrified to be seen struggling, already so conscious that my disability alone placed my mothering ability under suspicion.

Like many mothers from oppressed groups, I was afraid to access mental health care, fearing that biased practitioners would find me unfit.

All mothers should feel safe to voice their mental health struggles with the confidence that they will be supported in their right to parent. I have since recovered and share a deep, joyful bond with my children.

This poem was written in the hope that more mothers, especially disabled ones, will be able to have the same outcome.

Works Cited

National Council on Disability. *Rocking the Cradle: Ensuring the Rights of Parents with Disabilities and Their Children. NCD.gov.* 20 Nov. 2017, https://www.ncd.gov/publications/2012/Sep272012. Accessed 11 May 2024.

6

Confronting Ableism as a Disabled Mom[1]

Debra Guckenheimer

S ometimes when you see me, I look like any other mom. But often, you don't see me at all. I'm the mom missing from in-person events. I'm the one asking for a virtual option. When there's a virtual option offered, I'm the one with her camera off, lying down with a toddler climbing on top of me. When I turn on my camera to ask a question, I'm smiling and also wincing in pain.

I miss out on so many aspects of mothering as I become more disabled. Granting moms like me access would take so little effort; instead, we get intense ableism hurled at us by well-intentioned people.

I am a single, disabled mom with multiple disabling chronic illnesses. Sometimes I use a cane, sometimes a walker, sometimes a wheelchair. I am writing this piece from my bed and an adaptive desk that allows me to type while lying down. Next to me is a standing desk whose monitor is connected to the same computer so I can switch back and forth between lying and standing as each position becomes too painful to bear.

Adding to this rollercoaster ride, I developed a rare chronic cerebral spinal fluid leak in 2020 after a lumbar puncture attempting to diagnose some confusing new symptoms of leg weakness and dystonia and worsening brain fog. Other than a six-month reprieve, I have been parenting from my bed or couch with severe pain and a brain injury for the last three years. It's hard for me to complete complicated tasks, fulfill parenting responsibilities, and keep up with the many demands of my health and health insurance. I had to give up my job that I loved to go on disability leave and then was fired for being on leave too long.

That I wrote this at all is a huge accomplishment, which I paid for in pain, money to a caregiver to take over household tasks, and time to address the chaos my medical crisis and ableism have brought to my life. (I can't get my insurance to process my MRI from six months ago or to approve my home physical therapy, nor could the person I hired to help.)

When my pain is high, it is difficult to be my usual warm and calm self. Anyone can see the pain and paleness in my face and the tension in my voice. Pain registers in the part of the brain that processes danger, so while my body sends danger signals, I have to find a way to send signals of safety to my children. I have light sensitivity, and it's hard to keep my eyes open sometimes. I get dizzy and drop things. I lose words. My children ask why I can't take them outside to play in our backyard.

It's hard to get help, especially with increased COVID-19 risk. Asking for help and getting turned down waste my precious spoons.[2] Hiring help is difficult, expensive, and adds to our COVID-19 exposure. One of my caregivers could not get vaccinated because of an underlying health condition is higher risk so would arrange to be here when my children were not. Caregiving companies serve either seniors or children and are not willing to provide support to a disabled middle-aged adult and her children—if you have savings to afford that.

Having a caregiver means giving up your autonomy and how you like things done. One person I hired left wet clothes in the dryer for so long that I got a fungal infection on my knees, which my body isn't powerful enough to fight off months later. Another shrank my clothes in the wash, which I couldn't replace easily because I am not able to go inside a store to try things on, and I gain and then lose large amounts of weight depending on what medication I'm on and my level of nausea. And for this, I will drain my children's college fund because my condition would worsen if I do it myself. I don't have family to help me, and I don't yet qualify for the limited underpaid help provided by the government.

Many people judge me and tell me everything I'm doing wrong to make themselves feel better subconsciously. There isn't much support for moms like me, and school communities are not well set up for us. For example, one of my children's schools has an equity initiative that only has in-person meetings and has announced that if you don't attend in person, you can't participate. They say it is because the meetings are interactive, gaslighting me that hybrid or fully virtually meetings aren't possible.

Ableism is not just discrimination against disabled people. It's the systemic erasure and dehumanization of disabled people. Ableism leads to the exclusion of not only me, but also my children. This chapter is an act of protest, challenging readers to rethink what makes a good mom and the painful ways in which we judge one another

For so very long, I have been too embarrassed by my story to share it. I tried to pretend that I didn't have these insurmountable hurdles. I worried that people would think that I didn't deserve to be a mom because of my disabilities. I've overheard teachers, other parents, and even my ex talk about me as a burden even in front of my children. They fail to see the amazing mother and human that I am. I realize that you, dear reader, may judge and pity me too when reading my story.

So I learn about disability justice to be able to let go of my internalized ableism and to fight for access. Disability justice is an approach to resisting ableism by recognizing that everyone has needs, disabled or not. Disability justice is a framework that allows rethinking motherhood and community altogether. When we honour the needs of everyone's bodies, we are all better off.

All moms have needs, and the more we focus on supporting the diversity of mothers' bodies, the better for us all.

I take a deep breath and vulnerably share my story in hopes of change.

The way the world responds to me as my disability changes is devastating. What my kids and I miss out on makes this very isolating and heartbreaking.

But it's not my disability that makes us miss out: It's lack of access. The community camping trip is held in a location that requires a lot of hiking, crossing water, and sleeping in tents. So many school events, afterschool activities, and other children's birthday parties are only held in person in spaces that aren't wheelchair accessible (I often look to see online if such spaces are available in advance, or I ask the host whose event I'm attending if they have space). The family members who won't visit here make my children navigate sometimes complicated relationships without me present.

And Then There Was the Camp…

When your kids have minority identities, it helps to build a community reflective of those identities. I work hard to ensure that my children are supported by using resources that fill in the gaps that I cannot because I take my responsibility as a white adoptive mom of Black Latinx children seriously. So, when I found a camp for adopted children of colour and their families, I knew I had to find a way for my family to attend.

We missed the camp for a couple of years, hoping my health would improve enough to attend the next year. Then my spouse took our child alone. When he returned home, he told me that the camp wouldn't work for me; he also told me how hard it was on our child that I wasn't there and that he felt our child needed my presence. (I felt pressure to either cause myself harm or be a bad mother.)

After a two-year pandemic hiatus, camp was held at a new location that was supposedly more accessible. Armed with a new electric reclining wheelchair (new to me because my insurance wouldn't cover the ten thousand dollars for a brand-new one), I decided to give attending a go with my now two children. Not able to do it myself, I asked my spouse to arrange accommodations, especially around food, since I have several severe food intolerances. Consuming the wrong foods could take away my ability to participate in camp.

People with disabilities often have to pay extra charges to access services; scholars call this the "disability tax." For our disability tax (Olsen et al.), we had to get a much more expensive room that was closer to the main building and had a kitchenette that would enable me to prepare some of my food, although I hoped that I could do well enough not to have to use it much. We also rented an expensive wheelchair van for the first time to bring my wheelchair to and from camp because the one (double the price of a regular van) I was buying wasn't available yet. The arrangements took hours and multiple awkward conversations.

I stayed in my room alone and rested while other parents were socializing and attending programs. When I did come out to socialize in my wheelchair in spaces that were hard to manoeuvre without good aisles, it was awkward. The one exception was that another mom who had an invisible disability found me and helped me feel less alone.

The camp was not accessible to me. Attempting to engage, I waited in line for food and felt countless stares for doing so in my wheelchair, only to find nothing labelled, so it was unclear if anything was safe for me to eat. Embarrassed, I wheeled out with a plate on my lap with little food. Because the camp was held largely indoors, sometimes in big groups with no social distancing, I didn't feel safe participating because three-quarters of my family was at higher risk for COVID-19.

Had I known this upfront, I would not have gone.

Someone else's child came up to me repeatedly, pointing and saying, "Your legs are weak." My child was humiliated.

I depended on my spouse to make arrangements for me, and when he didn't, and I experienced harm, I felt hurt. My marriage was already strained from the pandemic and years-long medical crises. This was yet another nail in the coffin of my marriage.

Some sessions were held over Zoom, but when I asked to watch them from my hotel room, my request was ignored. Eventually, I got an email saying I would get a Zoom link to the program; I prepped to attend, waiting for an email with the link while refreshing my email as the program started and then ended. I asked my spouse to get to the programs early, ask for permission, and call me with his phone close to the presenters so I could listen. Each time, I would sit in grief and anger that I didn't even get an acknowledgement that a link or phone call wasn't coming.

Desperate to participate in the camp, I attended a smaller group discussion even though it was indoors. I had difficulty entering the room with my wheelchair because the entrance was blocked by a chair holding the door open. Chairs were arranged in a circle for participants, and I had to move a chair to make space to join the circle. Since this was one of my first times using my reclining power wheelchair, and I suffer from dizziness, I was quite clumsy about it and felt awkward stares. After a few others entered the room, some without masks, the leader suggested, "Let's make the circle smaller, so we can be more intimate." *But doesn't that increase our COVID-19 risk?* I thought to myself as the leader passed out pens and paper so that we could write down our hopes for the discussion group. I wrote, "I hope I don't get COVID."

She collected the papers. We took turns reading anonymously. When mine was read out loud, the group laughed as though I was making a joke. Was I glad it was anonymous! I felt mortified that my need for precautions was being mocked.

When someone in the group said that it was important to meet accessibility needs and suggested we move outside next time, I held my breath. Then, a man said, "I would be more comfortable staying inside." And the discussion ended there.

But I wouldn't let that stop me. I reached out for help. I wrote to camp staff again asking for more COVID-19 precautions and reminded them of my request for Zoom links to attend sessions. Staff either ignored me or told me that I would get a link soon. They said they weren't used to Zoom, were unsure how to do it, and were too busy to figure it out. I suggested that I help find someone at the camp to help.

I wrote to an ally involved in the organization who was not at the camp that year to help me strategize. She also helped me contact my small group discussion leader and asked her to move our group outdoors.

The move outdoors was quite awkward. From the looks I got, I feared that my peers in my small group knew it was me who made the request. I got the sense that many were not happy about meeting outside. The space was not well thought out, so it was difficult to hear everyone. Instead of having one larger group, led by a leader, we self-led ourselves around three tables but were so close together that we heard everything said at the tables next to us.

I felt like an outsider in the discussion. I felt different because of my disability. I felt isolated because my children's adoption stories did not seem to fit within the group's experiences, and the facilitator was at a different table, so she couldn't help us navigate this.

After the group ended, it was time to pick up my child from their program. I wheeled to a space outside the room where my child's program was being held. I felt so awkward until one of the participants from my group, a Hollywood actress whose work I admire, came over and chatted with me for a bit, making my day. For a moment, I felt like a person.

As the space became crowded, another mom standing next to my chair said, "I wonder why they don't let you pick up your child from the other side, since it's not crowded there at all." I replied, "I haven't been successful at securing accommodations so far, so I don't feel like I can ask, but that would be amazing." These two conversations with other parents were some of the only ones I had at camp, so I felt pretty proud of myself until I heard that the head of the camp talked about the importance of apologizing when mistakes are made. She then apologized for a racist interaction between the hotel staff and the children from the camp. When my spouse told me this, we were surprised she saw the lack of access that largely kept me out of camp as not apology-worthy.

One of my children caught a mild cold that caused a sudden severe asthma attack while the two of us were alone in our hotel room. I injured myself trying to find and administer the hidden inhaler while the poor kid was vomiting from trying so hard to breathe. Ironically, this was why I asked for virtual participation, and I still had not gotten a link to participate virtually. I felt neglected.

During the final program, all the children performed outdoors. The space was crowded, and chairs blocked the entrance. I handed over my youngest kid to my spouse to move closer so they could see. I found my way to the back of the space, the only option with my wheelchair, but balloons blocked my view. I hoped someone would take a video for me. The physical barriers felt like a metaphor for my camp experience. I felt heartbroken and wanted to cry.

When everyone went to take a camp photo, I hung back and waited, saving my spoons for the trip home. Why pretend I was a part of camp when I hadn't participated despite all my best efforts?

A few people approached and told me they were disappointed at the lack of accessibility, including the mom of a disabled child. A woman told me that she had been alienated from the camp because of her queerness, but that with advocacy things did change and would around disability as well. While I heard from these allies, I never received an apology from the organizers other than a gaslighting email with some recordings after camp was over. If they could record the session on Zoom, why couldn't they send me the link to listen in real-time or acknowledge that was their plan earlier?

Most people walked by me as if I wasn't there, increasingly so as the camp continued. I felt ashamed and unseen. Most people didn't respond to the camp Discord conversations, where I asked for more access. I felt unheard.

Allies at the camp told me that my access issues were viewed through a lens of white privilege without accounting for ableism. Some participants and staff felt that white parents take up too much space at the camp and saw my requests for accommodations within that framework of a privileged mom taking attention away from the kids of colour. I have experienced this pattern in spaces for kids of colour when I bring up access issues.

By the end of the camp, I had spent a lot of money at a time when I had huge medical bills; my pain had become more intense, and my family felt traumatized. The following year, our application to attend the camp was denied. This experience was not unusual for me. The following years, our applications to attend the camp were denied.

Ableism: Not an Uncommon Experience

I know that my experiences are not uncommon: paying a disability tax, experiencing countless instances of inaccessibility, feeling invisible or judged, and navigating ableism while mothering amidst severe health issues and pain.

I know that ableism is the root of the harm and barriers that keep mothers like me out of events, not our disabilities. It is a double-edged sword because when we are not there, we are judged as incapable mothers not worthy of being included.

I know that the first step in reclaiming the narrative and beginning to dismantle the ableism that interferes with our ability to mother is to find our collective, share our stories, stand up for our rights, and work to dismantle oppressive systems. And so, I begin.

I connect with other moms with disabling chronic illnesses who willingly share their experiences with me; I also draw from online posts revealing the complexities of motherhood experienced by chronically ill people. Sharing these stories sometimes brought tears, anger, and guilt because of the intensity of these struggles, especially when experienced in isolation.

I discovered that many chronically ill moms face ableist ideas coming from their families, contributing to feelings of guilt and shame around internalized ableism. If families focus on what we cannot do and overlook the many things we can do with adaptations and support, day after day, this can lead to internalized ableism no matter how strong and resilient we are. Sometimes, it's overt, as described by one mom in a Facebook group: "Your children just think you're lazy, and they see you in the same horizontal position day in and out." Other times, it is more subtle, as this other mom describes:

The guilt is sometimes worse than the rest of the symptoms combined.... One day, I was bed-bound—pain, unrelenting, and overwhelming fatigue, and a thick brain fog. I don't remember what brought on the flare, but I suspect it was me overdoing it because of choosing to do something extra for my children's school. My oldest... his friend was urging him to come over and play. My eldest came into my darkened bedtime, and I replied, "I can't do that today." ... He told his friend, "My mom won't take me today." That was a decade ago. The sting of me saying "can't" and him saying "won't" is still painful. That story sums up life with ME/CFS [myalgic encephalomyelitis/chronic fatigue syndrome] while being a parent.

Many disabled parents do not have the necessary support from family or friends, and the government rarely provides caregivers. But imagine how different that last story would have been had the mom had someone she could ask to give her child a ride to his friend's house.

Trauma from ableism and sexism experienced in the medical system affects disabled moms' ability to mother. This occurs particularly in cases of invisible disabilities, as expressed by one mom: "I want people to know that when those of us with invisible neurological conditions/diseases/ ailments go misdiagnosed, undertreated, gaslighted due to unfounded old judgmental stigmas, it's not only the mom that impacted but it's her family too. It's her children. It's her whole livelihood. Unnecessary traumas are created."

Women who have health problems—especially related to pain, fatigue, neurological disorders, and other rare conditions—are likely to go undiagnosed or be misdiagnosed with the modern-day hysteria diagnoses of functional neurological disorder or anxiety. (Not that some people do not have anxiety, but it is not the cause of diseases like endometriosis or Ehlers-Danlos syndrome.) Doctors offer only antidepressants, referrals to therapy, and recommendations to practise yoga or meditate. Many diseases affecting only women lack research and are not well understood. The lack of medical treatment and the resultant stress and trauma are hard on moms and their families.

Moms without savings or families to financially support them struggle to survive. It's difficult to get disability benefits, and disabled people report the process taking years. Some are denied benefits despite needing them. One mom posted begging for money from strangers in a Facebook group: "Hey mamas, I'm beyond embarrassed to ask. I have been sick...off and on colds that turned into sinus infections and Lupus flares, so I haven't been able to gain many hours at work. I'm going to be short on rent.... I've never been late on rent, and I'm feeling beyond defeated." In desperation, several moms shared staying in abusive and/or unhealthy relationships out of necessity to survive financially.

Lest you think it is all doom and gloom, disabled mothers report that their children develop high levels of emotional intelligence. For example, one mom noted, "Being so sick in front of my child is causing her to develop so much empathy at such a young age. It's beautiful to see." Similarly, another mom said,

I do find a little solace in the fact that they have grown up to be quite empathetic, thoughtful, helpful children who are grateful (most of the time!). I think (hope) that they will have better relationship skills in adulthood than most men do. I also think they've gained a sense that people get sick unexpectedly and early on in life sometimes—that illness is not just a problem for the elderly. They are aware of invisible illnesses that people often have struggles that we know nothing about when we interact with them. They know that self-care is sometimes really difficult, but they also know how important it is to have a healthy life, physically and mentally.

Despite the guilt and shame thrown at us for not being enough, disabled moms raise some amazing children who are better for having us as their moms.

By naming and calling out ableism and sharing my story along with reflections of other disabled moms, I take back our power, and I position us in the broader experience of motherhood in a predominately ableist world. As I conclude this piece, I enter the space of maternal activism by offering a challenge to the ableist world to treat disabled moms with empathy, compassion, and equity.

Dear Ableist World

I need you to know that disabled moms can be amazing moms. Our kids can be more empathetic and just. When I encounter ableism, my children help me name it, which allows them to understand that sometimes when I am unable to show up (at all or in the way that I want), it is not because I don't want to but because there are outside forces and systemic barriers to mothering while disabled. My children are creative at finding ways to play with me and are powerful allies.

Disabled moms like me need acceptance, love, and support. We need not be judged by others. We need to let go of our own internalized ableism that makes us feel shame and guilt. Supporting moms like me need not be difficult, but it does take some planning to ensure we can fully engage. Learning about ableism and disability justice can help. If you think that a chronically ill person is being rude to you during a conversation, consider that they may be struggling with some severe, distracting symptoms that feel like a loud ringing in their ears and electrical shocks being sent throughout their body.

Know that we want to participate in family and school events, but we need accessible options. Resources are limited, so while you may not be able to make things completely accessible for every person in the world, small things can make a huge difference for the people in your community. If you don't know, please ask. We can let you know what we need. Everyone's needs are different, and sometimes these needs are in opposition, so when in doubt, have a conversation with the disabled people in your community. The easiest way to find out the needs of your community is to have an accessibility coordinator whose information is included in publicity about your events so there is a point person.

You probably already know of some ways to make your events more accessible, such as having virtual participation options with captions, labelling food with common allergens, having an ASL interpreter, and ensuring in-person events are wheelchair accessible with masks required.

Small things you may not have thought of can make a huge difference, such as offering to drive or pick up our kid and sharing photos of events to help with the feeling of missing out. Some moms at my kid's preschool take photos of the classroom board and the nap log for me. That makes me feel so included and parent better.

Even offering to go grocery shopping for us when you go to the store can be huge. One friend texts me a few days before she goes to the store, asking me what she can pick for me. I send her a list, and she drops off the groceries on the ledge next to my front door. I pay her back in an app. It helps so much and makes me feel so loved.

Be proactive and helpful to the chronically ill moms in your community. Invite our children to a playdate or offer to watch them at our place. Share an art or craft kit that our children can do independently. Some friends send me encouraging texts or little gifts. Offer to mask when you are with us or our kids and make sure your kids are masking at school. Advocate for policies to continue mandatory masking, at least indoors or during COVID-19 outbreaks.

Try to avoid giving advice about our health or our parenting. If our accommodation requests are being denied, don't justify that; instead, say what you will do to include us in the future. Many justifications are ableist. For instance, if you say that masking won't be required because many are annoyed with the practice, you are putting the feeling of annoyance over the lives of higher-risk people. If you feel frustrated, angry, scared, judgmental, or critical, deal with that by talking to someone who is not us. Ask us, "How can I help?"

Most importantly, accept us for who we are. We are doing the very best that we can with the resources we have available to use. We are experiencing more pain and suffering than we let on, and that has nothing to do with you. But if you are silent in the face of the ableism in our shared spaces, you are a part of the problem. I invite you to become a part of the solution.

Endnotes

1. Thank you to Shifra Pride-Raffel and Jennifer Brown for their help with edits. Michelann Parr was an amazing editor to work with and significantly improved the piece. I'm so grateful to all of the moms who shared their stories with me.

2. Spoon theory is a concept created by Christine Miserandino. Spoons are a metaphor for the energy that a person has. A chronically ill person has fewer units of energy than others. We need to be strategic about how we spend our limited number of spoons.

Works Cited

Miserandino, Christine. "The Spoon Theory." But You Don't Look Sick, https://butyoudontlooksick.com/articles/written-by-christine/the-spoon-theory/. Accessed 12 May 2024.

Olsen, S.H., et al. "The Disability Tax and the Accessibility Tax: The Extra Intellectual, Emotional, and Technological Labor and Financial Expenditures Required of Disabled People in a World Gone Wrong… and Mostly Online." *Including Disability*, no. 1, 2022, pp. 51–86.

Sins Invalid. "What Is Disability Justice." *Sins Invalid*, 6 June 2020, https://www.sinsinvalid.org/news-1/2020/6/16/what-is-disability-justice. Accessed 12 May 2024.

7

I Am a Mother. I Am an Artist

Claire Haddon

I have worked as an artist and in education for over twenty years. I have always maintained a portfolio career to leave space for art. My prac-tice has centred around photographing familiar situations and changing them. Influenced by structuralist- and process-based ideas, my practice is an inquiry into perception, the process of photography, and often abstract ideas that didn't feature other people. I realize now that my concerns prechildren could be described as quite male-centric; I never felt so female as when I had kids.

I now find myself at a point when I realize that I haven't made the time, space, or opportunity to make art for ten years. But that's not true either. I have worked, just slowly, imperfectly, and have continued to make art for wider purposes, for example, wedding presents for friends, pieces for children, workshops with schools, and some work for myself or an exhibition. Yet I wonder: Where is the proper artwork? Some are in progress, stalled until I find time/space to realize it. Anything relating to my experience as a mother, I haven't shown in public; I felt embar-rassed, isolated, unsure, and so vulnerable. I realize that I have been playing the role of mother while forgetting about my artist-self, deeming it incompatible with family life.

It's not easier not to make art though; although I have been suppress-ing that side of myself, it has been coming out in my dreams and the odd set of photos that I haven't done anything with, beyond take. If we are transformed when we become mothers, my art-self has been in its chrys-alis, struggling to get out. Yet, again, perhaps I need to set aside, or bracket, my preconceived notions and assumptions about life and art and motherhood.

Bracket Life

Imagine my surprise to find myself, as a mother of four, questioning whether, I am, in fact, an artist anymore. Or whether I am creative at all.

It didn't happen as a big whoosh.

In labour, my artist-self was there trying to take
last-minute photos of my pregnant belly before it was no more.
(I subsequently had three more pregnancies so needn't have bothered!)

I took my baby out for walks with my camera.
I took my camera out for walks with my baby.

I took my toddler—sleeping—to my studio.
I lugged the buggy up the stairs.
Fifteen blissful minutes of silence until she woke.

I contributed to a blog *Missing in Action/Mothers in Art*,
discussing and suggesting creative ways to work.

I exhibited artwork and seriously considered each invitation to
Enemies of Good Art gatherings,
even though I couldn't get to any of them.

I fell asleep reading books, visited exhibitions,
and watched children's responses to artwork.

We installed an exhibition with three children in tow,
found a doctor's surgery in an unfamiliar place
because one of them developed a rash
in our very limited set-up time.

Meanwhile, in real life, Dad got ill and passed away, and I lost the one day of childcare that had enabled me to get to the studio.

The needs of my growing family and rigid timetable expanded.

I had to leave my studio as I wasn't using it enough.

We moved to a different house to get studio space at home.

And then, we had another baby.
SURPRISE!

Mum had a stroke; we moved her into a long-term care home and cleared her house of forty years.

And then the pandemic hit.

"Bracket Life" is a prose poem that documents the day-to-day struggles of an artist-mom. I wasn't sure whether to include the poem in my submission but decided to keep it because it shows the self-editing we do as mothers, writers, and artists. I played with inserting and crossing it out, settling into bracketing these bits of life to keep the personal and professional separate.

For many years, I have not been working in the way I would like and because I could not reconcile my new role as a mother with a way of making art, I developed a resistance to making it—not snatching the small amounts of time I did have. I was plagued with questions of

What for?

What's the point?

Is it valid?

How and where will it be seen?

It's too hard. I'll do it later.

Art Outcomes

Outcome 1: Moved studio

Outcome 2: Research

Outcome 3: Sketchbook Work

Outcome 4: Attended Conference

Art Outcomes is a series of images documenting the results of my artistic practice; it sets up an opposition between the positive language of success (as an artist) and images of failure (as a mother). The word "outcome" has become all-pervasive in art, education, child development, and elsewhere. I would love to have a tidy kitchen and engage fully with my children, and often I do. Here I give visual space to the direct results or unintended outcomes of my art practice: showing my neglect and making the invisible labour visible. I find it amusing that I am spending time photographing the mess rather than automatically cleaning it up, but that's the point. Should I be embarrassed or proud? Perhaps I should put the photographs on Instagram.

Abbreviated Curriculum Vitae

Abbreviated Curriculum Vitae: Course of Life

I am a mother	Year	I am an artist	
	1998	BA Hons Fine Art; Exhibition: Glued	Studio Assistant
	1999	Exhibition: Fields of Vision on Land	Darkroom & Studio Assistant
	2000	Exhibition: Street, Eden Project, Resolution	Teaching Digital Photography
	2001	Exhibition: Annual Exhibition	Tutor-Technician
	2002	Exhibition: Glasslight, Les Femmes Digitales, Out There, Bethnal Green Festival	Honorary Fine Art Practitioner
	2003	Exhibition & Community Workshops: Ringing, St Augustine's Tower	Workshop Facilitator
	2004	Commission & Exhibition: Blood & Flowers, Slowfall and Barbican Gallery	Secured Studio
	2005	Exhibition: Siege, Measuring Trees, Intercede	Arts & Crafts Programme Manager
Married	2006	Exhibition: Measure Workshop: Teen Mum's Project, Pump House Gallery	Admin Assistant, Teacher Artist Partnership
Maternity Leave TRL born	2007	Commission: Face to Face, Creative Partnerships Project	Trip to Japan & New Zealand
Returned to work	2008	Exhibition: Open Studios	
	2009	Publication: Blog for MiA (Missing in Action/Mothers in Art)	
Maternity Leave EiL born	2010	Exhibition: Psychometry, NepArtism	Moved Studio, Absorb Arts
Dad died, Returned to work	2011		
Maternity Leave RPL born, TRL starts school	2012	Exhibition: There is a Shadow	Moved Studio, storage
Returned to work	2013		Art & Photography Teacher
	2014	Commission: Photography Collaboration - Black Chronicles, Autograph ABP	
EiL starts school	2015		
Moved house RPL starts school	2016		Art & Photography Teacher
Maternity Leave EiL born	2017		Moved Studio
	2018		Visited Gallery, Shape of Light, Tate
Mum's stroke TRL starts secondary school	2019		Photography Tutor
Covid 19: Homeschooling	2020		Art Tutor
Covid 19: Homeschooling EiL starts secondary school	2021		Missing Mother Conference
Clear & renovate Mum's house EiL starts school	2022		Proposal : Pain Mothers Must Never Expose

Abbreviated Curriculum Vitae (Course of Life) is the result of trying to frame my accomplishments to reflect my life experience: to explore the prominence, emphasis, and narrative we use to present ourselves. It started as a practical exercise to fill in the gaps, reminding myself of all the things I had accomplished (even, as a traditional CV, it would look thin or incomplete). It then developed into an exploration of more conceptual concerns. I am interested in the gaps on the page, how much space the words take up, the structure, and the editing process. Of course, there is a metaphoric element, elevating the status of my work as a woman and mother. I am struck by how little space and language I have given to the gargantuan task of motherhood, yet keeping to the traditional CV format and weight given to such tasks, it is all I can do.

8

Motherlines and *Maternal Entanglements*: Unravelling and Embracing the Multiplicity of Abortion, Embodiment, and the Maternal

Kate Antosik-Parsons

As a multimedia artist concerned with female embodiment and memory, much of my recent work uses photography and performance, focussing on becoming and maternal subjectivity. For me, becoming a mother has profoundly affected how I perceive my identity and my relationship to my body. As an artist in my early twenties, I moved from California to Dublin, Ireland, where I experienced an unwanted pregnancy, or as it was termed in Ireland, a crisis pregnancy and was forced to travel abroad for an abortion. Up until January 1, 2019, Ireland's strict laws forbid abortion in all circumstances, unless continuing the pregnancy would lead to death. Under Article 40.3.3, the Eighth Amendment to the Irish Constitution, the life of the unborn child was equal to the life of the mother. This restriction on the female body is part of a culture in which sex and sexuality are taboo topics.

Historically, women's roles in Ireland have been defined largely by their capability to reproduce within the right circumstances. For me, choosing to terminate an unwanted pregnancy not only transgressed the

KATE ANTOSIK-PARSONS

boundaries of what the perceived status quo deemed acceptable but also contributed to feelings of marginalization and erasure: People who had abortions in Ireland were shamed into silence. During this period, my artmaking felt angry, as it was the only means I had to express the complex layers of emotions associated with not being able to access abortion in the country in which I lived. I painted several works exploring my anger; I recall one large-scale painting on which I scrawled: "Poison, from my bitter mouth." This one, I destroyed.

When I became pregnant by choice years later, I felt an othering—that my abortion had marked my sense of self and my experience of pregnant embodiment. I felt this most profoundly at my first maternity hospital appointment with my eldest child. When the midwife asked about previous pregnancies, I told her about my first pregnancy that ended in abortion. She stopped writing on my form, looked up, and said, "We don't need to mention that." This made me pause: Why wouldn't my reproductive medical history be recorded in my medical files? Just because abortion wasn't legal in Ireland didn't mean that it didn't happen. On two subsequent pregnancies, I made the point of bringing up my abortion when giving my medical history, and I was astonished that these responses bore a remarkable similarity to the first. Was abortion so taboo that I couldn't even mention it to a midwife?

In these two series of works—*Motherlines* and *Maternal Entanglements*—my explorations sought to unravel and render visible the complexities of these entanglements and subvert celebratory or essentialist ideas about motherhood while insisting the need to embrace the layered, multiple, intersecting, and at times messy versions of the maternal. The translation of these artworks from full-colour photography to the monotone reproductions in this text means there is an element of loss to the image; hence, the rich descriptions offered below aim to account for this.

Motherlines

Birthing, 2015

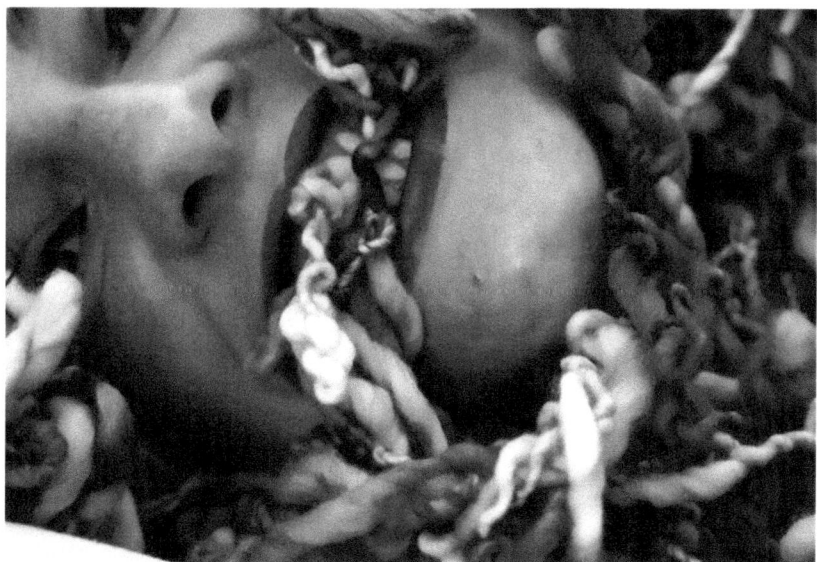

Clenching, 2015

...

Silencing, 2015

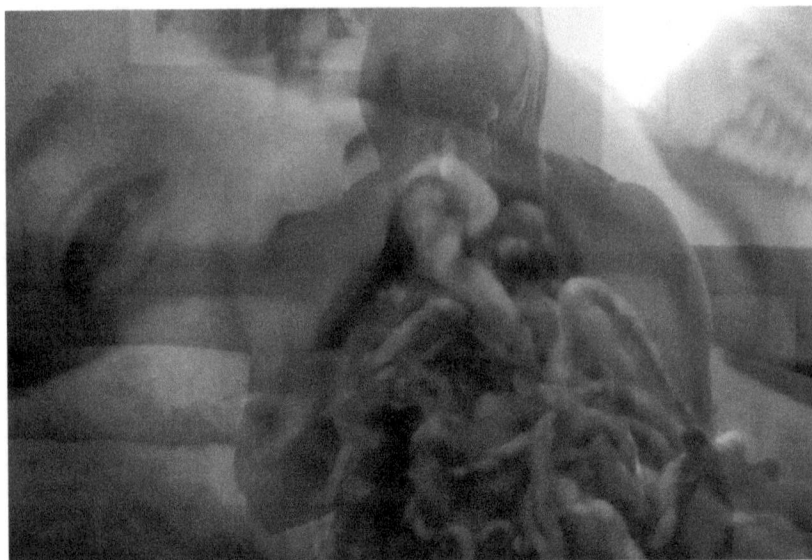

Othering, 2015

Mother and Daughter, 2015

Motherlines (2015) is a series of works in which I consider my fertile body, becoming a mother, and my embodied relationship with my children while engaging with the body's materiality. The origins of this work are found in a poem I published on breastfeeding called "My Maternal Stigmata" (2012), which explores the difficulties I experienced feeding my child. At a spoken word performance event in 2013, I read that poem to a gathered crowd. After my performance, a fellow performer (published in the same collection) took issue with my reference to nipples in front of children. Another writer argued that my poem was about feeding a child, a natural process. This seemingly inconsequential exchange high-lighted how conflicted discussions about the maternal body continue to be, and this experience became a touchstone for thinking about the complexities of what cannot be spoken about.

In the beginning, *Motherlines* (2015) was a series of performative photographs in which I wrapped and revealed different parts of my body with yarn. As the work (un)ravelled, I experimented with yarns dyed in rich colours of yellows, pinks, and purples. Increasingly feeling some-thing deeply umbilical about the work, I began to vary the thickness of the yarn. Ultimately, *Motherlines* centres on becoming and the physical-ity of the maternal body, the marks it leaves on the body, both visible and hidden, and the idea of connections made through the body.

As a mother, I embrace what Andrea O'Reilly terms a matricentric feminist approach as I seek to create social change through my childrearing. Part of this work is actively trying to counter the silences around abortion and different experiences of reproductive healthcare. In 2017 and 2018, I was a feminist community organizer to repeal the Eighth Amendment in the Irish Constitution that prohibited abortion: I canvassed voters in my locality, asserting my overlapping identities as a mother and a woman who had an abortion. Canvassing entailed going door to door and talking about the issue of the constitutional referendum. It meant arriving on people's doorsteps and not knowing whom I would meet on the other side and how they might choose to discuss the issue. By openly talking about my personal experience, I deliberately sought to skew people's sense of abortion and motherhood as incompatible. Alongside this, I was actively engaged in ongoing conversations with my children about the law in Ireland, explaining how it was unjust, what it meant for someone who needed to access abortion, and why I was so personally involved in campaigning for it.

Maternal Entanglements

Elegy, 2017

Ageing, 2017

Roots, 2017

Blood, 2017

Maternal Entanglements (2017) is a series of works borne out of a sense of the slippage I felt between my identity as a woman who chose abortion and a mother at a time when I was thinking intensely about the possibility of change in Ireland. Its origins were in performative experimentation for a commissioned book cover for an edited collection on reproductive justice and transnational feminism. I began by making performances with a pomegranate. First, I cut it open and squeezed the arils between my fingers, their blood-red juices staining my hands, and then I photographed my daughters holding the pomegranate. Later, I left the fruit out to weather in my back garden and then hung it on my washing line next to my laundry. I forgot about it for a while, and when I went back a week later, it had withered; its skin began to take on a leathery texture, while new life, albeit mould, had started to grow on the arils. This became the basis for *Maternal Entanglements: Elegy* and *Maternal Entanglements: Ageing*.

For this project, I used a root ball from a vegetable I had nurtured from seed. I left the root and stalk of the plant in the ground long after it had died, and when I pulled it out of the earth, I was surprised at how large the root ball was and how delicate yet strong its tangled roots appeared. Sourcing other things from my garden, I cut forget-me-nots, the seeds of which were a favour from my friend's wedding.

When I travelled to have my abortion, my friend's mother took care of me so lovingly and gently afterwards. She died of cancer a few years later, and as a remembrance at my friend's wedding, my friend gave out forget-me-not seeds, her mother's favourite flower, in honour of her dear mother. After the wedding, I shook the seeds into my garden, and they spread and returned each year. Forget-me-nots are a symbol of mothers and daughters, interdependence and care. The red string and unfinished quilt have personal significance, as they were inherited from my grandmother; intuitively, I brought them into dialogue with the root ball.

The day after my abortion, I cared for my grandparents. Although I hid my pain well and they never knew that my body was aching and bleeding, it struck me that as I was caring for them, I wished they could reciprocate that care. As I worked with the materials I gathered, I accidentally pricked my finger with a pin and was amazed at the quickness with which the red blood swelled, surging from my finger to drop onto the ground where the root ball lay. The beauty of the pattern of blood droplets around the gnarled roots, coupled with the pain in my finger, felt strangely cathartic.

Works Cited

Antosik-Parsons, Kate. "My Maternal Stigmata." *Embers of Words: An Irish Anthology of Migrant Poetry*. Edited by Theophilus Ejorh. Choice Publishing, 2012, p. 37.

O'Reilly, Andrea. "Matricentric Feminism: A Feminism for Mothers." *Maternal Theory: Essential Readings*. Edited by Andrea O'Reilly, 2nd Edition. Demeter Press, 2021, pp. 457–75.

9.

Pandemic and Pandemonium: Emerging from Emergency

Alex Maeve Campbell and Terry Anne Campbell

Introduction

This is a conversation in prose, poetry, and image; it moves between us, from daughter to mother, and back again. It is set in the context of mothering and daughtering through medical emergencies experienced individually and jointly. The large world context is a global pandemic; the small world context is comprised of events involving immediate family members—a daughter, Alex, and a mother, Terry. Ironically, the medical emergencies did not involve either of us contracting the COVID-19 virus; they occurred during the pandemic and were therefore affected by the pandemic pandemonium of restrictions and chaotic hospital conditions.

Through conversations with one another, we provoke and probe the pain of the serious health problems we have encountered. We examine, explore, and understand these problems and hope to emerge from them into ongoing states of healing, health, and power.

The common threads braiding together our near encounters with death include our voyages into the land of pain; the frustration of being the objects and subjects of medical services that often demean and rarely heal; and our shared love of "The Love Song of J. Alfred Prufrock"[1] by T.S. Eliot.

We take lines from Prufrock as threadings and respond to them by feeling thinkingly and thinking feelingly.

Some emerging themes include the pressures of daughtering and mothering, especially from places of pain, the performing and persuasions inherent in these roles, and, finally, the power that can be plumbed when we go deep enough.

Through the depths of poetry, we seek to uncover, discover, and re-cover our power.

We hope to show how transpositions or transformations from and through pain are temporary but laden with meaning.

Let us go then, you and I,
When the evening is spread out against the sky
Like a patient etherized upon a table... (p. 3)

Threading 1: *And How Should I Begin?*

As we record our conversation, it is February 2023. Some are calling this the postpandemic period, although COVID-19 variants still circulate the world, including our world in North Bay, Ontario. The events we discuss happened during the pandemic dominated by its lockdowns, restrictions, and mandates, such as mask wearing. Our experiences were not directly caused by the virus but were tainted by the timing and circumstances we found ourselves in.

Danger: Falling Rocks by Alex Maeve, 2021

Alex's First Emergency

I know the voices dying with a dying fall
Beneath the music from a farther room.
So how should I presume? (p. 5)

In December 2020, with the pandemic in full swing, I got sick. Various confusing symptoms worsened, and I spent about a week in bed, listening to preparations for the holiday season carolling from a farther room. When it finally became too painful to move, let alone breathe, I did what years of unconditional support told me to do—I reached out to my mother. I texted her, asking her to come get me, ending the message with "It's an emergency." Time would tell just how much of an emergency this moment was. When she appeared at my door, I asked to be taken to the hospital, saying, in pandemic paranoia, "I think I have it." After a tense car ride, we arrived at the hospital, where she physically supported my weakened, staggering body to the door of the emergency room. But due to COVID-19 restrictions, I was forced to continue alone. Beyond the intense physical pain, I also felt intense feelings of separation. Over hours, I was put through a battery of invasive questions, tests, X-rays, and extended periods of waiting, by myself, in a claustrophobically small and seemingly isolated room at the end of a long hallway. As pain shot through my body and I struggled to breathe, at times I wondered if I had been forgotten there. Finally, with difficulty and errant blood that would stain my clothing, two IVs were inserted, and the clothes that painfully hung from my illness-ravaged body were exchanged for a hospital gown. I was brought on a stretcher to a communal room full of other, masked patients in various states of emergency.

And I have known the arms already, known them all—
Arms that are braceleted and white and bare. (p. 5)

Somewhere during this period of flux, I was told that I did not have COVID-19 but a case of acute pneumonia that would keep me in the hospital. After I begged various doctors and nurses for something to ease my body's pain, an obliging nurse finally gave me a dose of morphine, which gave me the strength to reach for my phone. Feeling a strange need to document my predicament, I took photos of myself IV'ed and hooked up to a heart monitor on the stretcher and sent them to my mother, telling her that I would not be coming home and would be transferred to critical care.

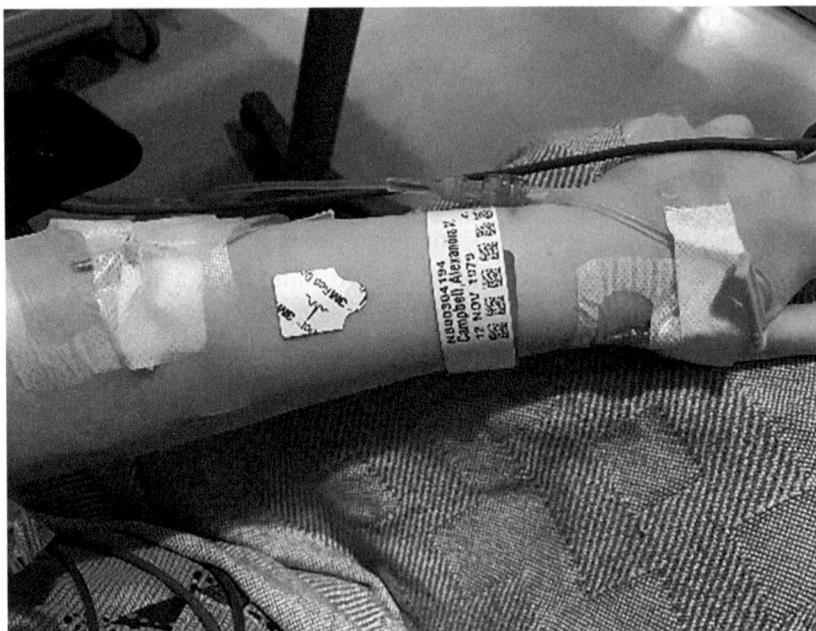

Arm Braceleted and White and Bare

It is impossible to say just what I mean!
But as if a magic lantern threw the nerves in patterns on a screen... (p. 6)

My memory of the next days and horrifying nights is clouded by the experience of the worst pain of my life—the pain of a body that, only later would I find out, was struggling not to die. This was compounded by the pain of a mind trying to make sense of torment in a state of forced separation, in which I cried out in agony for the first time in my life— agony that was met with what can only be described as dismissiveness, bordering on contempt, by nurses stationed in the critical care unit. Unable to reach out beyond my hospital bed, hooked up as I was to seemingly endless IVs and monitors, the only recourse my mother had was to call the hospital to ask what had occurred. These inquiries were met for days with the enigmatic response that I was merely stable.

Weak Signal, by Alex Maeve, 2021

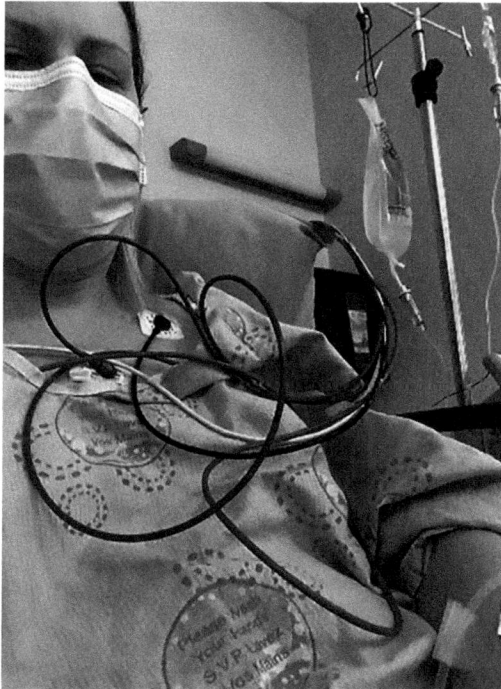

Alex with IVs/Monitor

Threading 2: *Let Us Go and Make Our Visit.*

After days of instability, there came a time that was, comparatively but not entirely, stable. I was moved from the critical care unit to a regular unit in an isolation room, where I was allowed, according to COVID-19 restrictions, one visitor during prescribed hours. Predictably, it was my mother who stepped up to the plate. I had recently turned forty-one, but there is no age when a mother stops mothering. Visitor mandates meant that visiting me involved not only putting on the usual mask, but getting dressed up in a plastic gown, medical gloves, and a visor—just short of a hazmat suit and a getup I joked added a Cronenberg-esque tinge to things. Again, I took photos.

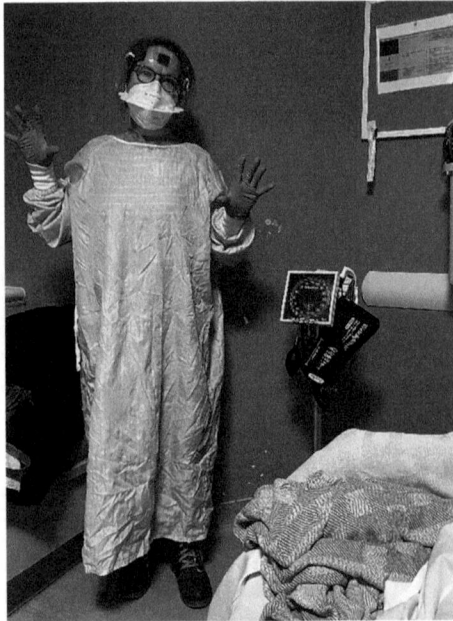

Terry in Hazmat

Just as there is an art to being a good patient, there is an art to being a good visitor, and in this case, perhaps the two combined with being a good daughter and a good mother. I had experienced being a visitor, having had both parents in hospital emergencies multiple times in years past, but this was my first foray as a patient. In this context, I was accustomed to worrying, not to being worried about. But there's nothing easy about being a patient (a title that insinuates an ability, or at least a need, to practise patience) or a visitor (a title that insinuates the very temporariness of that position). I was accustomed to entertaining, not being entertained, yet I learned that as a patient, there is something of the entertainer engrained in the role—you are necessarily on display, being bed and hospital-bound—and I found myself in my weakened yet recovering state slipping somehow easily into that role. Yet there were times, particularly during my second (yet to be explored) emergency stay, that the pain and discomfort of being a patient overcame my ability to be the entertainer. I was forced to experience my mother's worry and care more directly.

Consequently, in our postemergency conversations, we have, on several occasions now, discussed whether it is easier to be patient or visitor and what we end up feeling in each of these roles innately requires of us as a mother and as a daughter. Essentially, no conclusions can be drawn, as both roles require certain types of strength during times of forced weakness and vulnerability, not unlike what the roles of mother and daughter require at various times throughout lived experience.

Let us go and make our visit... (p. 3)

Terry's Notes

After Alex's stint in the ICU, where I was provided with a succinct response to my frequent telephone queries to the nursing station (the desk nurse always fetched Alex's nurse to answer my questions), I was finally allowed to visit my daughter, from whom I had received increasingly alarming texts filled with fear of death and reports of unspeakable pain.

To gain entrance to the hospital, I had to get through the first gatekeeper, who supplied me with a fresh mask. I then had to answer the standard questions about possible exposure to COVID-19 (Do you have sore throat?; shortness of breath?; Have you been in contact with a person with COVID-19?; Have you travelled outside of Canada?... etc. No, No, No...). Next, I had to sign in at the visitor's desk, where I identified the patient I was visiting. (They looked the name up and then phoned the correct unit to see if such a person existed and whether they were allowed visitors.) I declared myself as the patient's "primary care person," signed my name, and agreed to abide by the hospital's two visiting hours—one in midafternoon and one in the evening. Next, I was allowed into the unit where Alex's isolation room was located. I had to present myself at the nursing station, where I was gowned, masked, gloved, and visored—all hazmatted up as Alex put it. I was then allowed into her room. I followed this same procedure for every visit.

Before entering her isolation room, I found myself pausing, taking time.

To prepare a face to meet the faces that you meet... (p. 4)

Each time I visited and saw her lying there, tubes attached and pale as fog, I found myself forcing a smile. (Would she see my eyes crinkle if not the mouth behind the mask?) Was I there to cheer up the patient? Let her know I was there for her? (Pray for her?). We talked. I asked questions, and I listened. (*Are you Lazarus, come from the dead?*)

Each day, she was closer to vertical. One day, I went in and lo and behold, she was sitting up in bed, cross-legged! Hallelujah! So, "*Are you Lazarus, come from the dead?*" I wanted to ask, but I was always worried. Would I seem too eager? Was I expecting her to reveal something, hoping she might say, "*I am Lazarus, come from the dead / Come back to tell you all, I shall tell you all—*? (p. 6)

And there was this thought: that perhaps she,
...settling a pillow by her head
Should say, "That is not what I meant at all;
That is not it, at all." (p. 6)

In short, the visits were fraught. But they were worth it, after all.

Threading 3: *Oh, do not ask, "What is it?"*

Terry's First Emergency

Terry: (from Journal Notes, 02/02/20—all the twos)

On Friday, Jan. 24, I received two pieces of news, one expected, one not:

1. My six-month sabbatical for the winter of 2021 was approved (YAY!)

2. My biopsy taken from my left-breast scar tissue (I had a mastectomy in 2011) came back positive. What? How much will things change? Once treatment begins, plenty, I assume...

Stimulated Emission of Radiation, by Alex Maeve, 2021

Treatment began in March 2020, with daily trips to Sudbury's cancer centre five days a week. Despite the pandemic lockdown, which began on March 20, 2020, treatment continued for eight weeks. I kept the pain hidden from family and friends, even Alex. I could tell she was worried. I didn't want to make it worse for her. (Or let's face it, for me. Better not to talk about it).

Going in and out of the treatment centre during the pandemic lock-down was a pain. Rigmarole getting in and out, questions, masks (I'm okay with those!), and no one allowed to accompany me. (Fine by me!) Other cancer patients wanted to talk. I used headphones to cover my ears and books to engage my eyes and mind. I barely spoke to the radiologists, technicians, and oncologist except to ask a few obvious questions (*Oh, do not ask...*). I followed all the procedures, rules, and advice for follow-up...

Deferential, glad to be of use,
Polite, cautious, and meticulous;
Full of high sentence, but a bit obtuse;
At times, indeed, almost ridiculous—
Almost, at times, the Fool. (p. 7)

I just wanted to get through it. Here I am celebrating successful treatment. The fool rings a bell and everyone in the hub of the cancer centre applauds.

Terry Ringing Bell in Cancer Centre

To be honest, I barely remember those months of treatment. I remember the car journeys to and from Sudbury, playing Leonard Cohen and Bob Dylan in the car, drinking tea from a turquoise thermos, and watching and listening to the ravens circling and calling in the skies above. And I would come home, exhausted.

> I should have been a pair of ragged claws
> Scuttling across the floors of silent seas. (p. 5)

Threading 4: *A Tedious Argument of Insidious Intent*

Assuming the treatment had been a ringing success, I went my merry fool's way. What a presuming fool was I. What was that transitional journey like? We were both recovering and healing both inside and outside our bodies. Alex was left with a chronic cough and damaged throat; I was battling extreme fatigue and burned skin requiring its own treatment. In our conversations, it was not lost on us that our troubles resided in (and on) our chests, the abode of the heart. In time, though, we each returned to work and our usual pursuits but with an obscure sense of dread.

> Let us go, through certain half-deserted streets,
> The muttering retreats
> Of restless nights in one-night cheap hotels
> And sawdust restaurants with oyster-shells:
> Streets that follow like a tedious argument
> Of insidious intent
> To lead you to an overwhelming question...
> Oh, do not ask, "What is it?" (p. 3)

Ask instead, "What is it—this time?"

Threading 5: *In a Minute There Is Time / For Decisions and Revisions Which a Minute Will Reverse*

Alex's Second Emergency

> And would it have been worthwhile,
> To have bitten off the matter with a smile. (p. 6)

Fast forward to February 2021. I had a root canal booked. Not great, but surely no one ever died from a root canal. Then again, nothing is sure. To make a long story shorter, the specialist who performed my root canal may or may not have drilled down too deeply, thus releasing the infection located there into the rest of my body—specifically, my lymph nodes—because about a week after the procedure, I had what I was half-comedically referring to as a goitre on the left side of my neck. I saw my general practitioner, and she sent me to the hospital for tests. Mere hours later, I was being told they would have to operate. Only two months after the pneumonia incident, I was told that I couldn't leave the hospital. Again, I texted my mother. Again. Disbelief abounded. The next thing I knew, I was on the operating table, about to be put under, and a doctor was explaining to me that I might wake up with a breathing tube inserted.

When I woke up, there was, mercifully, no breathing tube inserted. However, I had a tube draining the lymph from the wound inserted into the surgical wound on the side of my neck—a wound that I would later refer to as my "Bride of Frankenstein" look. My neck was so inflamed it started to dwarf my head. Not a cute look. And then there was the pain, which barely made it possible to speak or function in any way, even from a hospital bed. I was being pumped full of antibiotics via IV to fight the infection as well. My body was full of things that it was fighting, and it was in this state that my mother then saw me, and I can only imagine how difficult it was to have a normal reaction to such a view. Being a good patient was all I could focus on, and being a good visitor must have been a challenge.

Once I was released from the hospital about a week later, I would spend the next month and a half regularly visiting a nurse-run clinic to have maintenance done on the massive wound on the side of my neck—gradually removing the draining tube and Bride of Frankenstein stitches and cauterizing the wound. It was in this state a month later that I ended up driving my mother back to the hospital for her life-threatening post-mastectomy. My health took a back seat, almost literally, as I drove my mother back to the hospital after discovering that her wounds were not taken care of as expected, as she was released prematurely from the hospital following her major surgery.

And indeed there will be time
To wonder... (p. 4)

Let us wait now for the next emergency...

Terry's Second Emergency

Almost a year to the day after treatment for the 2020 recurrence of cancer, in March 2021, I underwent mastectomy number two. (Yes, I should have had a bilateral done in 2011, goddammit! And yes, I was right in the middle of that well-earned sabbatical!)

This time, Alex became very much involved. Thank gawd!

In the room the women come and go
Talking of Michelangelo. (p. 3)

So, the date was set for a second mastectomy: let's call it the Ides of March. Unlike 2011, when I was kept in the hospital for three days after that mastectomy (and yes, it was painful in many ways!), this time, in 2021, I was sent home the same day—surgery at 8:00 a.m. and discharged at 3:00 p.m. As before, I had the throbbing pain just barely under control. Alex and I were eating toast and drinking tea in the living room at home (at tea time, around 4:00 p.m.) when I felt something wet and warm down my right side. It was blood. A lot of blood. Alex immediately drove me back to the hospital. We lived not five minutes from the hospital, so this was more convenient than calling an ambulance. My husband (and Alex's father) Keith had gone to the pharmacy to fill my prescriptions.

Due to COVID-19 restrictions, I staggered alone into the Emergency Department. I explained to the triage nurse the basic facts of my predicament. I was taken inside the big double doors immediately. (WOW! I didn't have to wait in the general emergency waiting room!) I was then left alone in a bare room on a bed of sorts, with one sheet, which became quickly soaked in blood. I felt someone would appear soon, but this was not the case. There was no call bell (as I said, the room was completely bare—no equipment, not even a paper cup of water). I slid off the bed, holding the sheet to my copiously bleeding incision, and went to the door. I called for a nurse at the station across the hall. There were several there, chatting it seemed. They all stopped talking and looked over at me. Finally, one of them, a male nurse, moved towards me, got some dressings and one of those large elastic bandages typically used for sprains, and wrapped me up tight. I had not yet been seen by anyone else. No checks on vitals, no conversations, nothing. I was put back on the bare rubberized mattress and stayed there, drifting in and out of consciousness. I really thought I might be bleeding to death.

> *The yellow fog that rubs its back upon the window-panes*
> *The yellow smoke that rubs its muzzle on the window-panes*
> *Licked its tongue into the corners of the evening*
> *Lingered upon the pools that stand in drains....*
> *Curled once about the house and fell asleep.* (p. 3)

When I woke up next (although I hadn't been sleeping), I was in a division of the Emergency Department I had not seen before—a basement, since there were no windows. There was one nurse at a large desk, and various stretchers filled with emergency victims, some with curtains around them, most without. One doctor saw me after several hours. He said the nurse would continue to keep my chest tightly wrapped and that he was trying to find a room to admit me. It was deep into the night by this time. I said that if the bleeding was under control, I just wanted to go home. He shrugged. He did not advise that. Besides, the bleeding was not under control. Did I detect some sarcasm? Then he (the only doctor in the Emergency Department) disappeared for some time. (Was it forty minutes, sixty?). Blood technicians came by periodically and tried to get some blood from my arm. Paradoxically, or perhaps ironically, with all that other blood flowing, they could not find a vein. I said something to this effect; they did not laugh. They poked my fingers. It was almost amusing. And oh, did I mention the pain? By now, the anesthetics and whatever pain meds they had given me that morning were long gone. Someone finally asked about the pain and said they would have to ask the doctor (that same one doctor!). I was given one tramadol.

I have seen the moment of my greatness flicker,
And I have seen the eternal Footman hold my coat, and snicker,
And in short, I was afraid. (p. 6)

But though I have wept and fasted, wept and prayed... (p. 6)

I stayed in that basement all night. I did not sleep. I did not eat. I was allowed one small paper cup of water. Was this in case I needed further surgery? I texted Alex and got the desk nurse to phone home so that I could talk to Keith. He was upset that I was communicating with Alex and not with him.

After that long night...

And I have known the eyes already, known them all—
The eyes that fix you in a formulated phrase,
And when I am formulated, sprawling on a pin,
And when I am pinned and wriggling on the wall,
Then how should I begin... (p. 5)

The following day, at 5:30 p.m., they told me they had to go back in. This was just over twenty-four hours after Alex had saved me—she literally saved my life—by taking me back to the Emergency Department. Yes, more surgery, opening the same incision to clean it all out. It? The hematoma. One nurse said this happens all the time. Her sister-in-law was sent home after a double mastectomy last month and had to come back and have emergency surgery to stop the massive bleeding. Before the first mastectomy, I felt many things but not fear. The second one, I felt anxiety but not fear. This time, though, in short, I was afraid.

I was allowed to stay two nights in the hospital in a private room, where I could have had Alex or Keith (only one designated care person!) come in all hazmatted up, but I declined visitors, opting to talk on the phone, mostly to Alex. During this time, I was seen by three doctors and given Tylenol (regular Tylenol) for the pain. It was a "significant discomfort," as the nursing staff phrased it, but eventually, the bleeding stopped. I was sent home to heal.

> *And would it have been worth it, after all,*
> *After the cups, the marmalade, the tea,*
> *Among the porcelain, among some talk of you and me*
> *Would it have been worthwhile?* (p. 6)

Final Threading: *There Will Be Time. There Will Be Time.* (Combined Poetry of T.S. Eliot, Alex Maeve Campbell, and Terry Anne Campbell)

From frozen, immobile, silenced states
To states of vigilance
To choosing a face,
a performance beyond pain
To power, which when expressed,
   dares disturb the universe
And sometimes,
We return to silence.... But a potent silence.

> *There will be time, there will be time*
> *To prepare a face to meet the faces that you meet;*
> *There will be time to murder and create,*
> *And time for all the works and days of hands*
> *That lift and drop a question on your plate,*
> *Time for you and time for me*
> *And time yet for a hundred indecisions,*
> *And for a hundred visions and revisions,*
> *Before the taking of a toast and tea.*
>
> *In the room the women come and go*
> *Talking of Michelangelo.* (p. 4)

So let us take our toast and tea.
We ask ourselves:
> *Do I dare*
> *Disturb the universe?* (p. 4)
We find the answer between us: Yes.

Endnotes

1. Please note that all italicized lines throughout this piece are quotations from T.S. Eliot's "The Love Song of J. Alfred Prufrock."

Work Cited

Eliot, T.S. "The Love Song of J. Alfred Prufrock" *Collected Poems 1909–1962*. Harcourt, Brace & World, Inc.

10.

Lingering Regrets Revisited

Mandy Fessenden Brauer

It is not always easy being honest, especially when I consider my role as a mother. Now as an octogenarian, eighty-two as I write this, and looking back on my two children's births over fifty years ago, I so often focus on unhappy times, guilt lurking beside the photos on my desk as I ponder what I did and didn't do, what I should have done and what I shouldn't have done. Words spoken in anger or frustration still echo in my thoughts. Do those same moments haunt my daughter and is that why she continues to be uncomfortable with me? Do other mothers feel this way but don't talk about it?

Peering back to those days, I was so filled with unhappiness and depression that I wasn't as aware of my children's emotional needs as I could or should have been. I know that has been the major source of my regrets. Or is it guilt? Perhaps I wasn't that unaware or that insensitive, but, with today's consciousness, I am painting myself in a bad light. I wonder as I explore poems I have written over the years, many of which today seem like personal confessions, if I will then be able to find self-forgiveness or self-compassion for my mothering choices and for the all-too-often feeling of resenting the role I was expected to play. I wonder if I can integrate the poems into a personal reflection, thus releasing myself from those lingering regrets. I begin with "Pity":

Regrets, like dumpy unattractive clothes
Wrap around memories of mothering, intensity
Longing for release, failures a heavy burden
Hanging like chains of irremovable necklaces
Too strangling to be worn for comfort...

Thoughts are my chains, especially those about my failures that sit on the surface, ready for me to pull out and examine. Sometimes, they are my constant companions, lurking just on the periphery of my vision, and at other times, they are present like an unwanted guest who simply won't leave. I tell myself that I wasn't *that* bad a mother. After all, I didn't yell or belittle my children or intentionally put my needs ahead of theirs. At times, I was so depressed that I often wondered how I could keep everything together. I wonder now, was I really that inadequate? Or am I just beating myself up again? After all, my children were safe, they were in school, they were fed and clothed, and they had fun times. So, what standard did I, or am I using, to evaluate myself? By what standard do any of us judge ourselves? I question myself, but still, there's no going back, no second chance.

Feelings change, of course, including those about myself and myself as a mother. Being a mother is a topic I no longer think about much, or at least I try not to, or at least that is what I tell myself when I am not deeply embedded in this reflective work. I can never seem to give myself praise for that role and vacillate from painful memories where I hear myself screaming and yelling critical, cutting remarks that sound just like my mother—to almost okay times that bring a smile or half smile as I recall a flash of laughing together with my children as we were driving someplace or taking a pleasant walk on the beach.

I wish I could say that time has changed my views of who I was and am as a mother, but it hasn't. I try to rationalize this by telling myself I was so depressed that it was all I could do to stay alive, let alone be a good mother. When my daughter was a young teen and my son was in elementary school, I even planned my funeral. "Remains" gives the details:

Lately, I have been planning my funeral,
first calling around to determine prices
but even that is not so simple, not quite
like buying pots and pans, for example,

where material, manufacturer, and place
of purchase seem the main criteria for cost,
although in this situation, there are similarities
because it does come down to container size.

just like saucepans, skillets, and kettles, death
divides into coffins, urns, or cardboard boxes.
... it's a messy, complicated, costly process
but still, there's no free exit.

Lived Context

A few important facts: My parents remained miserably married and raised four children until my mother committed suicide at age sixty. I was raised in an elite boys' boarding and day school where my father worked and which my grandfather founded. My mother had a sign attached to her bedroom mirror that said, "I like all children except girls." I suppose it's not surprising that I've had issues all my life about not being that revered male child. I've had three marriages and two divorces and two children and two grandsons. I've lived basically in the Middle East since the late 1980s and have been dividing my time between Egypt and Indonesia more recently. My daughter's father left when she was less than a year old. She's now in her late fifties. My son, eight when his father and I divorced, died in a plane crash when he was twenty-nine. My hope in writing is to help others understand and do the job of caring for children with the knowledge, confidence, and kindness I too often lacked to accept and forgive themselves—something I am still hoping for—and to know that it is never too late for growth and change, which can happen throughout a lifetime.

So let me travel back in time. After getting divorced from my first husband, I went back to school and completed undergraduate and graduate degrees before eventually becoming a licensed clinical social worker. I worked first with foster children and then in medical social work. Somewhat later, I returned to school to pursue a doctorate in psychoanalytic psychotherapy with children; I was truly curious whether early interventions could help unhappy young children. The short answer is yes, they can. I moved into private practice where I specialized in working with children, particularly those who had been abused. In the process of studying and working, I learned a great deal about children and parenting, most notably the importance of understanding how young children feel about things—feelings they are more apt to show through play than words, feelings they don't understand. And I learned that I was not alone in not knowing much about mothering and that it is not an easy job.

Remembering Mother

Looking back at when I was a little girl, I remember how much I wanted a real, live baby. When my mother would take her brood to the department store for anything, I would disappear into the children's department to look at all the tiny clothes and pick up one of those free baby magazines full of articles and advertisements. I would stare at the baby carriages and bathinettes, imagining they were for my baby. Later, my younger siblings were born. I enjoyed them when they were dependent but found them less interesting when they had their own wants. Nevertheless, I spent a lot of time hurrying them through their baths, helping with homework, and reading to them before bed. I realize now that I had no idea what they were thinking about anything, and I really didn't know that I should have been aware of them to that extent. After all, if I had been petrified when my mother was on a rampage, weren't they? But in those times, as I was hurting, it never even crossed my thinking that they might be hurting. It just was part of life.

Of course, I knew I would be the best, kindest, and most successful mother. I would be different from my mother as portrayed in the following poem, "Image of Motherhood":

Craziness spilled like a pitcher of water
dropped, splashing all over the house,
drenching everything while bits of broken
glass glistened, sparking escape, which
to follow became not game but a necessity
soaking into the image of motherhood
where safety is not found in insanity
nor comfort in chaos...

Just surviving in my childhood home became a difficult enough job with my mother screaming and raging, sometimes twisting my limbs but more often hurting with raging putdowns and words that destroyed any self-esteem I might have gleaned. Sometimes, she went after my father with a meat cleaver, hurrying upstairs after him and yelling obscenities and phrases like, "God damn it, I want to kill you!"

While I was in high school, I worked in my free time—cleaning houses, waitressing for small parties, babysitting, and doing office work to pay for college—and hoped I could get a scholarship, as I sought to get away from that miserable house. Thoughts of becoming a mother faded and did not resurface until I was a freshman in college and began discussing marriage with a tall, dark, handsome man, who would become my first husband.

Husband Number One

I was eighteen when we married, and we immediately moved from the East to the West Coast. My husband was in the navy, so he was often at sea, and I was like a duck out of water. I had no idea how to cook, how to shop for food or anything else, and I had no idea at all about how to be a wife. I also was a virgin bride and had no idea that any physical pleasure was supposed to happen until years later.

When I finally became pregnant through fertility work, after miscarrying at five months due to an incompetent cervix, I knew it was my physical problem that had caused the miscarriage, which I then internalized as a personal failing. The ordeal was difficult physically: I needed two transfusions and stayed in the hospital for a few weeks. Of course, I felt guilty. My religious, hospital roommate fed my guilt by saying that because the baby was not baptized, she was going to hell. My husband, who professed to know a lot about psychology because he'd studied it at university, told me that unconsciously I hadn't really wanted a baby, so the loss was my fault. I left the hospital feeling physically uncomfortable and thinking of my baby in eternal hell.

As I write this, I realize that I still think of that little, unborn girl whom I secretly named, and I still wonder what she would have been like.

At home, our dog had just had puppies whose eyes hadn't even opened. I thoroughly enjoyed playing with their tiny, wiggly bodies, and when my milk came in several days later, I nursed a puppy, which I wrote about in "Thank-You Note."

> I once wrote thank yous to those who
> understood the agonizing, blinding
> pain of an infant born too early
> for any future.
> My husband said my nightmares
> must have killed her.
> Dripping with guilt, I attached a newborn
> puppy to my breast and wept...

A year after that painful miscarriage and with more fertility work, I gave birth to a healthy daughter. Thrilled and wide awake for the C-section, gazing upon her, I exclaimed, "She has her father's big feet and my big mouth."

Returning home, I struggled as my husband expected me to do everything: cook, clean, shop, and entertain. Meanwhile, I couldn't nurse properly, and my breasts stung. When the paediatrician said she was losing weight and suggested I use formula, I chalked it up to another glaring example of my inadequacies. Not only could I not give birth normally, but I also could not breastfeed either.

I felt like an abject failure even in those first few months of motherhood even with an easy and peaceful baby. One day when she was bathing, she smiled. To her, I was obviously okay, so I decided "to fix myself up" with a few sessions of therapy. Little did I know that I would be embarking on a journey that would last for many years—one that would also set the foundation for my career as a therapist.

After a few months of my therapy, my husband began to come unglued, and in a psychotic rage, accused me of sleeping with his father, my gynecologist, and a local firefighter. He said he intended to beat me until I told him the truth. The beating went on and on, even involving a gun, which I threw down the hillside so that he could not find it. I kept believing he would stop, saying to myself, "Forgive him for he knows not what he does." But he did not stop. It was only when he hit me in front of our baby that I scooped her up, ran out of the house, and fled to a neighbour's.

On My Own

My husband flew to his parents on the other side of the country and filed for divorce, something I didn't want but eventually had to accept. He was diagnosed as paranoid schizophrenic and spent many years in a residential mental health clinic in Switzerland. Years later, I tried to write about him in "Unpredictable":

> You are hiding but then, you always have,
> or maybe that's just my perception,
> you, who had such a pained childhood
> and such a wasted life, concealed so well
> behind brilliance, wit, and paranoia.

I used to ponder what fed your feelings,
what propelled actions that took such
sudden leaps into places I couldn't follow,
but no matter what I did, you remained
lurking in some sort of darkened corner...

There I was, with an infant, no family support, since they were all on the other side of the country, with no idea about how to do much of anything. I had to learn quickly how to handle a chequebook, keep track of bills and taxes, buy and cook food, and deal with life on my own with an infant.

I was fortunate that she was a happy, easy baby, besides the frequent ear infections that required me to juggle my budget to accommodate visits to the paediatrician and expensive medications. When she was about six, the doctor recommended a tonsillectomy and myringotomy (tubes in her ears). Her father feared surgery would kill her so took me to court to try to stop it. He was unsuccessful, but the surgery was a success.

Meanwhile, I was so depressed that I wasn't comforted by the fact that I had enough financial resources to live on because of part-time jobs and child support. I also had a place to live and a lovely little daughter. I felt exhausted, anxious, and scared. I resented the consequences of my choices and believed everything was my fault. I couldn't keep a husband, and now, if I were truly honest with myself, I even resented my daughter. I tried to compensate for those feelings by buying her little European-smocked dresses that hung in her closet until she outgrew them. While I have been writing this, some pleasant memories have surfaced. We had a wonderful collection of children's books, some from my childhood; we would buy others at library sales and thrift shops. We read them together and delighted in discussing the illustrations, which usually enhanced the story. These books took on a life of their own as my daughter shared them with her children.

Juggling part-time work and parenthood, and since I had only finished freshman year at university before getting married, I decided to go back to university. School had always been the one area of my life where I received praise and felt some sense of self-worth. But of course, I had to think of my daughter who needed babysitters. First, I hired a trained nurse who was wonderful with children but constantly criticized my parenting skills and various decisions I was making. I suppose, in retrospect, I shared too much about my personal life with her. Time and trial and error helped me learn how to set such boundaries. Eventually, the nurse-babysitter was replaced by preschool, and I would hire other babysitters as needed. As I think back on that time, I probably gave little thought to my daughter's emotional wellbeing, more preoccupied with her more obvious physical needs.

Things, though, were not smooth. Two of the babysitters exposed themselves to her: one was an elderly neighbour, and the other was the brother of someone I was dating. "Mommy, he wanted me to lick cookie crumbs off his pee-pee," she told me. My therapist cautioned me about going to the police. She said it would be ineffective legally because an attorney could easily destroy the child's testimony, and it would likely be traumatic for her. So, my daughter and I talked about people with "'crazy thinking' who wanted to do sick things," and we talked about how she could stay safe. I also praised her for telling me.

I followed the professional advice but now wonder whether I should have done something more, legally or illegally. She didn't seem upset, but hidden feelings surfaced later. In one of her gripe sessions as a teenager, she said she felt so confused and vulnerable at the time and wondered why I hadn't done more. "Wasn't I important too?" she asked. I just stared blankly and said nothing.

Suicidal thoughts continued to dominate my inner world. To say I was depressed is putting it mildly. One of my friends said, "You don't have the luxury of suicide. My God, do you want her father to raise her?" Truthfully, though, I was often suicidal and would fantasize about how I could be successful. It seemed to me that I had always been depressed, even contemplating the act from the time I was a small child by jumping off the balcony, but, fearing failure, I collapsed into feeling imprisoned by life, my failures, and my daughter.

I once read about a hotel in Canada that had a full-time service for parents who wanted to leave their children for lengthy periods of time. There was no way I could put that into my budget, but I fantasized about it. Looking back at those early years of being a mother continues to be painful for me even some fifty years later. I was so involved trying to get my own life together and managing to stay alive that, at times, I stepped off the beaten path.

At university, I was introduced to drugs by one of my professors who said, "If you don't, you're a baby." I've never done well with dares. And this was in the sixties—a time of free love, flower children, hippies, and "sex, drugs, and rock and roll." I tried lots of drugs, discarding angel dust, which was my favourite, because it was so dangerous. Despite what I was doing, I continued to get good grades and had some semblance of a social life, but resentment was there because motherhood was always interfering with the life I felt I wanted to lead.

In my memory, I hear myself shouting and criticizing much more than praising or just planning to have a good time being a mother. And I was an uptight, New England prude springing out of self-imposed constraints or restraints and trying to be less depressed. My life was chaotic and lacked much caution or discretion. I struggled to let go of what no longer served in much the same way as I resisted getting rid of my "Green Robe":

"Why don't you get rid of that ugly old thing?"
asked my lovely daughter, pointing in disgust
to a tattered and faded green robe,
complete with a grinning frog on the front.

"You've had it since I was a child: it was hideous
then, and it's even worse for wear now!"
How do you tell a grown-up child that an old robe,
like an old body, is full of interesting memories?

The frog and I once weekended on a Spaniard's yacht,
went to the desert with a cat and a record producer,
I, thinking one would legitimize the other, which
of course, was either naïve or creative rationalization.

Together we wrote papers for ourselves and others,
payment being dinners, dope, and sometimes
delicious hours of carnal delights, not suitable
to be discussed with a daughter.

The bulging-eyed frog and I even wrapped up
Together after a rape,
Followed by a suicide attempt,
Fortunately, unsuccessful ...

Husband Number Two

My daughter found my second husband while I was in graduate school. He lived in the complex behind our apartment and was not the first man she brought home, another being the elderly man who molested her. The real estate broker whom she found and who became my second husband also became her psychological father. He was an excellent father, but we were very different. He was Orthodox Jewish from an immigrant, Midwestern family, and I was from an old, New England, WASP family. Regardless, a strong attraction was there, so we married.

Shortly after our marriage, when my daughter was about four years old, her birth father kidnapped her and took her across the country to his sister and her husband's place. At my lawyer's suggestion and with all the papers needed, my new husband and I flew immediately to pick her up. She was traumatized because she had been told she was "now safe from her bad mother." I later found out I was "bad" because I'd married someone Jewish. My daughter adored her birth father who doted on her and was generous with toys and trips.

My new husband and I tried to explain what had happened, telling her that her father had confused thinking. I look back at that time, and I realize that I failed to understand how traumatized she was. I cuddled her and tried to comfort her, but it was difficult for me to be there for her. During the plane trip across the country, I was more worried about the exams I'd missed than what happened to my daughter. Again, this was another instance where I put my needs ahead of my daughter's. Or were my feelings so intense that I was powerless to integrate her feelings with the same intensity? Or did I confuse worry with guilt? Maybe I am just beating myself up again.

In "Daughter's Father," which I wrote years later, I write from my daughter's perspective about the confusion she might have felt at the time about her father. Now, I not only carry my pain but that of my daughter as well.

> The voices in his head
> are speaking to him again
> and taking over his brilliant brain,
> leaving no room for him to listen
> to me, his little princess, his child.
> Where do they come from, those others

who give him such terrible thoughts?

...

Are they from his distant, formal parents
whom he despises and who look at me
as a result of his momentary mistake
in marrying my mother?

...

How can I rescue him from them
so I can have a father?

My second husband and I also sought fertility help, and it worked. When I threatened to miscarry, I was on bed rest for three months. When my son was born, I was thrilled. My in-laws hired a baby nurse for two weeks, and I made sure she cooked special dishes for my husband while I took full care of the baby. I adored him from the beginning, relaxed with him, breastfed him successfully, and momentarily, at least, felt fulfilled. He was a delightful infant, active and interactive—everything I ever wanted in a child. But still a child. Still needy. When he was less than a year old, I went back to work as a social worker, working with adoptive and foster children. My son had a young Guatemalan woman taking care of him. She was marvellous with him, and they adored each other. He became fluent in Spanish, speaking it much better than English for a while. I, however, could not understand him. I didn't even understand he was speaking until a friend recognized it. Unfortunately, my son's caregiver was more than caring for my husband. By the time I learned about it, it was like an unread footnote, of no use.

Social Work Insight

What I saw in my social work caseload was eye-opening. A four-year-old told me about hiding under a table when her daddy and mommy were fighting and daddy shot his gun. She said it went "bang, bang." It scared her, so she closed her eyes. She said this while hugging a soft toy dog in my playroom. "Where is Mommy now? Why doesn't she come to see me?" she asked plaintively. Put yourself under the dining room table with her while her parents argued for the last time. Imagine how frightened she was. Unfortunately, her mother was dead.

Or the boy in residential placement for stealing, whose uncle thought he'd spoiled a drug deal, so he hit him in the head with a claw hammer, causing brain damage.

Or the cute redheaded boy who went home after school to find the place empty, empty of everything, and whose family left no way for him to contact them.

The list of cases of abused children was endless in the foster care system.

Why could I hear and see those children's emotional needs so clearly when it was so difficult for me to see them in my children?

Was it like seeing our problems clearly in others while we can't see them in ourselves?

My Son

It is hard for me now, so many years later, to describe my son as a little boy. He loved life and doing what he wanted, even if it was dangerous or unacceptable. At just two, he manoeuvred a chair onto the kitchen counter, climbed on it, and then perched himself atop the tall refrigerator. Dangerous! He also climbed a tall palm tree and laughed and laughed until crawling down. In restaurants, he loved to make loud, gleeful sounds and then look at all the people staring at him. I had no idea how to handle him. Perhaps I was in awe of his maleness. I'm not sure. The truth is, I loved his maleness and probably envied him.

But I found him challenging and felt incapable of keeping him safe, let alone getting him to behave. I couldn't understand his baby-talk Spanish and certainly couldn't control him. I would even spank him, but then I started to use a wooden spoon. One day, when he had done something he knew I wouldn't like, he brought me the wooden spoon, and I was shocked. What was I doing? Was I a child abuser? I was horrified.

A parent in my office once said, "I know it's wrong to hit them, but it feels so good to slap their soft little bottoms." I understood that sentiment. It seems that we are all capable of being child abusers. Parenting is hard and confusing, but that is no excuse for hurting a child. Eventually, I took the spoon to my office where it became part of my playroom equipment.

That long-gone son was also somewhat quirky at times. For almost a year, he didn't want to eat anything but white bread and bologna sandwiches, and since he was healthy, the paediatrician said to let him. For a time, he didn't want to bathe. He claimed it took too much time when he could be doing something better, such as building with Legos or reading about history. I recall his head smelling slightly sour and fruity, almost like what lingers in an empty locker room. And of course, I remember too well battling and yelling and pulling him into the bathroom for a shower because I was larger than he was and still could.

How I would love to smell that odour again.

He was an inveterate reader and retained what he read, but he didn't want people to know how smart he was. I never knew why. I remember when he was seven. I took him to a local community event against the advice of friends who thought it might be traumatizing for a little child to see a movie about what would happen if a nuclear bomb fell on San Francisco. He said the following to a group after seeing the film: "Of course, it was scary for a little kid like me to know this could happen, but it wasn't scary enough. They didn't even discuss the water table, which would be radiated for years!" I remember not dealing with the emotional component of what he'd said. Maybe he was scared of what the future held. I didn't pick up on that. Instead, I commented on his knowing something I didn't know and was proud of him for that.

When my son graduated from the sixth grade, his father and I sent him to the boarding school where I'd grown up. Less than a month after he arrived, he was on final probation for a year. His crime was "forging" a teacher's signature so he could use the library. Yes, that was the only reason! I was commanded to fly across the country to meet with the headmaster about this serious infringement; unfortunately, I supported the school and expressed great disappointment in my son "who had brought such dishonor on the family," all for going to the library. How I regret my stance! How I wish I had stood up for my son, for his desire to learn. But I didn't. Who hasn't made the wrong choice viewed in retrospect? After he died, I mentioned the boarding school in "Objects of Grief."

... Pictures of you at all ages
fill and frame long days:
here, on the mahogany table
is one of you climbing a palm tree,
diapers ditched, naked as a jaybird

and laughing as if you'd just
conquered that cage of a crib

while nearby is another of you
wearing a favourite Dodgers cap,
toothless smile well captured,
juxtaposed with a serious stance,
corduroy suit reminiscent of
the hated boarding school,
which I now regret demanding...

My Daughter

With the agreement of her birth father and my second husband, my daughter went to boarding school for her benefit, and I was able to arrange a scholarship as I later did for her brother. Although I went to public schools, I believed in that form of education, perhaps because I had grown up in a boys' boarding school where my father worked for his entire life. I was also concerned that my daughter was more social than academic, and I convinced myself this would not be a great loss to either of us. We did have a somewhat stormy relationship, not to mention I had no idea how to handle her after she was no longer a cute, little elementary school pupil. She was overweight, and since I had struggled for years with weight issues myself, I harped on her to eat correctly and to get more exercise. My approach was, of course, unsuccessful. As a young teenager, she sometimes got drunk with her friends, pilfered small items from stores, and lived a life I knew little about. For her sake, I was glad for her to be in a good school, and for myself, I was relieved to have her out of my hair.

One time, when she was home for spring vacation, we decided to work on our relationship by going canoeing on the Colorado River. It was a several-hour drive to what seemed like the middle of nowhere where we were given our canoes. It was blisteringly hot, and after a short time, my arms started to hurt, and I was paddling inconsistently. My daughter announced, "If we were a married couple, I would divorce you when we got home!" "Indifference" is about what I felt about my daughter that day:

Indifference is not what I now feel...
nor was indifference in the canoe when
our gawky girl-child and I were trying
to communicate on the Colorado although
it may have clung to the gunnels when
I dropped my paddle overboard and
silently watched it drift behind us
like a downed kite drowning...

I recall how wonderful it felt as I watched my paddle drift away. It was the least motherly emotion I could have possibly conjured up, but I felt terrific at that moment, even though my arms ached, I was sunburned, thirsty, exhausted, and worried that we would never see civilization again. As I stared at my daughter, now responsible for getting us to a campground, I wondered why I wished to be anywhere else with anyone else. What was wrong with me, I asked myself when the guilt kicked in. What kind of a mother was I? I have become more in touch with her feelings, which I ignored then. Did I see her as a rival? Do teenage girls see their mothers as rivals and treat them that way? Did she see us as rivals? Maybe.

Divorce Number Two

My son's father and I got divorced but continued to coparent both children. Before he went to boarding school, our son sometimes lived with me and sometimes with his father, who took him for his first airplane ride when he was six weeks old and taught him to fly when he was old enough to get his license. Both children graduated from college, and both stayed on the East Coast. My daughter became a teacher, and our son became a commercial pilot. I didn't approve of his flying but knew that he loved being up in the skies, as I wrote about in "Spending Money":

Spending money is fun,
but usually I try to feed the poor,
help the homeless
or save the whales.

Today I bought my son a necktie,
bright yellow airplanes

flying whimsically across
exquisite, pale blue silk.

No doubt he'll tell me
it's a sign of creeping senility
while secretly bragging to his friends
about his mother's bizarre taste.

Meanwhile, anxiously awaiting
the thank you that never comes,
I wonder if a tie can make up
for so many mistakes.

He flies through the skies
not knowing that my offering
was so much more,
seeing only a tie he'll never wear.

Death of My Beloved Son

And then came the phone call from his father. "I have bad news. It's our son..." I was home alone, since my current husband was on a consulting job in Kuwait. Alone, I paced and cried, screamed, shouted, sank to the floor and huddled there, making sounds like a wounded animal. The following day, I flew across the country to say goodbye to my son, and my third husband soon joined me. To discuss how much that good man has helped me mature and begin to feel good about myself would be another chapter.

The death of a child is a mother's nightmare. It never goes away and is always present. Sometimes, I can't even think about him without tears coming to my eyes; other times, I can discuss him with almost no emotion. Overall, it was devastating. I was consumed by my sadness and overlooked how much his death affected my daughter, who was close to her brother. I have never really mourned the life he might have had or what he missed out on having. It saddens me that I find it hard to imagine what he could have done. I know he wanted a family with several children.

I have written many poems about his death, some more comforting than others. Reading "Further Accolades" now, written three years after his death, I can see him driving with his arm resting on the open window, the sun glistening on the car. And when I said the same words as in the poem, I can see his huge grin and still feel the warmth of his hand as it reaches out to touch mine.

"I'm so proud of the man
you've become."
At least I told you that
before a plane crash
put an end to any
further accolades.
I burn with a sense
of my inferiority:
all I didn't do—
all I ignored.

I could have been
such a better mother
if only I hadn't had
such needs of my own.

For months after he died, I seriously considered suicide, my old companion. I was sixty years old at the time, the same age my mother was when she chose to die with pills and alcohol. I expressed this wish so openly that I was asked not to return to a church-sanctioned, grief group. Later, when I felt emotionally stronger, I met as a licensed therapist with the group leader and her supervisor to discuss how to deal with such similar situations in a more professional and effective way. I also read articles about people who had succumbed after the death of a child and those who had thought about it but made another choice. Words I'd heard sometime, someplace, echoed in my thoughts: "Suicide's always there, but first check out other options."

A few months later, I recall sitting in a library and wondering how to make my life worth living. I knew it would involve doing something different, ideally something I hadn't done before, something that would honour my son's memory. Since he loved reading, I thought about writing, and I then began to crank out stories for young children, many of which were eventually published in Arabic and English in Egypt. While

I was writing, I was enjoying the feeling of being a child again, like reading to myself; in retrospect, I realize I was writing to help children better understand themselves and their world. And I was writing to get away from my grief. Here's part of a poem I wrote, "On the Anniversary of My Son's Death":

I write for you, my son.
Every character has you
As a hidden role model
Rich with authenticity.
Infectious laughter bursts
Indiscriminately, words
Pounding reams of paper.

Just last week you were five,
Today a gawky teenager
Whose bantering arguments
With your older sister
Sizzle across the pages.

Another page to be filled,
Another memory recalled
Partially disguised as fiction
To share you with others...

Lingering Regrets

Regrets linger. Words spoken to discipline, belittle, and castigate flow to the surface when I write, when I remember mothering both children. But I also realize that mothering is learned intergenerationally, and I did not learn about good mothering from my poor mother. I also believe I had impossibly high standards for judging myself as a mother, not surprising given the patriarchy that was alive and well at the time. No one is as perfect as I imagined I should have been, no matter what, and I feel a huge disservice was done by those baby magazines we all read when we were younger, that did not discuss the difficulties and the almost overwhelmingly profound feeling of responsibility for raising children. They never seemed to have articles about the difficulties. As I attempt to reconcile and forgive myself, I realize that I experienced motherhood in a time and place that is much different from today. Fortunately, that's changed. But who really feels prepared for motherhood?

I take time to remember good times with my son, and sometimes, I can almost hear his laughter. I have come to understand more why my daughter and I haven't been close. I see she is a caring person, who has dedicated her working life to teaching in low-income areas. She has long-time friends, a good marriage, and is a wonderful mother to two remark-able young men, my grandsons. Today, I can even tell myself that maybe she received some good things from growing up with me after all. Perhaps I did not do quite as poor a job as I imagaine. As I sit here now, I see that we are more like peers than mother-daughter, and perhaps that is as it should be. "Choices" demonstrates my pride in her independence and her ability to make better choices than I did:

> There comes a time to call a halt to dreams.
> The fat little girl will never be a ballerina.
> The boy with one leg won't win the race.
> My daughter will probably always resent
> the mentally crippled father I gave her and
> the next one she found whom I divorced
> for having more women than his wife
> and daughter whom he always protected
> from his notoriously blatant philandering.
> Now that she's an adult she sees such issues
> as less important than I did at the time
> although such matters require choices,
> and she disapproved of the ones I made,
> not realizing all the steps required
> to make such magnanimous moves.
> She is very sure of herself, my daughter,
> and I am pleased that she has the strength
> to deal differently than her mother. Still,
> no one can truly wear another's shoes,
> can they? Her feet are much bigger
> than mine anyway.

I am proud of the way she has lived her life, and I have told her so. I am not sure how much she hears me because she usually jumps to other subjects. Nevertheless, I am glad I have shared such genuine feelings with her as I am glad to remember sharing warm feelings with my son.

Turning Eighty

Two years ago, when I turned eighty and was residing in Indonesia, I wrote about this chronological milestone in "Reflections on Turning Eighty." I am surprised now when I read it that I made no mention of being a mother. None. Isn't that odd? I thought of trying to add a verse about being a mother, but I decided that the poem would not be as honest as if I left it the way I had written it. I think it is significant that I left out the mothering part of my life entirely. But I did. Maybe, though, it has to do with my mothering days being essentially over. Maybe it has something to do with unresolved feelings about my mother or maybe I did not feel that I had the right to claim motherhood at eighty as there was still so much left unsaid. One child has her own life, and the other is long dead. I am still a mother, of course, but now my role is more concern and curiosity than active engagement. I see this as an improvement to the seeming indifference of much of my active engagement years.

Turning eighty was a milestone I didn't expect.
At first, it was rather depressing; looking back,
all the mistakes crowded to the present and
what I'd left undone didn't seem interesting.

Then I glanced at the near future, seeing
decrepitude creeping ever closer, like several
college friends slipping off the curb as dementia
or Alzheimer's become constant companions.

Time, time is running out I moaned, wallowing
in my misery before an inner voice was heard:
"Get busy, make the most of now. Otherwise,
your work will die when you do."

No longer racing to Tijuana on the back of a Harley
or sleeping with strangers met in a parking lot,

140

I sit with my husband, a cat purring on my lap and
contemplate which project to do next,

making the most of what I have, not focussing on
incipient forgetfulness, sagging skin, or opportunities
lost but on the now, what's around. It isn't that
the future's present but what I'll do flounces forward

and there isn't enough time to write all I want,
to read what is already piled up and slipping out
of the overflowing bookcase. But that's alright.
Each breath, each moment, is mine to take,

to shape, to waste, to do with whatever I choose
and, like the cat, I live immersed in the now,
smelling orchids, fragrant frangipani, endlessly
watching small rice shoots mature

and finally, as an octogenarian, I've decided
at last, no matter what happens, I will accept,
enjoy, leaving depression in the bag outside
the thrift shop because I am, at last, acceptable

even to myself.

Being a mother for me is a chapter already written, whether I like it or
not, am proud of it or not. Life has moved on, and writing this personal
essay has helped me realize that I did the best I could, and it was what it
was. I also have come to understand through this writing that my children
were satisfied with the lives they carved out for themselves. My daughter
has a fulfilling, happy life, and I shall continue to praise her for the
wonderful mothering job she has done. My son loved his life as a commercial pilot, which gave him the time to do what else he wanted, like
read, fish, hike, and visit his sister. My son and daughter adored each
other, and I now understand her sense of loss is as painful as mine. We
have been getting closer by talking more about her brother and grieving
together.

I think I am still, and will like always be, trying to nurture and heal
that little child in me who was so hurt. Gained from a lifetime of strug-

gling, I wish someone had better understood my needs as a child because, like all children, I needed to be treasured and reassured, listened to rather than lectured at. I wish someone had told me that mothering was hard work and we do the best that we can. I wish someone had told me it was okay to be selfish sometimes and that mothers need time to relax and refuel. And I wish we were taught to forgive ourselves for the mistakes that we will surely make, as I am now learning to forgive mine

Most importantly, I hope as I finally learn to forgive and accept myself that this is not lost on my daughter and together we can work to help each other heal. Perhaps together, we can tackle some of the greater problems by working towards a common cause to make things a little better for everyone and for this world in which we live, as I describe in "Mother Earth":

Oh, Mother Earth,
What is happening to you?
Day after day your body is abused
And your sagging tits no longer
Drip with thick milk. Your scarred belly
No longer holds the promise
Of tall sons and fertile daughters
Bursting forth from those hidden
Places from which all bounty emerges.
We have accepted without question
Your endless gifts, arrogantly believing
We can sup forever at your battered table
While we gorge without ceasing,
As if mothers are meant to be ignored,
As if all we desire will flow forth
Forever.

Part III

Destabilization: Reimagining Non-normative Mothering

11.

Pain's Wisdom: From Normative to Relational Mothering

Gertrude Lyons

Westerners have strayed far from a healthy relationship with pain. Few places is this clearer than in our relationship to birth. Women need to know options exist to normalize pain experienced during conception, pregnancy, birth, and motherhood. It's not all bad. We don't have to be afraid. This chapter discusses what is possible when we reframe pain and foster an inclusive relationship with strong physical and emotional sensations that we have been programmed to fear. When women are presented with choices to express their pain, they can rewrite their mother codes and end the suppression that silences us from our wisdom and locks us into a role that denies a full developmental experience as a mother. I argue that the old model has been built on a false foundation of fear that systematically blocks us from our innate power to ride the inevitable waves of pain towards positive outcomes. The chapter explores how women can break free from this restricting paradigm and enjoy developmental and transformational opportunities. I conclude with a future outlook of the broader implications when women are empowered to follow the wisdom of the pain of childbirth.

As a motherhood scholar, feminine leadership educator, woman, and mother of two adult daughters, I came to focus on the transformational opportunity of mothering for personal reasons and because as a life coach and educator, I wanted to bring my research findings into the mainstream (Lyons, *Expanding Motherhood*; *Rewrite the Mother Code*; "Mothering in the Balance"). My work can be distilled into a single phrase: rewriting the mother code. This speaks to the reality of the family and cultural programming laid down during our formation (Mezirow), which is perpetuated by our current culture and will remain our operating system unless we reprogram it. Along with Andrea O'Reilly, I conceive of the necessity of moving out of the programming of patriarchal mothering and creating new tracks leading to "empowered mothering" ("The Baby"). Note that my scholarship is anchored in motherhood broadly conceived and that the indoctrination I speak of—the cultural coding—takes place to varying degrees among all of us. Motherhood is at the root of the Mother Code, but the code itself is universally inculcated, albeit to varying degrees.

Old Model: Pain is a Four-Letter Word to be Avoided

> I will make most severe your pangs in childbearing;
> In pain shall you bear children.
> —*King James Bible*, Gen. 3.16

Within a Western cultural context where religion meets the scientific, mechanical, and masculine (Rich), pain is inherently profane and is to be avoided or numbed. Conception, pregnancy, birth, and new motherhood occur in a backdrop of fear, which is instilled in virtually every area of our lives: These messages are delivered by our doctors and other authorities, presented and consumed in the media, and observed by our family and friends. It is not surprising that our fear of pain looms so large.

With conception, the current dialogue is shrouded in doubt and fear of infertility (Martin). Many women experience the inability to be productive—or reproductive—as a fundamental spiritual failing to not procreate. In a woman's childbearing years, she might hear: Your eggs will dry up; you have a family history of challenges getting pregnant; you better start trying because the clock is ticking; and the list goes on. Fear is internalized and has women running to fertility doctors even before an issue has been encountered. Women fear that their bodies may not perform and do the job they are purportedly put on Earth to do. For women who are fortunate enough to get pregnant but suffer the loss of the fetus, the unspoken dictate is that nature has a way of taking care of itself and that we should mourn in silence (quickly please). In the modern era, mothers are doubly damned. Painful birth is a legacy of Eve's sin, whereas not being able to be pregnant is another level of judgment—a divine declaration of unworthiness.

A pregnant woman hears more about the downsides of pregnancy than the celebration. It quickly becomes obvious that pregnancy, labouring, and childbirth are to be tolerated and that discomfort is a negative thing. Avoidance of pain is the dominant message, which has little to do with the experience of mothering or even with bringing a healthy baby into the world. We fall prey to countless messages surrounding the pain of birth. It is a wonder that generation after generation, women continue to bear children.

The Myth of Pain in Childbirth

There is merit in exploring these myths no matter where we find ourselves on the mothering continuum, as the silencing of pain that begins in childbirth lingers and touches us all. Not unlike the rest of Western culture, women are subject to the masculine model of controlling, compartmentalizing, and mechanizing what should be natural as a pretext to save women from the pain of childbirth—or maybe it is to ensure that the pain of childbirth becomes a distant memory to facilitate higher levels of procreation. Yet we have been trained to fear pain. We crave comfort and ease. The good life is pain-free. The medical system promises to rid us of our pain, which is synonymous with illness and death—a fate sealed by Eve who proudly and powerfully chose for herself and was, therefore, cast from the garden and punished with the pain of childbirth. What a clever way to strip women of sacred tools and symbols. (*King James Bible*, Gen. 3.17–19).

We find ourselves trapped in a model where the wisdom encoded in a woman's pain is silenced by the beeping of a fetal monitor and numbed by medication intended to ease our suffering. We are shamed and ridiculed for uttering our cries—cries full of the intelligence that signal the progressing stages of birth. Perpetuating the myth, women continue to mute their voices, leading to a separation of self, loss of agency, and a terrifying apex of obstetrical violence being committed, predominantly, to women of colour (Fraker). Women who have been shamed about their bodies throughout their lifetimes and culture will likely experience shame in the bodily sensation of birth (Kitzinger). It is more convenient for the doctors and staff who are under pressure to move women through than it is to be in rapport with women who are not only feeling physical pain but also deep and unconscious emotional pain. Good intentions are tested when there are quotas and women waiting for beds.[2] Women express pain, terror, and pleasure every day, but their voices are often silenced by the boom of patriarchal constructs. It is not for women to shout louder to be heard. Rather, it is only when we value ourselves and our experiences—be they pain or pleasure—that the oppressive noise will subside, and women are given back their birth experience. Birth must be returned back from a medical event to a sacred one, where a woman reconnects with her innate wisdom and is celebrated beyond her function to produce a baby.

Birth as a Medical Event: Perpetuating the Myth

Birth is unequivocally a sacred event—at once mundane and wondrous. It perpetuates the human race and has the power to reveal the mysteries of creation and cycles of life. Women are a sacred vessel in partnership with the child they carry for months. Birth is also a medical event, a Western and masculinized cultural construct (Odent), the beginning of which is marked by the gleaming sign as she drives up to the hospital— EMERGENCY (Downe). For eons, birth was held in the highest regard and a symbol of a woman's power and creation manifested in physical form (Prinds et al.)—that is until it was subjugated by patriarchal thinking and behaviours that cast it into the dark shadows to be experienced as punishment for alleged sins against a masculine god (Rich).

As the story unfolded, women suffered in childbirth, until one day a man (think superhero in a cape) came to save the day with his science, prestigious medical knowledge, and fancy devices and potions to rescue the poor, helpless woman (think damsel in distress) from her terrible lot (Odent). Just as problematic as the technology and the myth is the prohibition from seeing this as anything but progress. The woman who questions the new mass-production system of birth becomes the mother outlaw, an apostate operating outside the accepted boundaries of motherly behaviour (O'Reilly, *Mother Outlaws*). Although medical technology has brought effective life-saving measures when needed, what women need rescue from is oppression, degradation, and the systematic rewriting of pain as the villain in the story. What is villainous is that women are conditioned to believe that they need an intercessor instead of being taught that they have internal power. This is not unlike many religious paradigms that have intermediaries to facilitate our experience of God. Surrendering our power and experiences to the powers that be is a devious and clever way to create a powerful dependence hierarchy. Women are not simply victims; they also share the responsibility for offering themselves up to be rescued. Retribution for Eve's sin of standing in her power translates into generations of programming and wiring of our brains linking birth and pain.

It is time to set aside the disempowering view of birth as a medical event and return it to a space where a woman connects with her divine wisdom encoded in her body that is supported by scientific knowledge, not run by it. At its best, the medicalization of birth has kept many mothers and babies alive. At its worst, the medicalization of birth is not without complication and destruction. Is one truly any better than the other? What happens when we support women to expose the birth pain myth and empower them to make choices for themselves?

Saniya's Birth Experience

Saniya (a pseudonym) was one of those people who turned her nose up to natural childbirth. She asked herself, "Why would you do that when you have medical science? What is any woman thinking that does that?" What Saniya realized was that she had a fear of natural childbirth. First, she was afraid to step out of what had been wired in as the "safe" way to give birth. After a deeper exploration, she found that she was afraid she would not be woman enough or would not be able to handle the pain. What was most sobering for Saniya was realizing how afraid she was that she would not be able to handle the vastness of the experience—that she would crumble. The roots of these fears can be found in the disempowering aspects of the medicalized paradigm. These insights opened the door for Saniya to consider first and then shift from her plan of a fully medicalized birth to a birth plan that called for no medical intervention unless needed. Three weeks before her due date, Saniya and her birth partner engaged in a dynamic breathwork[3] session. This experience took Saniya out of her head and into emotions and unconscious wiring, where she realized she did have it in her. She came to understand that her fears were based on her past wiring, and she was able to transform what could have been paralyzing and limiting fear into the excitement of being fully conscious during labour. She flagged that her fear was really about her aliveness and noted that she felt more alive during childbirth than in anything else she had done. In the end, it was scary, exciting, and thrilling, but this is the kind of aliveness that Saniya has chosen for the rest of her life.

Rewriting our mothering codes has the potential to explode the myths surrounding pain and birth just as Saniya chose to do. This is not about seeing women suffer needlessly, nor is it about seeking superwoman status. Rather, the point is to examine and critically think about how the birth pain myth conditions us to believe that others have deeper and better knowledge than women when it comes to birthing a baby, and this is inclusive of medical experts, friends, family, and even media moms. Unsuspecting and accepting mothers internalize the idea that if we follow outside directives, it will all be fine; women's inner knowledge, the wisdom of pain, is both dulled and minimized leaving women stunted, frustrated, and lacking in agency over their bodies and their experiences. Once the pain myth is exposed and new models are put in place, we may find a more empowering mothering experience.

New Model: Fostering an Expanded Relationship with Pain

> Turn your wounds into wisdom.
>
> —Oprah Winfrey

What if we flipped the script and looked at the value, potential, and positive possibilities of women's pain (Leap and Anderson)? What if some of the pain was not only inevitable but also good? Pain doesn't have to be solely scary and bad, nor do experiences involving some measure of pain. A growing body of literature supports the idea that a new view of pain has tremendous potential for mothers alongside child development, which is considered the mission of mothering (Leap and Anderson; Downe; Prinds et al.). Mother and child are inextricably linked, and pain experienced by mothers who feel as though they cannot freely express their feelings is a barometer of a missed—and essential—development opportunity (Trad); this in turn might perpetuate a similar perspective of pain for their children. As the wellbeing of mothers shifts from a false presumption of unimportance to a central part of childrearing, a more sophisticated understanding of human development becomes possible (Trad), which opens the doors to more honest portrayals of pain and suffering between mothers and children.

This rethinking of the meaning of pain must be accompanied by reconstructing the matrix of life-giving, both the reconnection of the pleasure of conception and the pain of birth and the dissolution of the strict separation of parent and child. Motherhood embodies the power of the entire life cycle and the interconnectedness of life. Barriers have been erected over time to introduce a narrative that controls and limits women in this process. Affirming the entirety of motherhood's domain begins with affirming the positive value of the birthing process.

Physiology of Emotions

A central premise of the medicalization of birth is that it is both an event too painful for women and all too emotional, especially too frightening. It is a narrative that seeks to render women powerless at a moment in which our potency is at its peak. Our response to this should be that we embrace emotion and feel our experiences. After all, emotions are a natural part of our physiology: Fear, hurt, anger, sadness, and joy serve a purpose just as blood flowing to and from the heart and breathing keep us alive (Pert). Our brain and the brain matter reside in our heart and gut, are part of our circuitry, and flow with energy (McCraty et al.). The most effective way to counteract the status quo of hiding and muting our pain is to feel it. To feel it fully. To surrender and dive right into its depths. Our pain takes us to the present moment and reminds us we are alive and living the human experience of which we are the author.

The Birth of My First Daughter

After a two-year journey of confronting deeply unconscious emotional pain during conception, I chose a home birth. It made sense to me, and I listened to that intuitive voice instead of the voices of my family and friends. This was a significant act of individuation on my part as my historical norm operated from an external locus of control (Rotter) and dependency on the authority of first my mother and then anyone who claimed expertise. Embracing my inner power and seeking to break free of traditional birth pain myths, I learned to identify and follow my deeper yearning (Lyons), creating a conscious, empowered birth experience where I could feel and express all of my emotions fully. When it came time to push, I froze in deep terror. My midwife looked me in the eye and told me to push into the pain. Was she insane? That was the last thing I wanted to do. Warnings from my limbic system came in fast and furious. Shut down! Run! Sensing my fear, my midwife took my hands tightly in hers and encouraged me with a demeanour that embodied fierce compassion and solid presence. As the next wave came, I chose to partner with the pain and push directly into the burning sensation. What a rush! I found myself on the razor's edge of pain and pleasure. Within two of these intentional pushes, our daughter was born. The moment she emerged my first thought was "I am a goddess!" My next thought was "I would do it all over again right then." It was as if all the pain associated with what I had just experienced vanished. I believe the same holds true with our emotional pain. If I had held back and succumbed to my fear and mistaken belief that I was not capable of expanding into the depths of this pain, I would have lost the opportunity to transform. I likely would have still received a healthy baby, but I would have missed an experience that forever imprinted and rewired my capacity to stay present to my pain and partner with it.

Opening ourselves to our pain's wisdom or growth potential is never about feeling less pain. As we let down our barriers, we feel more pain more deeply and intensely. What is left out of the pain myth is the potential for cleansing, renewal, and release of old hurts and trauma. Because our fear of pain is learned, we can unlearn it. Textbooks and Western medicine may appear to be the authority on childbirth pain and the need to numb the pain; the embodied experience of so many women suggests otherwise (Boucher et al.; Farrish and Robertson; Lothian). In one study of 160 American women who had opted for home birth, safety and avoidance of unnecessary medical intervention were the two most common themes in their explanations of their home birth choice (Boucher et al.). There was also a common refrain among the participants that they trusted the birth process and did not approach it as something to medically manipulate (Boucher et al.). In another study, of twenty-five Black American women who chose home birth, the idea that pain should be feared or numbed was explicitly rejected: A common explanation for their home birth choice was to avoid pharmacological pain relief (Farrish and Robertson).

What is often left out of the discourse on pain avoidance is quite possibly that the way you bring a child into the world may be a sign of how you might face the challenges of motherhood. Yet we are taught to believe that if we avoid the pain of childbirth (that being whatever everybody adheres to, including looking outside yourself for the answers, not trusting your body, and turning to medication as the first and only line of relief), it will all be fine. Our first thought when pain arises is to get rid of it, and we suffer, which often causes more distress than the actual pain of childbirth.

Implications: Pain as a Conduit for the Development of Self as Mother

> It's never too late to have a happy childhood.
>
> —Tom Robbins

The Path of Pain

When we choose to be a mother, we choose a path of pain; this may or may not be a conscious choice. There are many schools of thought that would suggest that we cannot know great joy without knowing great pain. If we choose to numb ourselves to that pain right from the start in childbirth, I wonder whether we are unconsciously sending ourselves a message that we are incapable of handling the pain of the whole mothering journey that follows. Understandably, it makes the experience more comfortable to use pain medication during childbirth, but in addition to the potential side effects (most of which are not shared with the birthing person) (Davis-Floyd), we need to understand that we are also disconnecting ourselves from the greatest source of comfort and wisdom we have—our fully conscious selves. We close ourselves off from connecting with the feminine mysteries and the path of rebirth that fully feeling our pain has the power to take us on. We are never the same after we surrender to our pain. Like a phoenix rising from the ashes, we are renewed and reborn. We discover new parts of ourselves that have been forged in the fire of our pain where a space is created that allows us to step beyond our familial and cultural codes that are attached to the pain of birth and rewrite them. We can rewrite our mother codes to reflect our story—the story that contributes to "herstory"[4] and compels others to do the same.

My dissertation focussed on raising women's awareness of the transformational opportunity in mothering. I check in with many of them periodically, often hearing how much our raw, vulnerable, and honest conversations about the role of pain in motherhood informed their mothering journey, expanded tools to deepen their thinking, and fostered discernment and empowered decision-making. Each path has been unique and ranges from making a conscious choice not to have children, to freezing eggs and later becoming a single mother by choice, to pregnancy loss. For one, breaking the myths surrounding pain had the greatest impact on fostering a growth mindset (Dweck), accepting challenges as they arise, and bringing new knowledge into new ways of mothering that build a redemptive narrative (Bauer et al.), one where she learns and grows with her children.

Future Outlook/Next Direction

> If we were forced to make love in public, and in the setting of the standard hospital delivery room, we would probably feel inhibited.
>
> —Sheila Kitzinger

When I first conceived this chapter, I thought my goal was straightforward: normalize pain by bringing it out of the shadows and into the light. As the process has unfolded, I am cautious that normalizing could be a disservice due to the risk of misinterpreting normal for what the current culture expects and accepts. Reclaiming pain as an acceptable and transformational agent in all aspects of motherhood requires envisioning a new normal. As women, we need to listen closely to pain's wisdom, don the raiment of the mother outlaw, and take this female-defined, female-centred reading of birth pain and pleasure to its next organic step; as mapped by Andrea O'Reilly: gender socialization. Let's assume that a steady dismantling of patriarchal constructs continues, what do we want in its place? While my list is long, a few possibilities include birth spaces that provide a clear positive message to the birthing woman and the newborn, opening ourselves to birth pleasure, and reclaiming pain in new motherhood.

Reclaiming a Positive Birth Environment

How is it that a cry from a newborn has come to be viewed as a positive sign of life when in reality there are gentler ways to allow for the adjustment of breathing outside the womb (Leboyer)? If we stop to consider what those first moments outside the womb wire into our consciousness, we should be concerned. Entering the world in an aggressive and masculine-value way, with the confusing complacency that it is safe and normal, we are sending a mixed message that this is what they can expect out of life—violence masked as love. Frederick Leboyer's position that a baby has rights was received as hostile by his fellow physicians but embraced by midwives and mothers. Something felt off to him about the pervading belief that a crying baby was a good sign, and it took years of observation and practice to show that birth does not have to include that moment of crisis. His premise was that a baby has feelings that should be considered. Birth is a memory buried deep in our unconscious. Interventions break the communication and relationship between the mother and infant. Labour, Leboyer contends, is a place of solitude and self-dependence where a mother is attuned with her baby in the act of giving this child its freedom. It is a powerful mystical experience: Women let go of the ego and become boundless and part of life force energy, which makes it frightening. The process is powerful, and we come face-to-face with death. There is death with every birth. It is not a death of the body; rather, what dies is our sense of connection.

We know much about the power of context and beauty in our physical spaces. We know much about how our surroundings can bring security and comfort. We know much about how sensitive a birthing woman is to the energy of the space and the people in it. I have been asked to assist with several births. I have no formal midwife or doula training, but I have worked diligently to honour the power of feminine values, and I bring my sensitivity to energy in a space. My job at the birth is to "create the space" by bringing beautiful fabrics, candles (electric of course), music, flowers, healthy food (available mostly for the attendants and after); providing support of the father; and most importantly, to be a guardian of the energy of the space.

Conclusion

My purpose in writing this chapter is not to advance a single, correct method of childbirth, yet I am aware that I emphasize the limitations of a highly medicalized framework and challenge the assumption that pain ought to be minimized or even deadened altogether when possible. Inasmuch as I am advancing one approach to childbirth over others, it is the aggregate of embodied experiences of mothers who have felt they did not need to be anesthetized but were overridden by doctors. It is the mothers who choose a midwife rather than a doctor. It is the mothers who choose to be at home, in a nurturing environment, rather than in a metal box with a screaming siren approaching a building with the word EMERGENCY written in large red letters who bring to the forefront that context and environment matter when a woman is tuning into the wisdom of her pain.

There is no one right way to birth. There is also no component of a typical childbirth that should be stigmatized or presented as a horrifying prospect. Birth includes pain, very often. What that means depends on how it is experienced. Promulgating a view that instills fear and dread helps nobody. In this chapter, I have challenged the assumption that pain is inherently bad and without value. In the end, however, the most important myth to be exploded in the discussion around birth is that any people other than mothers are the ultimate experts on the subject or should be the final architects of any birthing experience.

Endnotes

1. I will in this chapter use the term "mother" in the sense that was outlined by Andrea O'Reilly in her 2016 address at the MIRCI Gala Conference—namely, "individuals who engage in motherwork or ... maternal practice" ("The Baby").

2. These conditions were eloquently described by an anonymous midwife: "The secret life of a midwife: I feel like I work in a factory, not on a maternity ward" (Anonymous).

3. Dynamic breathwork is a holotropic breathing technique that facilitates self-exploration and allows a person to experience deep emotions (Morningstar).

4. Believed to be coined by Robin Morgan.

Works Cited

Anonymous. "The Secret Life of a Midwife: I Feel Like I Work in a Factory, Not on a Maternity Ward." *The Guardian*, 21 Mar., 2016, https://www.theguardian.com/commentisfree/2016/mar/21/secret-life-midwife-factory-maternity-ward. Accessed 15 May 2024.

Bauer, Jack J., et al. "Narrative Identity and Eudaimonic Well-Being." *Journal of Happiness Studies*, vol. 9, 2008, pp. 81–104.

Boucher, Debora, et al. "Staying Home to Give Birth: Why Women in the United States Choose Home Birth." *Journal of Midwifery & Women's Health*, vol. 54, no. 2, 2009, pp. 119–26.

Davis-Floyd, Robbie. "The Technocratic, Humanistic, and Holistic Paradigms of Childbirth." *International Journal of Gynecology & Obstetrics*, vol. 75, Suppl. no. 1, 2001, pp. S5–S23.

Downe, Susan, Editor. *Normal Childbirth: Evidence and Debate*. Elsevier Health Sciences, 2008.

Dweck, Carol S. *Mindset: The New Psychology of Success*. Random House, 2006.

Farrish, Jasmine, and Ray Von Robertson. "A Qualitative Examination of Factors that Influence Birthing Options for African American Women." *Critical Sociology*, vol. 40, no. 2, 2014, pp. 271–83.

Fraker, Carolyn. "Racism in the Birth Room: Obstetric Violence in the U.S. Context." *Obstetric Violence: Realities, and Resistance from Around the World*. Edited by Nicole Hill and Angela N. Castañed. Demeter Press, 2022, pp. 109–110.

Kitzinger, Sheila. *Birth & Sex: The Power and the Passion*. Pinter & Martin, 2012.

Leap, Nicky, and Tricia Anderson. "The Role of Pain in Normal Birth and the Empowerment of Mothers." *Normal Childbirth: Evidence and Debate*. Edited by Susan Downe. Elsevier Health Sciences, 2008, pp. 27–29.

Leboyer, Frederick. *Birth without Violence*. Knopf, 1975.

Lothian, Judith A. "Questions from Our Readers: Why Natural Childbirth?" *The Journal of Perinatal Education*, vol. 9, no. 4, 2000, pp. 44–46.

Lyons, Gertrude. *Expanding Mothering: Raising a Woman's Awareness of the Opportunities for Personal and Psychosocial Growth and Development in Mothering—A Curriculum Evaluation Study.* 2017. Wright Graduate University, PhD dissertation.

Lyons, Gertrude. "Mothering in the Balance: Rewriting the Mother Code to Serve the Whole Family." *Care(ful) Relationships between Mothers and the Caregivers They Hire.* Edited by Katie B. Garner and Andrea O'Reilly. Demeter Press, 2024.

Lyons, Gertrude. *Rewrite the Mother Code,* 2022–2024, https://www. drgertrudelyons.com/podcast. Accessed 15 May 2024.

Martin, Lauren Jade. "Anticipating Infertility: Egg Freezing, Genetic Preservation, and Risk." *Gender & Society,* vol. 24, no. 4, 2010, pp. 526–45.

McCraty, Rollin, et al. "The Coherent Heart: Heart-Brain Interactions, Psychophysiological Coherence, and the Emergence of System-Wide Order." *Integral Review: A Transdisciplinary & Transcultural Journal for New Thought, Research, & Praxis,* vol. 5, no. 2, 2009, pp. 10–115.

Mezirow, Jack. "Transformative Learning Theory." *Contemporary Theories of Learning.* Edited by Knud Illeris. Routledge, 2018, pp. 114–28.

Morgan, Robin. *Sisterhood Is Powerful.* Washington Square Press, 1970.

Morningstar, Jim. *Break Through with Breathwork: Jump-Starting Personal Growth in Counseling and the Healing Arts.* North Atlantic Books, 2017.

Odent, Michel. "The Masculinisation of the Birth Environment." *Journal of Prenatal & Perinatal Psychology & Health,* vol. 23, no. 3, 2009, pp. 185–91.

O'Reilly, Andrea. "The Baby Out with the Bathwater: The Disavowal and Disappearance of Motherhood in 20th and 21st Century Academic Feminism." *The Motherhood Initiative for Research and Community Involvement (MIRCI) 20th Anniversary Gala Conference.* Toronto, Ontario, Canada, 2016.

O'Reilly, Andrea, Editor. *Mother Outlaws: Theories and Practices of Empowered Mothering.* Canadian Scholars' Press, 2004.

Pert, Candace B. *Molecules of Emotion: Why You Feel the Way You Feel.* Simon and Schuster, 1997.

Prinds, Christina, et al. "Making Existential Meaning in Transition to Motherhood—A Scoping Review." *Midwifery,* vol. 30, no. 6, 2014, pp. 733–41.

Rich, Adrienne. *Of Woman Born: Motherhood as Experience and Institution.* W. W. Norton & Company, 2021.

Robbins, Tom. *Still Life with Woodpecker.* Bantam Books, 2003.

Rotter, Julian B. *Social Learning and Clinical Psychology.* Prentice Hall, Inc., 1954.

Trad, Paul V. "On Becoming a Mother: In the Throes of Developmental Transformation." *Psychoanalytic Psychology,* vol. 7, no. 3, 1990, pp. 341–61.

Winfrey, Oprah. "Commencement Address." Wellesley College, 30 May 1997, Wellesley, MA.

12

Dragon Mothers: Possibilities and Experiences of Mothers of Children with Incurable Diseases

Júlia Campos Clímaco[1]

> Today, I understand what motherhood is about: not expecting
> to feel like the proudest mother because of my daughter's
> achievements, simply feeling her by my side, learning to enjoy
> her as she is. Moreover, to know that this little scene is full of
> something that I don't know if I would dare to call happiness but
> that I would undoubtedly call fulfillment.
> —Beatriz Fernández Domínguez

Introduction

During my postpartum period, I heard about the perils of not sleeping—the fear that nothing is quite right, that there is no time, and there are so many things to do. Over and over, I heard almost mantralike, "This too shall pass." I heard that mothering always presents new challenges, but even this came with the promise that this too shall pass. On a personal note, I have yet to return to prebaby sleep. Every day and night with my daughter symbolize a nonlinear future, but futures arrive each morning, like a version of *Groundhog Day*. I know that

I can get things with her right, or I can get it wrong, but one thing is for sure: Each new day offers a fresh opportunity to do it all again.

My motherhood mingles present and future, calling forth the past as more than memory and a hint of what is yet to come, as small bricks in an infinite construction. This construction can be anything, from Niemeyer to Gaudi to Escher, but it is always something. In my imagined future, this construction will never be destroyed. I know this is an illusion, a story I insist on telling myself with the dawning of each new day. I know this because there is no way of knowing what will happen, only a constant promise of life.

Normative motherhood is like this and is typically associated with a long and prosperous life for children, with mothers active and doing what it takes to ensure survival.

But what of those mothers who experience motherhood alongside a degenerative childhood disease with no cure? With no certain future? With no awareness of how many days and nights they will have? What of those who do not have the promise of constant life? Mothering in the context of incurable disease shatters the dominant view of normative motherhood, leaving the future impossible to imagine. The focus shifts to the now, the every day, and the urgency of life with an awareness that this will likely not pass. The reality is that there are no second chances, and harm reduction becomes as important as survival along with the desire to live life as fully as possible in the continual face of death. When motherhood loses its perhaps most central task—that of ensuring survival, each day is difficult to face without turning to stone as shared by Emily Rapp:

> What could I say about my son, about being a mom in the wake of Ronan's diagnosis? ... How do you parent without a future, knowing that you will lose your child, bit by torturous bit? Could it even be called parenting, or was it something else, and if so, what? ... For parents of terminally ill children, parenting strategies incorporate the grim reality that we will not be launching our children into a bright and promising future, but into early grave. The goals for our children are simple and terrible and absolutely grounded in the everyday: dignity and minimal discomfort.
>
> This was absolutely depressing ... the experience of being Ronan's mom was not, I grew to learn, without the wisdom, not without—

forced and unwelcome as it might be for those of us going through it—a profound understanding of the human experience, which includes the reality of death in life that most parenting books and resources fail to acknowledge. Parents with dying kids have *insights* into parenting and they are hard-won, forged through the prism of love. These women had learned lessons not just about how to be a mother but how to be *human*. (11–12)

Two Nonnormative Motherhood Experiences

This chapter offers the experiences of two women who mothered children diagnosed with Tay-Sachs disease, a neurodegenerative disease with no known cure leading to early childhood death. Emily Rapp and Beatriz Fernández Domínguez documented their stories in a published book or public blog, which are available worldwide. As a mother seeking to understand nonnormative mothering, I read their stories. I was careful to read for subtleties and discrete linguistic contours for the following themes: the relationship between mothers and dragons, pain and biosociality; narratives as possibility and experience; the diagnostic experience; the mothering experience; multiple meanings of hope and cure; and narrating an open future to memorialize children's lives. In *The Still Point of the Turning World*, American author Emily Rapp narrates her experience with her son Ronan from the time of diagnosis, aged nine months in 2011, until his death in 2013.

Spanish activist BF Domínguez, founder of Asociación Acción y Cura para Tay-Sachs (ACTAYS), narrates her experiences with her daughter Isabel in the blog Tal Vez Isabel (http://talvezisabel.blogspot.com.br), beginning eight months after diagnosis in 2012 until Isabel passed away in 2014.

As I read these mothers' narratives, I understood that reflexive narratives are an exciting space for interpreting the self (Mattingly). Historical contexts separate these writers, yet others separate us from them. I honour the voices and experiences of Rapp and Domínguez by using extensive excerpts from their writing; their narratives speak to mothering in the margins of the institution of motherhood through which mothers attempt to make sense of their experiences (Badinte; Del Priore; O'Reilly; Rich; Scavone; Zanello).

From the time of their children's diagnosis, Rapp and Domínguez found themselves in what could best be described as the diagnostic experience of motherhood, which isolated them from the normative experience of motherhood. This may have made them more empathetic to other mothers who shared similar experiences, as imagined by Domínguez:

> I wondered about the different lives Romina and I have led and how this strange destiny has crossed us on a perfectly symmetrical frequency. About how two people so different can have such a similar story. Characters and stories. And how in the end, we are not so different. Today I understand the mechanism that determines it: someone from another culture, from the other end of the planet, with another lifestyle, with such different ambitions, and yet so alike, so human, so condemned.

On Mothers and Dragons, Pain and Biosociality

E. Rapp and Domínguez connected with mothers who had also experienced the loss of a child due to illness. It is possible that this connection helped them find meaning in their experiences, thus redefining themselves as mothers They called themselves "dragon mothers," a term proposed by E. Rapp, to capture the strength and magical quality needed to redefine motherhood in light of such experiences. The dragon, a strong and mythical symbolical creature, might give meaning to the experience of motherhood in the face of impending death and daily conversations about palliative care and death-related decisions:

> What creature symbolized this modern love story of which Ronan and Rick and I and others were a part but whose roots were as ancient and mysterious as the Tay-Sachs gene itself? ... Dragons are creatures of myth and legend, beasts with the magical power of unicorns but made of much tougher, less ethereal stuff.

> What I came to understand was that mothers and fathers who take on the qualities of dragons feel as though parenting were our only task, and yet none of the parenting resources were written for us .... dragon parents have a lot to say about parenting. Why? Because we've had to redefine the act: parenting with no thought to that dreaded future when there will be no child—parenting without a net (E. Rapp 17–18).

The origin of the word "dragon" in the expression "To see clearly" is exemplified by E. Rapp's statement: "No one wants to see what we see so clearly. No one wants to know the truth about their children, about themselves: that none of it is forever" (18). This is especially significant in this time of medical advancement, where no one wants to hear about the body's fallibility, only about ways of controlling and stretching life for themselves and their children. Mothers of children with incurable diseases experience a pain they consider so primal that it forces people to see their fears reflected in the scary dragon scales: "Our narratives are horrible and the stakes are impossibly high" (E. Rapp 19). Domínguez dislikes the feeling of belonging to this category, but finds that it represents her like no other:

> A new character to play in my life. Dragon mother. I hate to admit it, I hate to be one, but I have rarely felt so identified with anything. Dragon parents have no worries about the future, development, or (obviously) health. We only have the present. And in this present, we spend our whole lives. Only we can understand the dark and pure sense of this vital state. Others try to be by your side, try to understand. Sometimes they cannot imagine, and sometimes they don't want to.

The diagnosis of rare disease redefined their lives and led them to seek out others who had similar experiences to understand and transform what they were going through. This might be viewed as biosociality, which involves localizing biological identities around DNA and mapping it rather than traditional categories of race, class, or age. Biosociality provides a space for bioactivism: making demands for diagnosis, solutions, and cures and accessing medications, therapies, or palliative care (Oliveira; Rabinow).

After her daughter's diagnosis and the doctor telling her nothing could be done, Domínguez felt at war with the disease, alongside other family members. She turned to maternal biosociality and bioactivism as she connected with other families with similar experiences and sought meaning and purpose in what she was experiencing. This offered feelings of belonging, mission, and community.

Community through biosociality is relevant for those parenting children with disabilities or chronic and rare diseases. Parents living with these conditions may not share meaning within their groups as their experiences may not be common, even within their immediate family, which can alter notions of kinship and disrupt the ordinary experience of kin (R. Rapp). In such horizontal identities, people may not be able to link themselves identity-wise even with their parents, unlike vertical identities, such as ethnicity, language, or religion (Solomon). The category of dragon mothers can provide a space of biosociality where mothers can see themselves reflected in others' stories and begin to deconstruct motherhood narratives that no longer serve them and serve to oppress and marginalize.

Narratives as Possibility and Experience

Our lives are lived in narratives that call forward previously lived experiences while seeing a possibility to remake them. New narratives emerge from the rupture of the ordinary, canonical plot. When something removes us from the ordinary, we create narratives about the lived experiences that take us out of the flow of chronological time (Bruner). Narratives of illness and suffering attempt to fill the gap between the ordinary and the new unknown that defies worn-out meanings. "Profound physical and mental suffering constitutes one breach that seems to demand a narrative shape" (Mattingly 1), insisting on new possibilities to reenvision the narrative with new endings. Narrative time is dramatic, allowing transformations in the dilemmas we face. Endings are uncertain, despite mothers' awareness that the death of their children would come much sooner than they had imagined and desired.

This may be why we try to move towards new endings and possible worlds, as we become readers and writers of our narratives. We accept that our story is never fully told, and we attempt to leave our narratives open and filled with possibility so that those who encounter them have the space to make them their own. There is no experience when we do not bind ourselves to what is passed on to us (Benjamin).

We are the products and producers of our lives, constrained by material and everyday situations but making moral choices that can create new possibilities and even start revolutions. These mothers created new possibilities for mothering, inviting others into their lived experiences in a way that inspired instead of drawing pity, sharing an experience but not a how-to guide. The challenge in reading these narratives is to avoid being sentimental or trying to find a lesson. These stories demonstrate the diverse and complex experiences of motherhood, leading to a (re)imagined future. We can understand experience as that which happens to me and us, taking us away from where we were, suspending us, and returning us different, transformed (Larrosa). I understand that what passes through me uncontrollably and what I can never absorb entirely allows me to look at the world with eyes that are not my own. Accepting this challenge, I intend to show the experiences and words of E. Rapp and Domínguez that passed through me while reading and opened a metaphorical space for imaginative experimentation with life's possibilities (Mattingly).

Even with their children's imminent death and uncertain lives, Rapp and Domínguez attempted to find ways not to lose hope. They reached for possible worlds that would welcome their children for a short time while trying to live their best possible lives. They played with different mothering practices, lived in the present, focussed on daily care, and continually rewrote their stories and possible endings. They reached for possibilities and (re)told their stories to keep themselves firmly anchored in the process and to preserve their meaning-making as mothers, which was often threatened by their experiences. By engaging life possibilities, they were also deconstructing their notions of self and motherhood and rejecting the hegemonic motherhood's telos of raising children for life.

The Diagnostic Experience

Rapp and Domínguez defined themselves as privileged, white, middle-class women from so-called developed countries, educated, married, with planned and desired children, and living as they thought they should. The diagnosis of their children brings a rupture, a previously unknown tragedy, as Domínguez tells us:

My story was that of any woman who grew up happy and had a life of opportunities.... Then came Isabel, the light, the rediscovery of the essence of things, the projection of myself, the future. Isn't that what children bring to a family? Future, projection, illusions, hope, plans, pride. And wonder. The marvellous wonder that brings us back to our original state invites us to appreciate things from a simple point of view. So much for a common story.

Before I digress, I want to clarify what my story is about. Today. At three and a half years old, Isabel was diagnosed with Tay-Sachs disease. A neurodegenerative disease that strips her of all her faculties and has no cure. The doctor who diagnosed her said she would probably live to be five or six years old. No more future, no more projection. It was all over. We were left with only amazement and, along with it, the pain, the impotence, the terror, and the exasperation of accompanying her on this journey. (Mar. 2013)

Domínguez's daughter Isabel had been experiencing a decline in her developmental abilities, and after many tests, she was diagnosed with a condition with no known cure. While this diagnosis was a relief for the doctors who had been trying to figure out what was wrong, it was devastating for Isabel's parents:

I don't remember the rest of the conversation well. I remember details but not sentences. I remember my mother's voice when she explained to me that it was a very serious illness.... She was direct; she told me that it was one of those very serious diseases, and that there was no cure. That Isabel would not survive, that children used to die as children. I stopped driving. The dimension of the car began to change abruptly; the roof and the doors were coming towards me without ever crushing me, like in a science fiction movie.... I kept walking, looking at my feet. I didn't understand how I could do it; how could the earth not open up under my steps? (Aug. 2013)

E. Rapp's son, Ronan, had been showing developmental delays, which his parents attributed to a sight problem. It was during a routine consultation with an unknown ophthalmologist that they received the diagnosis. This is how she describes the episode:

"I was tested!" I shouted. "I had the test." I remembered the genetic counselor asking, "Are you Jewish?" and shaking my head. "I want the Tay-Sachs test anyway," I'd said. Or had I? Had I, in this moment, instantly generated a memory to try to mitigate the present horror? ... I had the urge to swallow him, to try to return him to my body, where he'd be safe, but of course he'd never been safe, not even there but I knew enough about Tay-Sachs to know there was nothing at all for us to do and that my life, the life as a new and hopeful mother, was over. When our son's diagnosis—his death sentence, really—was delivered, I felt all of the known world was unraveling, everything splitting apart. The walls of the doctor's office were no longer beige, but purple, glittering, melting, closing in. (3–5)

E. Rapp writes about her son's illness and death to create a narrative for him and to ensure his story does not end in tragedy. The certainty of her son's death forced her to relearn how to live and be a mother, as motherhood is future-oriented, and thus, there were no narratives to mirror her experiences. She knew of no motherhood other than preparing her children for life:

Opening my eyes on that January morning after Ronan's diagnosis was like waking up in an alternative universe—a silent world, mindless and still and as bleak and vast as the desert I lived in.... We didn't know what to do, how to be with each other, with ourselves; we couldn't think of a thing to say.... We had no narrative anchor, no arrow to point us in any direction that didn't promise misery as its endpoint. (41–42)

Facing a vast desert of narratives and absence of meaning, Rapp understood that in addition to physically caring for her son, she should tell her story—not just so his life would live on just a little longer but also to construct a narrative of a mother's experience of the uncertain life of her child:

My other task beyond physical care, I began to realize, was to find Ronan's quiet, gap-ridden myth, his idiosyncratic narrative—to interpret it, share it, and learn from it. Mythology was the only solution.... In the gap where he existed there was no map for his meaning. But there will be, I thought. If Ronan needed a myth, I would write one. If the only way to stop being divided from him, if the only way to dwell in his space, even for a moment, which I ardently, desperately wanted to do, was to stare into that silent world and make it speak, then I had work to do. (48)

He had, literally, no future. How did we understand the meaning and purpose of Ronan's life in a society—like most societies—that was dedicated to progress and achievement, where going back was synonymous with failure? Where the longer life was seen as the more successful one, the one worth fighting for? If you were unable to tell your own story, did it mean you didn't have one to tell? (53)

Domínguez's journey towards activism began when she realized the impossibility of diagnosing and curing her daughter's condition. She felt powerless against her daughter's genes and sought comfort with other families who had gone through similar experiences. At first, she did not feel the need to connect with other families as she had her family, friends, and Isabel's therapists. She felt the loss of connection due to the lack of shared experiences and words. If there are no shared words, how can they continue the conversation?

From this position of loneliness, Domínguez began contacting other affected families, especially other mothers, inviting them to participate in online groups and attend family meetings. Ultimately, seeing a gap in Spain, she founded ACTAYS and dedicated herself to this association after Isabel's death. The only escape from her daughter's life impossibility and her own as a mother was to fight for Isabel, other affected children, and herself. Her daughter's diagnosis and her activism did not fit within pre-established and conventional boundaries for motherhood. With no available narratives, Rapp and Domínguez faced many trials in their attempt to live this new life; sharing their stories helped them assign meaning to their experiences, make sense of the illness, and point to a need for a new narrative with many possible endings. These narratives were experiments and opportunities to reenvision the self.

Mothering Experience in Everyday Life

Mothering in the context of dominant narratives was not easy and there was no clear pathway to make sense of the expectations and health projections for their babies that were not only imagined but lived daily before the inevitable deterioration of their health. E. Rapp notes:

> Living in the midst of the knowledge of Ronan's inevitable death forced me into a new kind of living. It was uncomfortable, a heavy and daily mental wade through some pretty difficult thoughts, but it was qualitatively different from the life I was living before—like a dream life, an alternative existence. It was a life of heightened presence and constant mourning, an activity of which I became a scientist. (177)

And Domínguez reflects:

Everything I learned during the pregnancy, my expectations and plans for this baby, all melted away. It does not happen in an instant, it goes on happening, it is a process. I learn to live each day, be reborn every morning, and reconcile myself with life (destiny, the forces of the universe, god, whatever you want to call it) every night. I have no more challenges ahead of me; my goal in this life is to make Isabel laugh, to give her all the chocolate she wants, and to exercise her body in the most fun way possible. Goodbye to the rest of my goals. (Mar. 2013)

Isabel has a rare disease and will continue to degenerate for some time until nothing can be done. In the meantime, I will ensure she is the happiest girl on the planet. This was the formula that I repeated in one conversation after another, trying to keep my voice steady and contain the atrocious crying that lived in my throat, whether on the phone or in a restaurant. This was my new reality I was re-learning how to live. (Aug. 2013)

E. Rapp and Domínguez wrote and narrated their stories during the experience of loss, illness, and death to find the myth or tragedy that their children needed, but also because they needed to tell their own stories as mothers in this journey. They reinvented themselves for themselves and for the world, setting aside familiar assumptions and expectations about motherhood. As explained by Cheryl Mattingly, both mothers imagined new lives and moral becoming, reinvented their daily lives to include therapeutic itineraries, and accepted mothering practices of present moments, in which each extra day may mean a day less:

"The sky was clear, the air was soft. That's Ronan's day of living in this world. One more alive day, and also another day—for both mother and son—closer to death. We could wish it weren't true, we could wish desperately, but we could not have one without the other" (E. Rapp 246).

The certainty of death and life seems to become the new horizon for their moral projects and care as a daily task and daily life as a life possibility. Not life despite death, but life with death on this horizon.

Postdiagnosis, life value became everyday life and daily care meant reinventing a good life. Despite deep sadness and constant mourning, this reinvention brought a feeling of unprecedented freedom, the unknown pleasure of living without expectations, and the desire to make every day the happiest day for their children: "It is a unique and terrible privilege to witness the entire arc of a life, to see it through from its inception to its end. But it is also an opportunity to love without a net, without the future, without the past, but right now" (E. Rapp 246).

These mothers reinforced the idea of finding happiness in their new experience of motherhood and rejected the idea of being pitied. They firmly believed that their children had their independent existence, despite their parents' sadness and that they should be valued for themselves, not as objects to teach lessons or make others feel good about their lives. As Domínguez shares: "I am because Isabel is." So life went on. Their children were still alive, and it was crucial to live each day. E. Rapp explains:

> My time with Ronan was short and beautiful and shot through with light, laughter and, above all, a kind of love that stripped me to the bone. A magical world, yes, where there were no goals, no prizes do win, no outcomes to monitor. Ronan was given a terrible freedom from those expectations that was searing, brutal and, especially, true. Ronan was mine but he never belonged to me. This was not an issue of ownership. (20)

> Tucked inside the moments of this great sadness—this feeling of being punctured, scrambling and stricken—were also moments of the brightest, most swollen and logic-shattering happiness I've ever experienced. One moment would be a wall of happiness so tall it could not be scaled; the next felt like falling into a pit of sadness that had no bottom. (22–23).

And Domínguez reflects on the following:

> Suddenly life turns into everyday life. The future is a blurry and almost non-existent idea.... And it's no use lamenting, it's no use asking. Because today she is here, beside me. And this, possibly, is the greatest gift that life gives me. (Mar. 2013)

> And I have to love her wildly; that is my main task, to love her bare-heartedly, no matter what, no matter how I feel, no matter what happens. The rest of the emotions are secondary, including the fear of losing her. (Mar. 2013)

Hopefully, I can communicate that these pages are not a lament about Isabel's illness but rather a proof of the transcendence of her life, of the freedom that resides in the small details that are still within reach of her hand. Her laughter, her discomfort, her relief, her calm, her peace, her pain, her deep sleep, her frustrations. (Jan. 2014)

The experience of living with death intensely present prompted Rapp and Domínguez to think about how we delude ourselves with the contemporary belief of control over bodies and the bodies of our children. Biotechnological advances lead us to believe that we have the capacity to keep our bodies young and healthy, to keep our children safe in utero, to avoid death or discussion of death. These mothers could not control the inevitable death of their children nor did they spend their time in avoidance. Instead, they constantly negotiated between possibilities for each moment they had with their children. The stories they shared encompassed daily care, love, sorrows, and joys, all part of living life as the world presents it and making a life that seemed worth living (Mattingly).

Multiple Meanings of Hope and Cure

Living life and death almost simultaneously is a moral dilemma. Domínguez clung to the hope that a cure would come within the time of Isabel's life, a wish memorialized in the very name of the blog: Tal vez Isabel (Maybe Isabel). She sought to envision ways to care for her living child while not clinging to the unlikely possibility of a cure that might interfere with this walk through of death and life:

Eight months have passed since then [the diagnosis]. A time that has given us the space to understand life differently. To move from mourning to hope, to find the strength to fight this adversity. To reorganize our lives radically, around Isabel, around her needs. And to learn to live with this pain that will hardly leave us someday but somehow gives a different value to our daily acts, intensifies them and gives us a survival instinct that we did not know and makes us find happiness in simpler things. (Mar. 2013)

This is my commitment, my hope. A miracle for Isabel. Maybe... maybe Isabel will be part of a generation of children who for the first time in the history of medicine, will survive the prognosis of this disease. Maybe. In the meantime, I will keep my commitment to not give up. (Mar. 2013)

And maybe those machines that hospitalize Isabel's room, machines that a parent should never have to learn to use, will mimic the butterflies on her curtain, and the dolls on her bookshelves, and cease to have meaning for a while. Just maybe. (Jan. 2014)

E. Rapp's memoir does not offer hope for a cure for her son's illness, as she was convinced of his inevitable death at the time of diagnosis. Her central dilemma was not about hoping for his survival but rather how to deal with life in the face of death and how to live with the knowledge that she would eventually have to say goodbye to her son:

That was my role as a dragon mother, as it is for others: to protect my child from wickedness and as much suffering as possible and then, finally, to do the hardest thing of all, a thing most parents will thankfully never have to do: let him go. (21)

[B]ut my task as his myth writer was still to understand my son as a person and being who was independent of me yet dependent on my actions, my attention, my love. I would not and will never do him the disservice of regarding him as an angel or telling myself God had "other" plans for him, and for me. (115)

Learning of the failure of a genetic therapy they were developing, Domínguez lost hope for a cure for her daughter. This felt like a second death sentence after the diagnosis and was the moment she decided to become more engaged with her association: "That day I lost hope. I began a very strong process of internal change. I faced myself in the open, I looked all my ghosts in the face, and I knew that no matter what happened, Isabel's life was the greatest privilege I would ever have" (Oct. 2014).

Hoping for a cure for such incurable and fatal illnesses is not about returning to a place before the illness that exists no longer. It is instead to remake life, find hope, and heal with open possibilities.

Rapp and Domínguez faced the dilemma of deciding what life-support interventions to accept for their children, such as feeding tubes, respiratory aids, and life-support equipment. These decisions were not fixed, and as the disease progressed, they required revisiting and experimentation. E. Rapp decided against force feeding her son and had to grapple with the guilt of potentially starving him; ultimately, she chose to respect his body and prioritize his comfort:

> As a mother I was charged with making impossible decisions about my child's right to life, and I argue that it was Ronan's right to live as fully as possible, in the world, with at least some of his faculties intact, and that it was my burden and my right to determine when his quality of life had become irretrievably compromised. When my son's brain was devastated and his body destroyed by this disease, to refuse to prolong his life through medical intervention would say nothing about how valuable he was to me, or how impossible it would be to quantify his loss. (110)

Domínguez found the decision about feeding tubes difficult to understand. When it came time to decide for her daughter, she could see how difficult it was for her daughter to eat. She faced daily moral dilemmas that challenged her and blurred the boundaries of what constituted a good life. She wondered when to move from the hope of life with her and start palliative care for her death:

> We also met the pediatric intensive care specialist. The first question he asked in our first interview was whether it scared us to cross that threshold of the hospital. The one separating normality from hopelessness, in a long, well-lit corridor with big blue letters on the back doors that composed a phrase that condenses everything: "Palliative Care." I feel like I am entering hell, every time I cross that door, that I am entering a land where no one will give me solutions, only vain consolations and pats on the back. Palliative Care. (July 2013)

When mothering a child with an incurable disease, a cure does not have a singular interpretation. Neither E. Rapp nor Domínguez desired a physical cure for their children. For Rapp, the cure would not be for her son to wake up without the disease but to have his place in the world. The cure would be for the world to accept people as they come: "The potential of Ronan to heal and be healed had little to do with his body and more to do with how he was accepted in the larger world. That, perhaps, was the healing task, and if it happened universally, everywhere we went, it would indeed feel like a miracle" (E. Rapp 150).

Domínguez will always draw on her daughter's strength in dying while still being able to see, hear, feel, and interact with the world; this was a reminder that she should also be strong. She now strengthens her association and fights the disease using what she learned from her experience knowing that this is her daughter's legacy and how hope will be sustained:

> I knew it was an honest and loyal way to pay tribute to her short but remarkable life and to spread the strong character she started expressing when she was only one year old and with which she left this world. She left this world prematurely, looking the Tay-Sachs monster in the face as if saying, "you won't get it all from me." Isabel never stopped smiling, seeing, and listening to her mother singing her songs, feeling her father's loving looks and hugs, going to school to have fun, travelling and seeing places. She left this world whole. (Oct. 2014)

> So I cannot but commit myself to fighting this disease.... Not to become an activist against this disease would be to despise my possibilities, not to listen to my inner voice shouting at me to go out and do something useful. Not giving enough importance to Isabel's life. (Mar. 2014)

> Isabel has had the magical virtue of leaving me fearless. My only fear is that her memory will enter an endless chain of fine threads of lives that are leaving, departing this world and that the passage of time will fade her life into oblivion. In our culture, we are accustomed to overcoming our crises and moving on. Now is when I most want to talk about her, to feel that her beauty and uniqueness reached many. Do not forget her, do not avoid her name in my presence; on the contrary: remember her, name her, speak of her. (Oct. 2014)

The experiences of E. Rapp and Domínguez highlight the continual negotiation between what is possible in the face of their children's illnesses—negotiating life, making the most of every moment with their children, and constructing a narrative of their own. Their stories keep their children alive and evoke their memories. Healing and hope may come in various forms within their narrative but not necessarily in a physical cure. Each new experience transforms becoming, and ultimately, their desire to keep their children alive with words and stories is what gives their experiences value and meaning.

Narrating Open Futures

Rapp and Domínguez write not to elicit sympathy or empathy, not to instruct their readers, nor to seek solace in their readers but to create new meanings, to change the dominant narratives of motherhood, to negotiate for themselves more open futures, and to memorialize their children's experience. They do not see their lives as tragedies, but they acknowledge their tragedy and willingly share their experiences so that others might imagine their experiences in a different way. E. Rapp openly admits:

> What I realized was that people across this country and across the world suffer from a lack of imagination when it comes to disability. Disability lacks a frame.... Most disturbing of all is a common reaction that is rarely questioned: what people view as the 'tragedies' of others makes them feel better about themselves. If somebody else has it worse than you, you can walk around feeling lucky for a few minutes. In the weeks following Ronan's diagnosis it upset me to think that Ronan and I had no purpose at all in this world other than to serve as reflections for situations other people feared. (29–30)

> The meaning of Ronan's life was not to teach me; we often say this about people who defy our notions of normal and I find it pathetic, patronizing, and a way of distancing ourselves from our own fragile bodies and tenuous lives. I don't believe that disabled people exist to teach people life stories—that is not their purpose. It isn't anyone's purpose. We are not 'the disabled', some shape-less, teeming mass of nonnormative bodies designed for teaching purposes, like some kind of pedagogical barbarian horde. So Ronan would have his own path that had nothing to do with me, and I would try to understand it in my limited way. (114)

Domínguez was uncomfortable that her life and that of her daughter were seen as tragedies with her positioned as a superheroine who could handle things that no one else could. Speaking directly to her readers, she said the following:

You would have no choice but to do the same as me: take care of your child and try to find the best specialists to look for a solution. But, above all, take care of your child, live day by day, and enjoy the routine together with them. This is what I do, enjoy each day I spend with Isabel, not thinking about throwing myself out of the window (even though this can sometimes be a temptation). (July 2013)

Every day of my life is a treasure, despite how hard they are. My life doesn't suck. Let no one feel sorry for me. My life is great. And despite the pain, I carry through the days, I am conscious of what my life means. And Isabel's. (July 2013)

Isabel is not just my daughter; she is not just a sick little girl. Isabel is not here for us to be taught a lesson or for others to "learn a lesson," as people sometimes tell me, so mistakenly. Isabel has meaning for herself. She has her own ambitions, however small they might be, and she has her own vision of the world. (Sept. 2013)

Saying goodbye to her daughter Isabel, Domínguez read the following:

When I was in India, I spent a few days in the holy city of Varanasi, where the Ganges flows. There, death is part of life and is continuously celebrated. Hindus lower the goths, wash their dead, cremate them and send them down the river. One early morning, I attended a ceremony in which someone explained to me that the last gesture when saying goodbye was to put a coin in their mouth to pay the passage to Jizo Bodhisattva, the boatman who crosses them to the other shore, the travelling partner between the two worlds, in the final transition of life. Tradition has it that he is also the guardian of the children. Would it be too much to ask him just to let me accompany her on this crossing? I would sit Isabel on my lap, let her feet out to the water, caress her hair during the journey, and upon arrival, I would hand the coin to the ferryman and let her go. (Oct. 2014)

Concluding Thoughts

I understand experience as "a territory of passage, something like a surface of sensibility in which what passes affects in some way, produces some effects, inscribes some marks, leaves some traces, some effects" (Larrosa 160). Possibilities and experiences marked these women's lives: possibilities to make their lives and their children's lives the best until their deaths and (re)imagined experiences in the world as women, mothers, and narrators.

I allow these narratives to pass through me and settle deep in my body. I use their words to find ways to transform the institution of motherhood. I spent time with these narratives and honour their pain, struggle, hope, ability to envision possibilities, and capacity to live each day fully accepting that no future is certain. As Jerome Bruner writes, "And this is, perhaps, what makes the innovative storyteller such a powerful figure in a culture. [They] may go beyond the conventional scripts, leading people to see human happenings in a fresh way, indeed, in a way they had never before 'noticed' or even dreamed" (12).

Endnotes

1. All translations were made freely by this author.

Works Cited

Benjamin, Walter. *Magia e técnica, arte e política (1892–1940)*. Editora Brasiliense, 1994.

Bruner, Jerome. "A Construção Narrativa da Realidade." Translated by Waldemar Ferreira Netto, *Critical Inquiry*, vol. 18, no. 1, 1991, pp. 1–21.

Del Priore, Mary. *Ao sul do corpo: Condição feminina, maternidades e mentalidades no Brasil Colônia*. Livraria José Olympio Editora, 1993.

Domínguez, B. F. "Tal Vez Isabel: el blog de Bubi." Entries from 20 Mar. 2013 to 31 Oct. 2014, http://talvezisabel.blogspot.com.br. Accessed 17 May 2024.

Domínguez, B. F. *Asociación Acción y Cura para Tay-Sachs*, http://actays.org/. Accessed 17 May 2024.

Larrosa, Jorge. *Linguagem e educação depois de Babel*. Autêntica, 2004.

Mattingly, Cheryl. *Moral Laboratories: Family Peril and the Struggle for a*

Good Life. University of California Press, 2014.

O'Reilly, Andrea. *Mother Outlaws: Theories and Practices of Empowered Mothering.* Women's Press/Canadian Scholars' Press Inc., 2004.

O'Reilly, Andrea. *Rocking the Cradle: Thoughts on Feminism, Motherhood and the Possibility of Empowered Mothering.* Demeter Press, 2006.

O'Reilly, Andrea. *Feminist Mothering.* SUNY Press, 2008.

O'Reilly, Andrea. *Encyclopedia of Motherhood.* Sage Publications, 2010.

O'Reilly, Andrea, editor. *From Motherhood to Mothering: The Legacy of Adrienne Rich's* Of Woman Born. SUNY Press, 2012.

O'Reilly, Andrea. *Matricentric Feminism: Theory, Activism, and Practice.* Demeter Press, 2016.

O'Reilly, Andrea. "We Need to Talk about Patriarchal Motherhood: Essentialization, Naturalization and Idealization in Lionel Shriver's *We Need to Talk about Kevin*." *Journal of the Motherhood Initiative for Research and Community Involvement,* vol. 7, no. 1, 2016, pp. 64–81.

Oliveira, Fernanda S. R. *Maconheirinhos: Cuidado, Solidariedade e Ativismo de Pacientes e Seus Familiares em Torno do Óleo de Maconha Rico em Canabidiol (CBD).* Master's thesis. Anthropology Department, Universidade de Brasília, 2016.

Rabinow, Paul. Antropologia da Razão: Ensaios de Paul Rabinow. Relume Dumará, 1999.

Rapp, Emily. *The Still Point of the Turning World: A Memoir with a New Afterword.* Penguin Books, 2014.

Rapp, Rayna. *Testing Women, Testing the Fetus: The Social Impact of Amniocentesis in America.* Routledge, 2005.

Rich, Adrienne. *Of Woman Born: Motherhood as Experience and Institution.* W. W. Norton & Company, 1995.

Scavone, Lucila. "Dar a Vida e Cuidar da Vida: Feminismo e Ciências Sociais." *Condições de Vida e Saúde Mental em Assentamentos Rurais.* Edited by M. Dimenstein et al., Intermeios Cultural, 2016, pp. 223–46.

Solomon, Andrew. *Longe da Árvore: Pais, Filhos e a Busca da Identidade.* Companhia das Letras, 2012.

Zanello, Valesca. *Saúde mental, gênero e dispositivos: cultura e processos de subjetivação.* Editora Appris, 2020.

13.

Imagining Motherhood in a Post-Apocalyptic World: Reifying and Resisting Normative Motherhood in the Climate-Change Novels *Clean Air* by Sarah Blake and *The New Wilderness* by Diane Cook

Andrea O'Reilly

Lamorna Ash begins her review of *The New Wilderness* by referencing the tagline of the British reality television survival series *Eden* (2016–2017): "What if we could start again?" She argues that this question is central to Diane Cook's 2020 novel *The New Wilderness*. This question, I argue, is also at the heart of Sarah Blake's 2022 novel *Clean Air*, which takes place a decade after deadly pollen from trees and plants overtakes the earth. The human beings who survive this disaster live in enclosed domes and cannot leave without wearing protective masks. A serial killer soon begins murdering families by slashing the protective lining of their domes, allowing in the deadly pollen. Similarly, in *The New Wilderness*, pollution has made the air almost unbreathable causing Bea and her partner to flee the polluted city to save the life of their daughter.

They are resettled with a small group of others in the Wilderness State, an experimental project designed to see if humans can live and survive in nature. Through the genre of environmental speculative fiction, each novel seeks to "imagine life post-climate change," (Goldblatt) and consider "the unforeseen consequences, innovative solutions, and the unintended outcomes of global climate catastrophe" (Rauch). While reviewers have taken up these speculations and questions in their readings of these cautionary narratives of "ecological horror" (Kirkus Reviews; Heng) and "biblical catastrophe" (Friedman), few have asked what future imaginings and starting again means or looks like for the mothers and their mothering practices in these two novels.

In "Resurgence of the Monstrous Feminine," Hannah Williams argues that "we retreat to fantasy when we want to escape from what we cannot change." Although in both novels there is a retreat to a fantasy of a better world, *The New Wilderness* imagines new and empowered mothering post climate change, whereas *Clean Air* serves to reify the normative motherhood of yesteryear. In *Clean Air*, life is not better for the mother protagonist nor does the fantasy provide an escape from the dictates of normative motherhood of the world before. Writing on *Clean Air*, Arianna Rebolini comments that while the opening scenes of the novel seem "familiar and mundane," we "soon find much of the new world is, however, profoundly changed." This chapter argues that little has changed for Izabel, the mother, of *Clean Air*, and that despite a climate apocalypse and cataclysmic societal upheaval, the patriarchy of yesteryear persists, and her life remains defined, structured, and confined by normative motherhood. In contrast, the mother Bea of *The New Wilderness* enacts maternal authenticity and agency to challenge the institution of normative motherhood and achieve empowered mothering. As Cook emphasizes in an interview with Diane Slocum, "I wanted to write a mother who was complicated and real and not an idealized version." Thus, while *Clean Air* presents normative motherhood as both natural and inevitable in a post-apocalyptic world, *The New Wilderness* imagines a mother outlaw who escapes from the normative motherhood of the destroyed old world to achieve maternal authenticity and agency in empowered mothering.

In her recent article, "Only Mom Can Save the World: Normative Motherhood in the Post Apocalypse," Katrina Millan analyzes the post-apocalypse films *A Quiet Place* (2018) and *Bird Box* (2018), arguing that both films "ultimately work to affirm or re-establish white, middle-class heteronormative motherhood as the most vital form of emotional and social connection in the face of world collapse" (1). More specifically, Millan argues that in *A Quiet Place*, the nuclear family is presented as the only visible—and therefore only viable—means of survival in an unfamiliar world, whereas the mother in *Bird Box* "is presented as an outlaw mother who needs to be corralled into normative motherhood" (2). Both films not only affirm the dictates of normative motherhood through the compliance of the good mother (*A Quiet Place*) or the nonconformity of the bad mother (*Bird Box*) but also serve to reify normative motherhood as not only natural but necessary for the very survival of the human race in a post-apocalyptic world. The two novels considered in this chapter similarly position mothers as either in compliance with or resistant to normative motherhood; however, in *The New Wilderness*, the nonconformity of the mother outlaw subverts rather than reifies the normative motherhood of yesteryear.

This collection aims to expose the pain of mothers, transform silence into action, and destabilize hegemonic institutions and structures. In its considerations of how normative motherhood is reified and resisted in two climate change novels, this chapter exposes and articulates the pain inflicted on mothers by the hegemonic institution of normative motherhood while considering how this institution may be destabilized through empowered mothering. Thus, I read the two novels as cautionary narratives about climate change and as necessary interventions in how new worlds are being imagined for mothers. I also consider how each novel, either its reification of or resistance to normative motherhood, exposes and articulates the pains of mothers to prompt action and change. As French writer Jean-Baptiste Alphonse Karr famously wrote, "plus ça change, plus c'est la même chose: the more things change, the more they stay the same" (qtd. in Hanley). In using Karr's oft-cited quote, Benet emphasizes, "A change of heart must accompany experience before lasting change occurs." Indeed, as the two novels reveal, any new imaginings or a true starting again must begin with a critique of and challenge to hegemonic systems, including patriarchy and its renditions of normative motherhood, if we dare to dream of a truly utopian future for women and mothers.

Clean Air: "Not How I Was Taught a Post-apocalyptic World Would Be"

A written letter that opens the novel signals a post-apocalyptic world ten years after an event coined "the Turning," when half the world's population was killed by tree pollen. This letter is later identified as written by the mother protagonist, Izabel, to her daughter Cami and explains that the signs pointing to the event were there but were ignored and that "most people's responses to catastrophe, as it approaches, is muted" (1). The letter concludes with Izabel's reflection: "That the resulting world, the world we built from scratch, it's not how I was taught a post-apocalyptic world would be. It presents itself like a gift" (1). I suggest that this letter, significantly written from mother to daughter, serves as the lesson of the novel: for women, and in particular mothers, the new world of *Clean Air* is not the ideal and perfect one that it is presented as, and just as people ignored the signs of impending climate disaster, they now are blind to the artifice of this newly created world that pretends all is good when it is not. I also suggest that the word "gift," though ambiguous, may be read as signifying possibility or opportunity. The line gestures to what Izabel must discover and act upon: Her life as a mother is not as happy and good as this society pretends it to be. Building upon a quote from the conclusion of *Clean Air*—"It's important for people to be the most happy they can be" (299)—Carolina Toscana argues that in the novel, this means "mothers must acknowledge and hold space for maternal anxiety, maternal ambivalence, maternal guilt, and imperfections within our definitions of mothering." I would add that Izabel's eventual understanding of the importance of happiness and how to achieve it only comes at the novel's conclusion, when she fully sees through the pretense of the supposedly perfect post-apocalyptic world and tears away its protective exterior, as the serial killer does, revealing the truths of her lived maternal life that are disguised and distorted by the normative motherhood she is required to perform. Indeed, as Blake explains, "I wanted Izabel to navigate her way through this new world, to help her feel agency in it, and belonging, and happiness" (*Crime Reads*). I also argue that while Izabel may find this agency and happiness to create a life outside of normative motherhood, the novel does not seek to challenge or change the institution of normative motherhood itself; rather, it only and tentatively provides this one mother, Izabel, a possible escape from normative motherhood to resolve her unhappiness.

Following the letter, the novel opens with a description of a typical morning for the mother Izabel as she pours juice for her daughter, packs up her lunch box, and organizes her backpack (3). Significantly, this normative rendition of mothering is immediately undercut by Izabel's reflection that "If she timed it right, the three of them would be in the kitchen together. Not that she didn't want to be alone with Cami [her daughter], only that she preferred not to be" (3). Later, we learn that Izabel is annoyed with her husband Kaito and wants to scold him for not backing her up in a disagreement with their daughter (7). That morning Izabel also decides not to eat breakfast with her husband as she normally does because she "knew she'd start a fight" (9). Izabel also reflects that while she was seen as the serious one in the family, she "didn't know if she would have been, if she wanted to be. If she started this way" (6). Once Cami leaves for school and her husband begins work in his home office, Izabel decides to "go to the mall, and while she didn't know what she would do there, it was better than staying at home" (9). At home, "the days dragged on until Cami back," and Izabel always felt that her husband "was critical of how she used her time" (9). Later, Izabel reflects that "even with the cleaning and laundry done, emails responded to, groceries ordered, and dental appointments scheduled," she questions what she is "doing inside her perfect life" (10). Although Izabel feels her unhappiness with her husband waning, she knows it will come back (10). This brief introductory chapter reveals and emphasizes that while Izabel cannot fully articulate the feeling, she knows she is not the fulfilled and contented woman and mother she is expected to be in her "perfect and comfortable life" (10). The chapter concludes with Kaito assuring Izabel that the air quality of ninety-eight percent in their home was fine and with Izabel, though believing it should be at one hundred percent, conceding, "I guess so." (11). Her husband's assurances and Izabel's reluctant agreement signify and symbolize Izabel's need to convince herself that all is happy and good in her life of normative motherhood.

The opening chapter also introduces the new realities of their post-apocalyptic lives: Cami putting on a mask and leaving the home through two sealed doors to an awaiting taxi, discussions about the home's air quality, and Izabel reading news from ten years earlier, before the Turning, on her app. The following chapter describes the changed reality of their new world. The air filtration system of their home fails, the family retreats to their safe room, and Cami is taken to the hospital by ambulance for breathing issues. In the hospital with her daughter, Izabel remembers the time she spent with her dying mother at the hospital in the early months before the Turning, "creating months of memories that she could look back on with guilt" (16). Following the death of her mother, Izabel tried going back to school but failed her courses, leaving her "not knowing what she wanted to do with her life; not knowing who she wanted to be" (18). Izabel's continuing remembrances of times before, during, and after the Turning that interrupt the present-day narrative, along with many references to the past—such as the reruns of old "feel good" television shows they watch in the hospital waiting room and Izabel constantly watching news from 2017 on her favourite app—suggest that the world created following the Turning is not that separate or different from the old world nor is this new world as perfect as they pretend it to be. Izabel remembers the building of their new world and the laying of hundreds of perfectly placed plumbing and electrical hook-ups—"making it look like nothing had been there before" and that history had been "wiped clean" (25). While Cami is in a coma at the hospital, Izabel first hears about the news of a killer who murdered a family of four by slashing the protective exterior of their home. This murder, the first murder since the Turning ten years earlier, soon becomes a series of killings as more and more families are murdered in the same manner. "Suddenly, like the taut plastic bubble of their living spaces," as Dan Friedman notes, "the fragile security of the new world has been ripped open." Significantly, as the novel unfolds, we learn that Cami, when she sleeps, sees each murder as they happen. Meanwhile, Izabel becomes increasingly fixated on the serial killer and begins to identify with him.

As the story unfolds, Rebolini observes that Izabel is "plagued by a suspicion that she and the killer might not be different" and questions why she cannot appreciate this clean world or why she seems to be the only one bothered by its superficiality. I suggest that Izabel identifies with the serial killer because both see through the artifice of the new utopian world, and both, as Friedman elaborates, understand that "the normalcy projected by Izabel's husband, and the town is deeply fake." More specifically, and in the context of Izabel's life, the perhaps ironically named "the Turning" changed little for mothers and their mothering, leaving Izabel unhappy and unfulfilled despite the social expectation to be otherwise as dictated by the new-world rhetoric that she has "a perfect and comfortable life" (10).

Although the new world may have changed how Izabel's mothering is lived and practised, it has not changed how it is defined, namely by the normative motherhood of yesteryear. As established in the opening chapter, Izabel is a stay-at-home wife and mother responsible for the childcare, housekeeping, and homemaking as delineated and dictated by normative motherhood. Reproductive and productive labour remain gendered in this post-apocalyptic world, and although the private realm may now be a pod, it is still women as mothers who are solely responsible for the reproductive and domestic labour of this private sphere. Here, we see enacted what I have defined elsewhere as four of the defining dictates of normative motherhood: privatization, individualization, idealization, and normalization (*Matricentric Feminism*). Privatization locates motherwork solely in the reproductive realm of the home. Individualization causes such mothering to be the work and responsibility of one person, and naturalization assumes that maternity is natural to women— all women naturally know how to mother—and that the work of mothering is driven by instinct rather than intelligence and developed by habit rather than skill. Idealization sets unattainable expectations of and for mothers. Normalization limits and restricts maternal identity and practice to one specific mode: the nuclear family. The mother is a wife to a husband, and she assumes the role of the nurturer, whereas the husband assumes that of the provider.

When Izabel first meets Andy, the mother of Cami's friend, she asks her what she does; Izabel responds, "Just a mother" (38). Izabel is bored and unfulfilled at home most days while her daughter is at school, and she continuously "tries to think of something useful she could do" (55). In her boredom, Izabel occupies most of her time watching reruns of reality television, reading news on her app, having pedicures/manicures, receiving acupuncture, window shopping at the mall, having her tarot cards read, and writing letters that are later destroyed in the privacy pods at the mall. One evening, as Izabel is watching another reality cooking show, she thinks that "she should never feel upset, not with a family as wonderful as hers" (58). Yet Izabel's internal dissatisfaction is evident: "She felt the ache in her back from bowing over a hundred little clothes like she'd said a hundred little prayers, as she arranged her head on a chintzy pillow that matched a vase and a throw and coordinated the room around a turquoise blue she once cared about, as she, Izabel, relaxed back into her life—she was upset" (58). Reading this passage, one is reminded of the dissatisfaction and boredom of stay-at-home mothers described in Betty Friedan's *The Feminine Mystique*, published in 1963. Friedan writes that "in lieu of more meaningful goals, these women spend too much time cleaning their already tidy homes, improving their already attractive appearances, and indulging their already spoiled children" (69–70). While a hundred years separate the mid-twentieth-century mothers of Friedan's book and Izabel in a post-apocalyptic world, the more things change, the more they stay the same.

That Izabel's life remains largely unchanged from that of her great-grandmother, despite the cataclysmic changes of climate disaster, is indeed confounding. Equally perplexing is how in this post-apocalyptic world, where most social ills have been remedied, the institution of normative motherhood remains unchallenged and unchanged. There is little economic inequity, and no poverty or homelessness, in this new world. Crime is all but nonexistent, and there has not been a murder in ten years. There are fewer illnesses, and people are eating more nutritious food. All citizens receive universal health care and a basic income. In the novel, as Friedman observes, "a purposeful cross-section of races and religions" suggests a world more equal and communal across cultural and racial differences. The women in this new world have what their mothers could only have dreamed of: free and universal childcare, after-school programs, children driven to and from school, remote work, and ample leisure time. Thus, while the novel is dystopian in its description of climate disaster, it is also, Katrina Millan argues, "a utopic novel where society has been rebuilt in a safer and more equitable way." Or, as Alexander Pyles writes, "The world of *Clean Air* features an encouraging vision of a future where humanity works together." Nevertheless, in this seemingly feminist and socially just utopian world, there remains the institution of normative motherhood and its patriarchal gender scripts and structures of male dominance. In other words, this new world seems to have corrected or eradicated all but one of the injurious institutions of yesteryear—that of normative motherhood.

Surprisingly, neither the novel itself nor the reviews of *Clean Air* acknowledge, let alone address, this irony: In a radically transformed and supposedly equitable world, little has changed or improved for the mother Izabel who, in both her marriage and motherhood, lives with gender inequality. Nor have reviewers asked what should be an obvious question: How could Izabel be so unhappy in this changed and just world? Nor have they questioned why Izabel is holding "a little anger that she kept and polished like a silver spoon" (42). So angry, as Izabel later tells her therapist, "that I could have been the killer because I'm angry about how we're living as if in some wild utopia now" (283). Izabel's discontent and rage are not permitted in normative motherhood and thus must be censored and concealed. Nonetheless, these feelings are articulated in the novel. To my knowledge, no review has identified this irony at the novel's heart: Although the world is is now equitable, it is not for mothers.

In the privacy pods at the mall, Izabel writes letters to the serial killer, reinforcing yet again, that like the serial killer, she sees through the artifice of the new utopian world. She wonders what "direction" her life should take: "to let it stand—that's where I am or to tear it apart, one home at a time—that's where you are" (74). In another letter, she admits to "imagining having sex with [him]" and although she hopes that she wouldn't enjoy "having sex with someone who's killed people," she admits she probably would (74–75). Like the serial killer, Izabel understands that the normalcy of the new world is all pretense but, at the same time, admits to her perpetuation of this artifice, as she explains to her daughter in a letter: "I want you to know that it wasn't hard to pretend for you that the world was well, normal, as it should be. My mother pretended with me" (76). Izabel must pretend all is good and normal for her daughter because that is what good mothers must do. This performativity of normalcy, I suggest, is hard for Izabel because it demands that she distort and deny the truths of her life and self. Here we are reminded of Susan Maushart's concept of the "mask of motherhood." The mask of motherhood, Maushart explains, is an "assemblage of fronts— mostly brave, serene, and all knowing—that we use to disguise the chaos and complexity of our lived experience" (2). To be masked, Maushart continues, is "to deny and repress what we experience, to misrepresent it, even to ourselves" (1–2). The mask of motherhood "keeps women from speaking clearly what they know and from hearing truths too threatening to face" (7). To borrow from Maushart, wearing this metaphorical mask, Izabel denies and represses the truths of her discontent and anger to project the happiness required from her in the new and ideal world. She must adhere to a rigid script with specific requirements, as she explains to her daughter in a letter: "[You must] wake up to your child and smile at them, despite yourself" (76). But like the serial killer, Izabel knows that all is not normal and that all is not new or just for mothers in this supposedly ideal world. I suggest that Izabel identifies with the serial killer's act of tearing open the exterior protective lining of the pod homes because it unmasks motherhood, revealing the truths of mothering disguised and distorted by the normative motherhood that Izabel must perform.

Early on, Izabel chooses "to let it stand"—live her life as if she were content—but as the novel unfolds, she increasingly identifies with the serial killer and begins to "tear it all apart"; unmasking motherhood to, in Maushart's words, "speak clearly what she knows." In her letter to her daughter, she explains: "I am not the person I might have been" (75). This is further emphasized later at a tarot reading—where the first card drawn, "the future card of what is already in you," which signifies "who you *could* become"—reveals Izabel as "Ambitious and Successful" (103). Significantly, after the reading, "Izabel felt the presence of danger. And she felt concern, too, because instead of fear *she was feeling a kind of power*" (105; my emphasis). Later, as Izabel goes searching for the serial killer, she imagines "a dozen women and how they might spend extra money on frivolity and extravagance. How they might create their lives to resemble something entirely out of place in the new world" (114). Following this imagining, Izabel witnesses the serial killer tearing open the protective exterior of yet another pod. As the killer flees, Izabel enters the pod, attempting to save the family but is only able to save the daughter. After she is interviewed by the police and Andy praises her bravery, Izabel looks in the mirror and realizes that "she didn't look the same as she had the night before ... her reflection suggested, if only slightly, that she was a changed woman" (131). The detective is so impressed with the detailed information provided by Izabel in the police interview that she tells Izabel "You're my star witness and hero" (185) and invites her to become involved in the police investigation. A few evenings later, Izabel and Jana—the young woman Izabel saved and who is now living with Izabel's family—see the killer on the street and chase after him with a gun. While they do not capture the killer, their pursuit of him prevents him from killing another family and prompts Izabel's husband to say to her, "You were very brave and I'm so proud of you" (228). To catch the killer, the police decide that they need to provoke him and set up a scene wherein the killer will come looking for Izabel. As Inspector Paz explains, "We will put it on the news—'the woman who faced the killer.' Really piss him off" (250). The plan is successful, and they capture the killer and learn that he is Patrick, a man Izabel knows and who works at the privacy pods she visited at the mall.

After the arrest of Patrick, Izabel's life resumes as it was with her watching yet another TV rerun and asking herself: "*Is this my now? Is this my life again?* (271). The inspector soon calls and asks Izabel to come to the station, leaving Izabel to admit, "I couldn't help but feel a bit of thrill" (271). The inspector invites Izabel to interview the suspect, and after a long and intense questioning, Izabel brings Patrick to a confession. Significantly, during the interview, Patrick asks Izabel what a typical day looks like for her, and she replies, "I clean. I shop for things I need. I watch old television and read old news" (280), prompting Patrick to question, "What would you even do with yourself—if you didn't have to clean?" (280). Following the interview and Patrick's confession, Inspector Paz invites Izabel to work for the police. When Izabel informs her husband that she will be taking the job, he says, "I think you've been looking for something you like for a long time. I'm glad you found it" (298). Izabel reflects: "That was true. Her life had been interrupted over and over by things she couldn't control. Sometimes she felt like she only *fell* into her life with Kaito [her husband], fell backward into it. And she wondered what her life would have looked like, if she'd been moving forward, toward one desire or another, never stopping and never stopped" (298).

The job requires Izabel to move to the capital, and her husband agrees to the move. When her daughter says she is happy staying in their current home, Izabel asks her, "Don't you think I will be able to make you happier if I'm happier?" (299). She asserts to her daughter: "It's important for people to be the most happy they can be. And for them to keep asking themselves what would make them the most happy" (299). With the capture and confession of the killer, Izabel learns that what makes her "the most happy" is meaningful work that she enjoys and is good at. With her decision to take the job, Izabel is "moving forward, toward that which she desires" (298). She has answered Patrick's question of what she would and could do if she didn't have to clean all day—create an identity and life outside normative motherhood.

The novel ends with Izabel finally becoming the person "[she] might have been" (75). This happy ending, however, does not unpack let alone resolve the novel's paradox: This new and equitable world is not so for mothers and the normative motherhood of yesteryear persists in its patriarchal gender scripts and structures of male dominance. Perhaps for Izabel, taking on full-time employment will eradicate the individualization, privatization, idealization, and normalization of normative motherhood, but this is left solely for the reader to conjecture. Overall, I argue that despite the novel's unmasking of normative motherhood to convey Izabel's anger and discontent, the novel's conclusion—wherein Izabel claims the agency to determine the direction of her life—does not offer a critique of normative motherhood, nor does it seek to counter or change it. Nor is any explanation given on why the novel does not or cannot take up these interrogations. Rather, the reader is left to ask: Why does the husband so readily accept Izabel following a career path at the end of the novel, even agreeing to move, when it seems like Izabel's role as wife and mother prevented her from doing so for most of their known relationship? Will Izabel still maintain the brunt of the domestic labour when she begins full-time employment or will her husband now equally share childcare and domestic labour? Will Izabel still be expected to do the impossible—to sacrifice one thing for the other? Or will she be deemed a bad mother for not doing so? Instead of exploring these questions, the novel leaves readers with an unsettling sense of déjà vu, as the normative motherhood of yesteryear is unchanged and unchallenged in its futuristic imaginings. In other words, and to paraphrase Izabel's lament, this is not how we imagined motherhood would be in a post-apocalyptic world. And that indeed the more things change, the more they remain the same.

The New Wilderness: "I Wanted a Mother Who Didn't Behave like the Culture Says Mothers Ought to Behave"

In an interview with Katherine Savage, Cook elaborates on her intent to write mothers who are complicated and real and not idealized versions:

> I wanted there to be mothers who didn't behave like the culture says all mothers ought to behave. I wanted mothers who behave the way I feared I might behave if I were a mother, ways I discovered I do behave now that I am a mother. I wanted the complexity of Bea's experiences to be on the page and not have it diminish her motherhood. I wanted everyone to get the chance to be human (qtd. in Savage).

In *The New Wilderness*, the mother, Bea, is indeed presented and developed as a complex and multifaceted character, and by "not behaving as mothers ought to behave," she interrupts and interrogates the scripts of idealized normative motherhood that Izabel enacts in *Clean Air*. In this way, Bea may be characterized as a "mother outlaw," as first theorized by Adrienne Rich in *Of Woman Born*. When discussing a vacation she took without her husband one summer, Rich describes herself and her sons as "conspirators, outlaws from the institution of motherhood" (195). Upon Rich's return home, the institution, in her words, "closed down on us again, and my own mistrust of myself as a 'good mother' returned, along with my resentment of the archetype" (195). Rich's reflections on being an outlaw from the institution of motherhood and the references she makes to being a good and bad mother are drawn from the key distinction she makes between motherhood and mothering. In patriarchal culture, women who mother within the institution of motherhood are regarded as good mothers, whereas women who mother outside or against the institution of motherhood are viewed as bad mothers. Significantly, Cook questions and reflects on this dynamic in an interview: "Would I be a good mom? Would I be the kind of 'bad mom' that Bea sometimes is. Maybe this is true for all parents and children: we're always trying and not quite getting there" (qtd. in Heng). When the interviewer comments, "I didn't think Bea was a bad mom. I thought she was trying really hard," Cook explains:

> I use "bad mom" with air quotes around it. To me, a bad mom means something like "more human than is permissible." I am fascinated by the idea of what mothers are supposed to be, and how that's at odds with what they are—the fact that they're just female humans who had a baby or are raising a child. I don't think Bea is a bad mom at all, but I know some people will think that. She makes some of the ultimate sacrifices for her daughter, she just isn't always happy about it... I wanted Bea to be complicated and have lots of realities within her, because I think that I do, my mom did, and we all do. (qtd. in Heng)

That Bea "isn't always happy about the sacrifices she makes" and that she is "complicated with lots of realities within her" positions her in stark contrast to Izabel of *Clean Air*, who not only performs the selfless happiness of normative motherhood but also disguises and denies the complicated realities of motherwork hidden by the idealized mask of motherhood.

Through her complexity and realness, Bea becomes that mother outlaw, described by Rich, to achieve empowered mothering.

In my work on empowered mothering (*Matricentric Feminism*), I define its overarching aim as conferring on mothers the agency, authority, authenticity, autonomy, and advocacy-activism denied to them in normative motherhood. Of particular relevance to Bea are the concepts of agency and authenticity that give rise to empowered mothering and serve to disrupt normative motherhood. "Maternal agency," as Lynn O'Brien Hallstein explains, "draws on the idea of agency—the ability to influence one's life, to have a power to control one's life—and explores how women have agency via mothering" (698). A theory of maternal agency focuses on, as O'Brien Hallstein continues, "mothering practices that facilitate women's authority and power and is revealed in mothers' efforts to challenge and act against aspects of institutionalized motherhood that constrain and limit women's lives and power as mothers" (698). "Authenticity," as explained in Elizabeth Butterfield's encyclopedia entry, "is an ethical term that denotes being true to oneself, as in making decisions that are consistent with one's own beliefs and values [whereas] inauthenticity is generally understood to be an abdication of one's own authority and a loss of integrity" (701). In the context of empowered mothering, maternal authenticity draws on Sara Ruddick's concept of the "conscientious mother" (Butterfield, 701) and my model of the "authentic feminist mother" (*Matricentric Feminism*), and refers to "independence of mind and the courage to stand up to dominant values" and to "being truthful about motherhood and remaining true to oneself in motherhood" (Butterfield, 701). Significantly, in *The New Wilderness*, this maternal agency and authenticity that achieves empowered mothering and counters normative motherhood is most fully revealed and enacted in Bea's relationship with her daughter Agnes.

It is Agnes's illness at the age of four that leads Bea to make, in the words of Téa Obreht, "the impossible and inadvisable decision to join an experiment in the Wilderness State to save her young daughter Agnes from the wasted City whose poisoned air has been killing her since the day she was born." While her partner Glen agrees with Bea that the plan "was crazy," he emphasizes that "If we stay, she will die" (72). Hearing his "flat and unequivocal words," Bea "felt like he slapped her" (72). Reflecting on his words, Bea admits to "wishing that she'd had better thoughts running through her head" (72); "Thoughts like, *I don't even need to think*—*of course that's what we'll do.... Whatever it takes.* But really, she thought, *So, we have to risk all our lives just to save hers? Is this the rule, or do I have a choice?*" (72). Thinking about the promising and fulfilling career she will leave behind, along with the close relationship she has with her mother who will not be joining them but whom she still needs in her life, Bea questions internally, "Did her needs not matter anymore?" (72). Bea begins hitting the side of her head "to rattle her humanity loose. To think of her daughter first" (72). She only stops when Glen grips her wrists and holds her in his arms leaving Bea with "bitter" tears on her face as she choked on sobs, "furious and brokenhearted," thinking, "*This is motherhood?*" (73).

Later, when the family is living in the Wilderness State and Agnes is still a young child, she asks her mother Bea: "Do you love me... Even when you're angry?" Bea lies to her daughter saying, "I'm never angry," because, as she reflects, "It was better if everything [I] did was labeled as love, wasn't it?" (69). As time passes and Bea reminds herself that her daughter is healthy, safe, and well in the New Wilderness State and that it was her decision to come that made this happen, she admits that it "only made her feel wistful" (117). Bea's sentiments articulate the maternal anger, resentment, and regret that Izabel in *Clean Air* diminishes in her performance of normative motherhood and position Bea as a bad mother by the dictates of normative motherhood.

As I explore in my work on maternal regret (*Maternal Regret*), the sentiments of maternal ambivalence, resentment, and anger are rendered taboo by normative motherhood because they challenge its dictates of essentialization, naturalization, and idealization—that all women want to become mothers, that mothering comes naturally to all women, and that women experience mothering only as fulfilling and gratifying. Indeed, as Orna Donath remarks in *Regretting Motherhood: A Study*, "It seems that there is no room for re-evaluation let alone regret [in motherhood]" (xv). However, in articulating the tabooed maternal feelings of ambivalence, resentment, and regret, as Bea does in *The New Wilderness*, these dictates are challenged and potentially disrupted, and these regretful mothers become mother outlaws who enact maternal agency and authenticity.

After several years in the Wilderness State, Bea receives a letter informing her that her mother has died and asking that she attend the reading of the will. When Bea, gutted with grief, shares this news with her daughter, she is enraged by her daughter's response: "Agnes was trying to take ownership of this pain, of this relationship. This important relationship that Bea had abandoned in order to care for her own daughter, a daughter who was strange and simpering.... Her own daughter who was looking for attention she did not deserve now" (132–33). Moments later, Bea leaps into a car that is leaving the Wilderness State, panting to the surprised driver, "Get me out of here" while her young daughter "stood, mouth agape, [with] confusion and fury dancing across her face as her mother drove away" (135). At first, Agnes cannot believe that her mother is gone, but as she comes to realize that "her mean mother has run away," she wonders if her mother had ever "been anything but a mean mother" and if "every kiss had been cruel, meant to eventually cause pain with its absence" (139). Agnes later learns, "There were other mothers [the women of the group in the Wilderness State] to be had. They stepped in right away and gave her more mothering than her mean mother ever had" (140). Unlike Izabel who performs normative motherhood despite her own unhappiness, Bea abandons her daughter to the care of others to act upon her own needs and desires. Leaving her daughter to honour the wishes of her deceased mother, Bea enacts a maternal agency that eludes Izabel in *Clean Air*, but in doing so, Bea becomes a bad mother, as maternal abandonment is the ultimate transgression of normative motherhood.

The following lengthy section of the book, "The Ballad of Agnes," is narrated from the perspective of the daughter Agnes, whereas Bea is absent in the narrative. Early in the section, Agnes reflects, "Having no mother meant she was an adult now" (143). Realizing that she could finally show how strong she was, Agnes "felt a lightning bolt of happiness that her mother was gone" (141). Living among the animals in the wilderness, Agnes "noticed that a mother would only be a mother for so long before she wanted to be something else. No mother she'd ever watched here remained a mother forever" (149). Thus, as Agnes later reflects, "She had been ready for [her mother's leaving] without knowing it" (149). The earlier sections of Agnes's narrative are emphatically daughter-centric in their privileging of the daughter's voice and enactment of mother blame. As the section unfolds, Agnes's perspective shifts to a matrifocal one, and she understands her mother in the context of her own life and appreciates how her mother loved and cared for her. When a group of newcomers arrive, and Agnes sees a young daughter with her mother, she feels an absence: "She remembered being that young, that easily safe. She was happy to be an adult now. But she missed feeling safe like that. It was gone from her life for good" (176).

Later, when Agnes is speaking to Celeste, a newly arrived young daughter, she remembers and describes to her how sick she was before coming to the Wilderness State. In reply, Celeste says, "So your mom brought you here to save you?" (182). Hearing her words, "Agnes caught her breath. She had not thought of it that way before. Her face burned, but she wasn't sure why" (182). Eventually, Agnes realizes and explains to Celeste that her mother left her behind in the Wilderness State not only because Bea's mother died but also because "[she] was pretty unhappy here" (183). Later, the ranger assures Agnes that her mother "is just in the city and that Agnes knows that" (207) and tells Agnes "That she misses you like crazy" (208). Hearing these words, "something newly bitter [was] released from her" (208), suggesting that Agnes has released the resentment she holds against Bea and has begun to understand her life.

As the section ends, Glenn shares with Agnes happy memories of their times together before they left the city for the Wilderness State and how her mother used to save orange lollipops for Agnes because she knew they were her favourite flavour. As Agnes listens to these stories, she remembers her mother putting her to bed at night with "feelings of sleep. Of warmth, of cool sheets, her mother's dry lips saying Good Night sweetheart" (220). She realizes then "how awful it must have been to leave such a nice life" (221) and that her mother did this to save her life. Agnes gets her first period, feeling at first excitement but then loneliness (233), suggesting that as a young woman, Agnes is better able to appreciate her mother's life and admit to how much she loves and misses her.

Almost immediately, as the new cold winds arrive, Agnes's mother returns (234). Mother and daughter are brought together in "Friend or Foe," a section of the book, wherein, emphasized by Carl, a member of the group, "Everything is different now" (237). Agnes is now a young woman, as signified by the start of her menses, and perhaps can understand better Bea's life outside of her identity and role as her mother and reconnect with her as a woman and person. When they first see each other, Agnes describes "her mother floating to her, drawn to her like a magnet" (238). In an interview, Cook explains that she "wanted to look at the ways that mothers and daughters come together and repel one another, like magnets.... I wanted them to share the story so that we could see how each of them sees the other, and how they misunderstand each other" (qtd. in Slocum). In another interview, Cook elaborates, "Magnets are usually thought of as attracting forces. Strong. But flip them and they repel. They are equally attracting and repelling" (qtd in Shekhar). Indeed, as the novel unfolds, Bea and Agnes, as Jessamine Chan explains, "are drawn together and repelled apart by the very relationship that binds them." As Agnes remains angry with her mother, not accepting her apology or trusting her, she is simultaneously drawn to the comfort of her mother's body and the warmth of her bed, "and [as] she curls herself into her mother, [she realized how much] she missed this feeling" (257).

When Bea tells Agnes, "I love you more than you can understand. I would do anything for you," Agnes resents her "mother's fierce love" and reflects "I wanted a mild mother, one who would love me exactly the same every day" because, as she reflects further, "*Mild mothers don't run away*" (260). During an altercation, when Agnes suggests that she and her father were better off when they thought that Bea was dead, Bea slaps her daughter and explains that the move to the Wilderness State, and the accompanying rules and restrictions, was all for Agnes's protection. In anger, Agnes proclaims, "I hate you," to which Bea replies, "Of course you hate me. I'm your mother" (267). Later though, when Bea tells the community members to listen to Agnes about what route they should take, Agnes reflects that "She hated how easy it was for her to love [her mother.] She would always love her mother. Even when her mother didn't deserve it" (300). Upon the death of Glen, an argument ensues between mother and daughter, and Bea declares to Agnes, "I love you. I know you love me" (338). Later, as Agnes swims with her mother, she "remembers feeling like ten of her could fit inside her mother. And then she is reminded that she had come from there. That she'd lived there, breathing water into her mother's guts" (343). Then "for the first time in a long time, the thought of her mother made Agnes happy" (344). Finally, as Bea, fully expecting an argument, tells Agnes it is time to leave the water, Agnes realizes the following:

> She didn't want to argue anymore. She let her mother tend to her as she slumped and stared into the fire [at the campsite]. It reminded her of being sick. Feeling this warmth... draping blankets across her shoulders, brushing the hair of hair out of her eyes.

> Wiping away droop or snot or blood if she had been coughing.
> Being sick had been awful but being cared for felt nice. She missed
> it. She knew her mother was still caring for her all this time. (346)

Although their mother-daughter relationship is like a magnet, Agnes understands and appreciates her mother's love, even if it differs from the love defined by and required in normative motherhood. Through her maternal authenticity, Bea speaks truths Agnes often does not want to hear. Through her maternal agency, Bea made the difficult decision to abandon her daughter to sort out her own life as a woman and daughter. This maternal authenticity and agency allow the mother and daughter to create a relationship of genuine love, care, trust, and admiration.

As the novel concludes, the state ranger informs the community that they must leave and return to the city, as the New Wilderness project has failed. Bea asks Agnes to leave with her in the hopes of finding and living in the Private Lands. But Agnes laments, "Why would I go any-where with you? You left me alone.... Mothers don't do that" (366). Bea succinctly replies: "Well this mother did. This mother loves you. And this mother left. And this mother came back. And this mother will never be forgiven for it" (367). Agnes longs for Bea to express remorse and admit that she should not have left, but Bea refuses: "I can't. Because it wouldn't be true. It was important for me. I never lied to you and I'm not going to start now" (367). Although Agnes wishes her mother would lie, Bea cannot and will not because she lives her life and mothers her daughter in authenticity and not, as Izabel does in *Clean Air,* through the pretence of idealized motherhood. Although never quite able to fully forgive her mother, Agnes can finally hold these seemingly incongruent truths together—her mother left, her mother came back, and her mother loves her—and she concedes: "I do love you, Mama" (368). As Agnes came to understand why Bea had to leave, Bea now understands why her daughter must stay. "Sobbing and beaming," Bea proclaims to the land and sky as her daughter walks away: "Look at the *wonder.* I was a *good* mother" (369).

Agnes chooses to stay in the Wilderness State and eventually meets an orphaned young girl, whom she names Fern and raises as a daughter. Agnes never sees her mother again but leaves notes in the trees, hoping that someday her mother will find her. Agnes and Fern are the last two to be rounded up by the rangers.

In the novel's epilogue, we learn that Agnes and Fern live in a resettlement complex but climb through a fence at night to return to the wilderness to "know the world as it once was" (391). There, Agnes tells Fern stories as her own mother had once done. On one such night, Agnes reflects, "I didn't understand [my mother] until I had the chance to care for this little Fern" (391), and then, "overcome with love, on the verge of crying and laughing, [Agnes realizes that] finally, finally, finally [she has] began to know [her] mother" (394). The novel concludes with Agnes telling her daughter stories of "complexities and complications" (395), "because that is what makes them true [...] it is the only way I know how to raise a daughter. It's how my mother raised me" (395). As a mother, Agnes is finally able to understand her mother's complicated motives and complex love, finally coming to appreciate how Bea lived and mothered with agency and authenticity. Agnes will now do the same for her daughter.

Conclusion: "Motherhood Felt Like a Heavy Coat She Was Compelled to Put on Each Day No Matter the Weather"

In an interview, Cook comments that "Motherhood felt like a heavy coat she was compelled to put on each day no matter the weather" (18) might be her favourite quote of the book (qtd. in Shekhar). I suggest this line is also an apt metaphor for the aim of this collection and my chapter. This chapter considers how two mothers Izabel and Bea wear this heavy coat of motherhood—the demands and expectations of normative mother-hood. Does the mother deny its heaviness, pretend it is lighter than it is, and seek to modify it ever so slightly to make it more comfortable as Izabel does? Or does the mother acknowledge and honour its heaviness, live with it authentically, and seek to fully refashion it so that it fits seamlessly with the body that is wearing it as Bea does? Each novel, in its futuristic imaginings, delivers two possibilities on how motherhood may be worn: in compliance with or in defiance of normative motherhood. I suggest that the maternal coat of authenticity and agency, worn by Bea and then bequeathed to her daughter, is the one we must dare to design as we live our lives today and imagine our future.

Works Cited

Ash, Lamorna. "Other Edens." *TLS,* 18 Sept. 2020, https://www.the-tls. co.uk/articles/the-new-wilderness-diane-cook-review-lamorna-ash/. Accessed 18 May 2024.

Blake, Sarah. *Clean Air.* Algonquin Books of Chapel Hill, 2022.

Blake, Sarah. "How Sarah Blake Turned Her Struggles with Allergens into a Dystopian Thriller Featuring Killer Pollen." *Crime Reads,* 18 Feb. 2022, https://crimereads.com/sarah-blake-allergies-dystopian-thriller/. Accessed 18 May 2024.

Butterfield, Elizabeth. "Maternal Authenticity." *Encyclopedia of Motherhood.* Edited by Andrea O'Reilly. Sage Press, 2010, pp. 700 –701.

Chan, Jessamine. "A Mother-Daughter Survival Story in a World Destroyed by Climate Change." *Electric Literature*, 31 Aug. 2020, https://electricliterature.com/diane-cook-the-new-wilderness/. Accessed 18 May 2024.

Cook, Diane. *The New Wilderness.* HarperCollins Publishers, 2022.

Donath, Orna. *Regretting Motherhood: A Study.* Berkeley, 2017.

Friedman, Dan. "Adrift after a Biblical Catastrophe, Trying to Survive a Flood of a Different Sort." *Forward,* 8 Mar. 2022, https://forward. com/culture/483593/sarah-blake-clean-air-naamah-noah-biblical-flood-climate-change-apocalypse/. Accessed 18 May 2024.

Friedan, Betty. *The Feminine Mystique.* W. W. Norton, 1963.

Goldblatt, Amanda. "To Imagine Life Post-Climate Change: A Conversation with Diane Cook." *Literary Hub,* 11 Sept. 2021, https:// lithub.com/to-imagine-life-post-climate-change-a-conversation-with-diane-cook/. Accessed 18 May 2024.

Hanley, Benet. "'The More Things Change, the More They Stay the Same...'—Jean-Baptiste Alphonse Karr," *ENIGMA People Solutions,* 4 June 2021, https://enigmapeople.current.jobs/blog/view/68/the-more-things-change-the-more-they-stay-the-same-jean-baptiste-alphonse-karr.aspx. Accessed 18 May 2024.

Heng, Rachel. "Diane Cook: 'Our Humanity Is What Makes Us So Particularly Wild.'" *Guernica Magazine,* 10 Aug. 2020, https://www. guernicamag.com/diane-cook-our-humanity-is-what-makes-us-so-particularly-wild/. Accessed 18 May 2024.

Kirkus Reviews. "This Ecological Horror Story (Particularly Horrifying Now) Explores Painful regions of the human heart." *Kirkus Reviews,* 18 May 2020, https://www.kirkusreviews.com/book-reviews/diane-cook/the-new-wilderness/. Accessed 18 May 2024.

Maushart, Susan. *The Mask of Motherhood: How Becoming a Mother Changes Everything and Why We Pretend It Doesn't.* Penguin Books, 2000.

Miller, Stuart. "'Clean Air' Is a Dystopic Serial Killer Novel, but Author Sarah Blake Says Joy Is Her Aim for Readers." *The Orange County Register,* 1 Mar. 2022, https://www.ocregister.com/2022/03/01/clean-air-is-a-dystopic-serial-killer-novel-but-author-sarah-blake-says-joy-is-her-aim-for-readers/. Accessed 18 May 2024.

Millan, Katrina. "Only Mom Can Save the World: Normative Motherhood in the Post-Apocalypse." Major Course Paper, GFWS 6214 Maternal Theory. York University, Fall, 2022.

Obreht, Téa. "The New Wilderness by Diane Cook review—A Dazzling Debut." *The Guardian,* 4 Sept. 2020, https://www.theguardian.com/books/2020/sep/04/the-new-wilderness-by-diane-cook-review-a-dazzling-debut. Accessed 18 May 2024.

O'Brien Hallstein, D. Lynn. "Maternal Agency." *Encyclopedia of Motherhood.* Edited by Andrea O'Reilly. Sage Press, 2010, pp. 697–99.

O'Reilly, Andrea. *Matricentric Feminism: Theory, Activism, Practice, The Second Edition.* Demeter Press, 2021.

O'Reilly, Andrea. *Maternal Regret: Resistances, Renunciations, and Reflections.* Demeter Press, 2022.

Pyles, Alexander. "A Gasp of What Could Be: A Review of Sarah Blake's *Clean Air.*" *Ancillary Review of Books,* 8 Feb. 2022, https://ancillaryreviewofbooks.org/2022/02/09/a-gasp-of-what-could-be-a-review-of-sarah-blakes-clean-air/. Accessed 18 May 2024.

Rauch, Marguerite. "*Clean Air,* by Sarah Blake." *Marguerite Reads,* 30 July 2022, https://www.margueritereads.com/home/clean-air-by-sarah-blake. Accessed 18 May 2004.

Rebolini, Arianna. "Sarah Blake's *Clean Air* IS a Cli-Fi Novel for Our Times." *Oprah Daily,* 24 Mar. 2022, https://www.oprahdaily.com/entertainment/books/a39491688/clean-air-novel-sarah-blake/. Accessed 18 May 2024.

Rich, Adrienne. *Of Woman Born: Motherhood as Experience and Institution.* 2nd ed. W. W. Norton, 1986.

Savage, Kathryn. "Beautiful, Hard, Elemental: Diane Cook Interviewed by Kathryn Savage." *Bomb Magazine,* 25 Aug. 2020, https://bomb-magazine.org/articles/diane-cook-interviewed/. Accessed 18 May 2024.

Shekhar, Gauraa. "A Very Different Landscape: An Interview with Diane Cook." *Maudlin House,* 2 Sept. 2020, https://maudlinhouse.net/a-very-different-landscape-an-interview-with-diane-cook/. Accessed 18 May 2024.

Slocum, Diane. "Escape to Wilderness Threatens Mom and Daughter Relationship." *Author Link,* 1 Nov. 2020, https://authorlink.com/interview/escape-to-wilderness-threatens-mom-and-daughters-relationship-2020/. Accessed 18 May 2024.

Toscana, Carolina. "Mothering, Masking Up, and Sarah Blake's *Clean Air*: A Maternal Ecocritical Reading." Conference Paper, *"Learning from the Pandemic: Possibilities and Challenges for Mothers and Families"* Remote Conference, April 2022.

Williams, Hannah. "Resurgence of the Monstrous Feminine," *Granta,* 12 June 2019, https://granta.com/the-resurgence-of-the-monstrous-feminine/. Accessed 28 Oct. 2022.

Part IV

Discovery—Transforming Intergenerational Pain and Suffering

14.

Letting Go: An Exercise in Writing through the Pain

Michelann Parr

Truth and Reconciliation

Living this chapter, reseeing my life's experiences, and piecing together these stories, I have come to appreciate the incredible gift afforded by my positioning as a white, able-bodied, and cisgender female—birth mother to three, nana to two, and mother-by-choice—with resources and room to call my own. My life is one of ordinary advantages and struggles. Today, I am better able to push back against structures that no longer serve, and I have done more than survive: I have rumbled with complex questions (Brown); I have lived an examined life (Hollis); I have thrived (Janisch); and I am living my way towards an undivided life (Palmer).

I would be lying if I told you I didn't have misgivings about sharing this chapter. I have been deeply troubled by the significance of my work and what might be perceived as navel-gazing within the broader context of the pain of mothers in "a viciously unjust world in a complete mess" (Rose 12). Ultimately, I find myself at a point of enlightenment: Those who can write should write. As we voice our ordinary taken-for-granted assumptions, microaggressions, and silencing, we begin to understand how experiences of extraordinary marginalization, oppression, and violence might play out in the world beyond our circle of influence, with unimaginable and unfathomable consequences.

With a heavy heart, I mourn with and for those who continue to struggle against a maternal ideal, who find themselves oppressed under persistent patriarchy, who are historically muted, who are missing or lost, and those whose pain is silenced, with stories left untold. To these mothers, I dedicate this chapter:

Missing, disappeared, dislocated, silenced
Gone...
Without a trace
Presumed dead, possibly murdered
Unsolved, devalued, unacknowledged
Epidemics of violence.

Haunting emptiness where once life was:
Soul-crushing, heartbreaking, violently hateful.
Horrible. Shameful. Terrifying.
Losses that echo for generations to come.

An enduring legacy,
A never-ending search,
A struggle to remember,
A tale of eternal love, loneliness, separation.

Tragic realities,
horrific endings.[1]

Re-Searching

Throughout the second chapter of my life as a mother, I have re-searched (Absolon) my maternal thinking (Ruddick), the self that mothers, the decisions made, and their lingering effects on the relationships with my children (see Parr; Martin and Parr). I've been to writers' and storytellers' retreats in Seattle, Guatemala, and Iceland; meandered for days along the Camino in France and Spain; participated in yoga and mindfulness retreats closer to home; explored motherhood within the context of educational sustainability; and during the COVID-19 pandemic, experienced stay-at-home encounters of what it means to live a feminist life

(Ahmed) and matricentric feminist life (O'Reilly). No matter where I go or what do, I am always pondering who I am and who I've been as a mother.

Hundreds of pages of travel logs—handwritten and password protected—have been reencountered, excerpted, and reconsidered to reveal to myself the hidden, less-known bits and release intense emotions that left unchecked keep me stuck and less than comfortable (see Bochner and Ellis; Heilbrun; Hollis; Murdock; Shields). Each encounter and revision[2] draws me just a little closer to fine (Indigo Girls), and in this silent retreat, I am left only with myself (Boyd; Chödron; Goldberg). The life of a mother, like the life of a writer, is mitigated and interrupted by life's concerns (Toewes).

Maureen Murdock's and Lynn Schmidt's *Heroine's Journey* are useful frameworks to explore my experiences and the stories I've told myself about my experiences. In the writing, I've learned that temporally organized stages do not work well to contain the life I've dreamed, lived, and storied. Dreams give way to life, writing gives way to story, and the result is far more organic than it is linear or even cyclical. I am far more at home in Bev Janisch's *Awakening a Woman's Soul* and Pema Chödron's *When Things Fall Apart*, which offer much to embody.

Paradoxically, while I crave wholeness in an undivided life, I find myself most at home in a fragmented structure[3] (Bonnaffons; Callahan; Elias; Parr) that mirrors my experience of mothering and the discontinuity of self often demanded by the institution of motherhood (Rich). I intentionally blur the lines of truth and fantasy, which frees me to write something closer to my experience; fictionalizing and layering of truths offer self-protection and confidentiality in a way that gestures towards open, yet-to-be-written futures and possibilities that shed the weight of the past. What follows is, therefore, not all truth, nor is it all fantasy. It simply is.

Truth. My Ruby Slippers.[4] 1. A verified, indisputable, obvious, or accepted fact or belief; 2. Sincerity in action, character, or word; 3. Perceptions or interpretations dependent on context, person, and experience. Synonyms: Actuality, reality, honesty, validity, authenticity. Antonyms: Fantasy, falseness, invention, lie, flaw.

Looking from the inside out,
I fear a muddy and dirty thaw...
Bound by quicksand that holds me still
In the stagnant water of doubt
Where cracks are quickly filled,
I stand alone on a solid bedrock of guilt and fear.[5]

*Fantasy. **Glass Slippers**.*[6] 1. Unrealistic, improbable, or unrestrained images in response to real and imagined need; 2. Acts of creative imagination, conceived, written, or expressed; 3. Pleasant yet often unlikely situations, enjoyable to think about, wounding when left unrealized. Synonyms: Pipe dream, illusion, invention, fool's paradise, delusion. Antonyms: Truth, realism, fact, reality, certainty.

Looking from the outside in,
I long for the purest of journeys...
Clear and crisp and refreshing
Where, in the deepest of cold, the air glistens with magic fairy dust
Where cracks in the icy exterior let the light in,
I hold a promise of a dream, a future, a hope.

Birthright

I often hear Charlene's song in my head: "I've never been to me." Originally released in 1976, the song sparked controversy. Maybe it was a little too feminist? Maybe there was a reference to abortion? Maybe the song drew attention to the seeming incompatibility of motherhood and paradise? Whatever the case, the world was not ready for this ballad... yet. Rereleased in 1982, the song topped the Canadian charts for four weeks. I was eighteen and attending a Catholic Girls High School that took a strong stand against the song: It was banned but never forgotten. Censoring is funny like that.

I still remember the lyrics by heart. Charlene sings to a discontented mother who is cursing her life and dreaming about things she'll never do; she sings of her own life in paradise and all that she has seen, bewailing that she is alone and mourning unborn children who might have made her complete. Motherhood is presented as truth: self-fulfillment and completion. Paradise, by contrast, is a lie: no more than a fantasy created about people and places as we'd like them to be.

I find myself deep in the paradox of motherhood. *I've been to so many places, I've seen so many things, I have children, and yet, I wonder: Have I ever been to me?*

Stillness

Deep in the entangled woods, alongside an enchanting waterfall and a babbling brook, surrounded by daisies and dandelions, amid the forest creatures, there is a magical place that only I can go: a space of renewal where time slows down and fear falls away. In stillness, I wander and meander, filled with openness and genuine curiosity:

> I begin this journey,
> On sacred lands,
> In traditional territories
> With all my relations.[7]

I whisper my question to the wind: "Is healing really possible?"
Resisting the urge to turn and run away...
I hear the gentle response of an ancient tree on my path,
"Sit with me awhile," it calls.
"Rest your weary bones.
Let me cradle you with my gnarled roots and strong trunk.
I am old and so very tired:
poked through to my very core,
Creatures nestled deep within my gaping wounds."

"Nevertheless...[8]
I am refreshed and renewed—
Lily-white blossoms adorn my dying branches,
Flourishing leaves reach towards the sky
Seeds of my potential fall to the ground."

"This cycle of life is a force to be reckoned with:
I am limber, never lost, always in process.

Sit with me awhile, and I with you.

We will share our energy, and hold this time and space and place

for us and all our relations."[9]

As I nestle into the tree's giving embrace, the pages of my well-worn, much-loved journal flutter open, beckoning me to enter its storied world. I am enamoured by its warmth, wide-open spaces, limitless pages, and hopeful acceptance yet gentle probing of all I have to offer. My eyes settle on an ever-familiar invocation: "There is always a refrain of 'Am I enough?' Ignore it as much as you can fellow Waterfall sister. You make do with one fork, one plate, one cup, one spoon... and feel rich. One writer. That writer is you. She is enough" (Anonymous).[10]

With a desire to heal, awaken, connect, and experience wholeness, I set aside a definitive that might leave me less than fine (Indigo Girls). I know that each time I sit down to write, each time I compose a phrase, sentence, paragraph, poem, or story, and each time I call forward a memory, thought, feeling, or experience, I put my composition of self, maybe even life as I know it, at stake.

Nevertheless, I begin.

Survival[11]

There were flashing lights at the end of the driveway last night. A police officer stood at my door. He showed me a driver's license. He asked if it belonged to me. I said it did not, but he did.

Her cell phone battery died; phone lines were down all over the city. She's still not home, and the sun is rising.

I can't see the floor. There are no dishes left in the cupboard. Wet towels are everywhere. Mildew is growing.

The lights are on, but nobody's home, except for the stranger sleeping on the couch.

Friends are here to clean. Where is she, and what happened here last night?

The hospital called. He has alcohol poisoning, needs eight stitches, and his shoulder is dislocated.

The neighbour saw her stumble at the door last night. But she is home. There was a bar fight. I saw the black eye, but I didn't say a word.

The school called. They need to see me. They need to see him. He's a semester away from graduating, but they haven't seen him in weeks.

She has been gone for a week. She didn't call. Her sister heard from her. She is okay. But she is not coming home. Her sleeping bag is missing, her backpack no longer hangs at the door, my new jeans are gone, and she "borrowed" money again.

The car was ditched and towed. I need a ride to work. Again.

It is her birthday tomorrow; she is a minor for just one more day.

The tickets are unpaid. They are registered to my license plates. They are now paid, along with the fine for unpaid tickets.

She came home yesterday. She slept. She showered. She ate. She left.

They won't come to church. They don't believe in God. They ridicule me for having faith. Little do they realize faith helps me to deal with the unanswered questions in my life.

We fight. The words fly in quick succession. More harmful than bullets, they leave gaping wounds in our souls and our spirits, scars that take years to heal. If ever.

I ignore, accept, and listen to everything—the good, the wicked, the fun, the adventurous, the truth, the fantasy, and the things that I would never do, not then, not now. I try not to judge. I try to understand.

They delight in shocking me, and I feel disrespected. They question my judgment, and I sense their doubt. They just don't bother, and I feel they just don't care. I wonder if I should.

I try to admit that once, I was just like them. But... I was not. And I don't understand.

I shift my gaze. I change my mindset just a little more. I get along by feigning a self that I'm not. I free them to make their own decisions, and I hide my apprehension and try not to alienate them or have the distance grow much further.

I take a deep breath and open the door. I give thanks I have faith to carry on—to shift my gaze and survive. I give thanks for the day they told me that it was okay to laugh through my sadness; they really were that funny.

I reach for peace within myself. I focus on what is important, essential, good, revelatory and what keeps me in this space.

I remind myself of Viktor Frankl's words that I have committed to heart: "Those who have a 'why' to live, can bear with almost any 'how.'"[12]

I now know why tigers eat their young (Marshall).

Denial

I wander from room to room, straightening a pillow, tidying a shelf, hanging a towel, depositing an errant glass in the dishwasher, swiping the crumbs off the counter yet again, throwing that last load of laundry on, and checking the details of tonight's party.

Ten precious minutes. The same ten minutes of solitude that I have borrowed, stolen, and cherished for years; they pass far too quickly, yet somehow, they seem like a lifetime. As always, I designate one minute to study the pictures on the wall—the first baby pictures, the impromptu snapshots, the professional portraits, and the traditional photos with Santa. We are a picture-perfect family with a beautiful home, meaningful family moments, and loving smiles. That is, at least, what the world sees.

This simple practice of gratitude usually grounds me.

But today, I pause at the door, scrutinizing what I find in the mirror. As memories of the morning stare back at me, tears well up and fine rivulets of hastily applied mascara run down my cheeks. I hate mornings, especially mornings like these. They weaken my resolve. They make me doubt the validity of my why. They make me wonder how much more I need to change and how much more I have at stake.

I get into my car and turn on the ignition. The radio is blaring... again. Some things never change. As the sounds of the morning show attempt to drown out the competing questions, demands, and statements that invade my reality, I feel a strange mix of pity, anger, determination, judgment, disbelief, and frustration. The constant barrage of emotions is ruthless. Maybe I really am crazy as I've heard over and over.[13]

What is it that I can't take? How much longer must I take it? Why now? Why can't I make it work? Why can't I wear sensible shoes like all the other mothers? Why can't I ignore it? What exactly can't I bear? Have I really done all that it takes? *Does it really matter?* Is my sanity, sense of self, happiness, and life worth it? What will the neighbours say? What will my friends say? What will my family say? What will my children say? *Do I really care?* What will I lose? What will my children lose? What will we gain? Where exactly is there to go?

I rest my head on the steering wheel, begging the arsenal of questions to cease and the thoughts to disappear into thin air. I command peace to soothe my heart's chaos, and for a moment, all is still. My inner retreat is soon interrupted by the voice of Shawn Mullins, singing it seems just for me: "Everything is going to be all right. Rock-a-bye."

I shake my head in disbelief. I am truly haunted by "Carl Jung's observation that whatever is denied within us is likely to come to us in the outer world as fate" (Hollis 3).

I wonder, *What exactly is this apparent hell that I've created?* Rock-a-bye.

Betrayal

It is so very dark.

Clouds pass by my window, more menacing than they were just five minutes ago. I imagine my children immersed in the storm as they always are. I wrap my fear of storms around me like a blanket, trying to rid myself of the icy chill that has settled deep within my bones. Freezing rain pelts my window as icy tears stream down my face. I wonder: Is this an ordinary storm that will do little more than disturb my environment, maybe offer renewal and refreshment? Or is this the type of storm that will render me broken, in search of another place to call home? How long can I stay in this darkness before someone notices I'm missing?

I'm so tired of dancing in the rain, pretending the loud booms of thunder and flashing lightning don't bother me. I spend so much time concealing and pretending I have become someone in the outside world I no longer recognize.[14] What is it about mothers/women like me who feel the need to be well put together, determined in all we do, competing to the death, unwilling to share our inner turmoil, and seemingly unshakeable despite the darkest of storms?

Maybe I can spend this one day in darkness and not let it take over my life. Just one day to retreat from the world and be one with the storm...

Most days, amid the carpools, laundry, and busyness of life, there is little time to give in to these long-drawn-out negotiations with myself.

Most days, I allow myself to be distracted by the rhythms of life.

Today though, I'll just survive. I will get up and do what it takes to feed my children (Dreamer). I will put breakfast on the table. I will call the school to set up that appointment. I will confirm the details for tomorrow's birthday party. I will make the VISA payment, the one I missed yesterday; interest is now accruing. I hate interest and freezing rain, particularly when the buses are cancelled.

Resisting a frigid stillness, I slip on my glass slippers. I accept the illusion. I paste on that smile and embody a picture-perfect stance. I will myself to see what the world sees; I will be open to where my glass slippers take me.

Today, if I cannot be the part, I can at least act the part.

Fate

My bags are packed. My books are not; they are too heavy to make the journey. I'm ready to go. I've waited for what seems like a lifetime for this moment.

I've left a note. I've left a schedule. I've left meals and snacks and fresh towels. The house is clean, the laundry is done, the dishwasher is unloaded, and the counter is free of crumbs. There can be no accusation of lack of care or abandoning my role as a mother. So then, why do I feel so guilty?

As I open the door, I take a breath. They will be just fine without me. How much can possibly change?

I grant myself time to be immersed in a journey of my own design, walk unknown roads and trails, and embrace the freedom of not knowing. I accept that she who wanders is not always lost.

Deep in Useless Bay,[15] I arrive at a crossroads face-to-face with a signpost that points the direction from here to there, from now to then, from somewhere to nowhere, and everything in between. The sign is intentionally incomplete and offers a simple invitation: "Add your sign here."

I catch my breath, overcome by the intense panic that drove me here, away from the uncertainties and ambiguities of ordinary life. Devastating moments leave little time, space, and energy to consider my children's realities. I have no idea where I am going, and no sign can point the way towards a journey with no destination. I am frozen by an invitation that I am not quite ready to accept.

I suppose I should have been wary of the sign I found just days before I left: "If you're looking for a sign, this is it."

So very ironic, given that for years, the sign on my porch screamed "keep out," the sign in my window read "lonely," the sign on my door advised beware, and the sign in my home insinuated no one knew me.

There were so very many signs, yet here I am. Unable to add a single word.

Seeking to ease my distress, I tap my ruby slippers.

The windows are dark, the doors are locked, no one is home, and my key no longer fits. The day has come when the risk of staying in this place is more painful than the risk of the unknown.

I leave behind my glass slippers; they'd grown a little snug anyway.

Discernment

Once upon a time, somewhere over the rainbow, a mother was searching for her heart's desire. Unaware that she had given her power away to others (Boyd), she was caught between acceptance and rejection, feeling and being, resulting in a dual existence of the good and wicked—a tale of conquest as old as time.

The good mother[16] did what needed doing, sometimes more than required, amid perceived threats and challenges to acceptance and belonging in her family unit. Sensing low relational value to her children, she felt perpetually in jeopardy, resulting in hurt feelings, jealousy, loneliness, shame, guilt, and regret (Leary; Martin and Parr). She did her best to hide her discontentment and fulfilled the roles assigned to her at birth to the very best of her abilities. The wicked mother, often feeling powerless and angry, secretly resented the good mother and offered a steady stream of internal criticism as she worked to cover up the inner torment that resulted in hostility, aggression, indifference, neglect, and undifferentiated rejection (Rohner).

More often than not, the mother found herself simply going through the motions, as flawless as possible, stacking up a long list of contingencies: If only this... when all these things... if she could just have... if her children would just... then she would be fine, she would belong, and she would be loved.

A years-long battle between the good and wicked ensued, leaving the mother disoriented, exhausted, unable to discern truth from fantasy, and utterly worn out by her old ways of being. The rapid, almost urgent, unconscious cycling of good and wicked kept her stagnant and trapped, sowing seeds of doubt, uncertainty, and ambiguity (Chödron).

Eventually, the mother fell into a deep slumber masking an inner life of quiet desperation and seeming indifference; nothing seemed to matter anymore. A shadow of her self[17] took over ordinary daily life and revealed her darker parts, which further troubled her concept of self, contradicted her professed values, and intimidated her already timid soul (Hollis 91).

Suspicion, confusion, misperception, contempt, comparison, competition, and mistrust began to play out in her relationships with her children, or at least that's how it seemed. Her greatest fears were invisibility and abandonment: nightmares her shadow was determined to bring to life.

In the dawning of the mother's consciousness, she explored "the nuances of [her] behaviour, the unintended consequences of [her] choices, and the pallid" life she had lived (Hollis 92). This discernment summoned more questions than answers: Does this make sense of my experience? Does it support my being and becoming? Do these values, practices, and expectations take me deeper into life, open new possibilities of relationship, align my being and becoming with the deepest movements of my soul and open me to the mystery of this experience of motherhood? "If not, then it is toxic, no matter how benign its claim" (Hollis 4). The mother realized that her challenge was "not one of conquest but one of acceptance, of accepting her nameless, unloved parts that [had] become tyrannical because she [had] left them unchecked" (Murdock 166).

Promises of healing, acceptance, and belonging awaken the mother from her shadow slumber, and she finds herself negotiating with the good and wicked: How can I convince my children that I have done my absolute best when I am not sure I believe it? How can I model for my children the need to examine their own lives and embrace growth when I have yet to begin? How can I cultivate respect with my children if I have not first claimed it for myself? How can I show my children how to live their truths when I have been so unmoveable and trapped in a forest of deep entanglement of my very own making? And how can I ask my children to do something I have not done myself?

Seeing wisdom and truth in all this, the good mother begins to cast away patriarchal values that suggest that there is no self, voice, and wholeness until the children are independent and grown. Hearing humility and courage, the wicked mother, still apprehensive in her resentment, bitterness, and anger, cautiously considers the space to be found by thinning out her need to defend, react, and conceal. Enlightened, embodied, and energized, the mother begins to weed out binary perceptions of the good and wicked, shadow and self, and truth and fantasy, which had been strangling her and the relationships she was trying to cultivate.

As the weight of her shadow lightens, the mother feels less divided and a little closer to whole (Chödron; Palmer); she realizes this was her choice all along.

She taps her ruby slippers, leaving behind her carefully constructed house of illusion.

Arriving home and knowing this place for the first time, the mother prunes back entangled vines to make space for new growth and establish better living conditions. She observes that this new landscape looks and feels a little sparse. Each day, she returns to the garden, watching for signs of growth and flourishing as she once did when her children were young. Accepting all as it is, she acknowledges her apprehensions, honours her fears, worries about the future, and revises her expectations for change. She plants seeds, and she waits.

Standing back to admire all that she has done, she knows—

It will take time to fill this fertile space.

To everything, there is a season.

Surrender[18]

Deep in a Guatemalan rainforest, my grandmothers visit me. On the first day, I find a dead butterfly; I let go of things that don't serve me— knowing that it is never too late. On the second day, a butterfly lands on my hand while I am eating breakfast. I awaken my soul. I am peaceful and mindful. I slow my life down. I accept all as it unfolds. I rest in stillness. On the third day, I spend time with glass-wing butterflies in a mystical garden. I am humbled by their ability to dance freely in the light and the shadows; I love that their wings allow light and sight all the way through, sometimes mirroring the environment. They are not threatened by would-be predators but instead find protection and safety in their transparency. A fellow traveller tells me that butterflies are a sign of positive transformation and that I am being called to make a dramatic change in my life. I wonder if this signals a move away from *what I should be and do* towards a life of *being and becoming*. It's not always easy to accept this call, and so

I surrender to all my relations, asking for guidance through
the darkness of my shadows
as I navigate this great gift of life with all its ups and downs,
twists and turns, ins and outs.

I surrender to the sky, a reminder of the expansiveness of the universe—
I am not alone. I was never alone. We all exist under the same
sun and the same moon.

I surrender to the land and rocks who ground me and catch me when I fall—
I will always have a solid foundation upon which to build.

I surrender to the waters who cleanse and keep our bodies nourished—
I will always have an opportunity to renew and wash away
that which doesn't serve.

I surrender to the trees who put down roots and reach their
branches to the sun—
I have shelter, even on the stormiest of days.

I surrender to the flora and the fauna, the ever-present life of the forest—
We share this place called home.

I surrender to the seasons of life that go round and round—
I accept that death and dying give way to new life and rebirth.

To all my relations, I say thank you; you are always with me,
keeping me grounded
and inviting me to embrace all that is with wonder and awe.

Hope

Any journey tale will reveal the same thing—we need shadow and wholeness, self and other, pain and joy, as well as time and space to grow, to
be, to become, to heal, and to find our way home (Boyd; Brown; Chödron;
Hollis; Janisch; Murdock; Palmer; Schmidt). Mothers have been conditioned to wait until the children are grown, to postpone their journeys
as some distant happily-ever-after, to give until it hurts. To do any less

is self-centred and runs counter to all we have been taught.

Today, I know differently, and with my enlightened consciousness, I accept mothering as a deeply relational practice that requires more knowledgeable m/others who have hoped, dreamed, lived, and storied their lives in truthful and authentic ways (Belenky et al.; Vygotsky). I am so very privileged to add my voice to a growing matricentric feminist collective that positions motherhood as individual and collective, practice not identity, socially constructed not objective reality (O'Reilly).

As we, who collectively mother, come to know our truths and change our own consciousness, we realize that we have the potential and the responsibility to "change the consciousness on the planet from one of addiction to suffering, conflict and domination to a consciousness that recognizes the need for affiliation, healing, balance, and *inter-being*" (Murdock 191 emphasis in original). In a world that continues to perpetuate patriarchal values, our matricentric feminist work requires continual re-searching (Absolon) and radical hope: "Hope gives us a sense that there is a point to working things out, working things through. Hope ... carries us through when the terrain is difficult, when the path we follow makes it harder to proceed" (Ahmed 2).

I am hopeful for those who push my buttons, most notably my children. Today, I recognize that they are the ones who truly help me to grow, albeit some days out of resistance. *Perhaps they see me and know me, after all.*[19]

> Through hope, we struggle,
> Through struggle, we hope.
> Wondering if ever we recover:
> What this new normal will be.
> Senseless acts that fail to protect and guard our spaces of motherhood —
> this place and this people we call home.

> Seven generations to effect change
> Unless,
> Someone like me, someone like we
> Care a whole lot.

> We tread carefully.
> We proceed with care.

We push back against inequity, oppression, violence.
We recognize the power of one,
We welcome the power of many.

We embody our inner work,
with action in the outer world.

Home

In the gentle embrace of my giving tree, I sit down and weep—for the many unable to expose their pain and for my self; for tragic realities, horrific endings, and hopeful beginnings. I stay as long as I need to stay. And I return time and time again. I allow memories, thoughts, and stories to wash through me. I reach out and I reach in. I connect. I relate. I retreat. I meditate. I breathe. I create. I hold space. I mourn regret. I accept silence. And I wander about in my garden of possibility. Someday, it will bloom, and the seeds I've sown will take root.

In the light of my consciousness, I set aside the pain, finding within myself what I was searching for all along: my "homeplace" (hooks)—my hidden wholeness (Palmer). What I needed most—what I thought was lost—had just gone underground; it was my job to nurture it, feed it, and invite it into the joy of my being and becoming.

Accepting all that I am gifted, I no longer fear putting my composition of self and life at stake.

One last time, I tap my ruby slippers.

I am m/other.[20] I am enough.

I am home.

Endnotes

1. Beginning this chapter was tough. As I reached in, I necessarily reached out finding intense distress, grief, and loss for missing mothers around the world. I found myself re-searching the internet. This poem is, therefore, composed of snippets of text that I encountered, suggesting that, in 2022, we continue to be plagued by the same assumptions and expectations that got us here in the first place.

2. Having encountered Lauren Berlant and Kathleen Stewart's *Hundreds*, I continued to write through the final edit, limiting sections to

multiples of one hundred (not including notes!). Accepting the challenge, I nurtured and weeded out words for clarity and depth. In the end, this type of revision was energizing and liberating—exactly what motherhood should be.

3. In this chapter, I have experimented with both writing a fragment and writing fragmentarily, drawing from Camelia Elias, who outlined two directions for modernist fragments: i) the juxtaposition of complete pieces of texts that close themselves around a particular meaning; and ii) fragments that break totality by juxtaposing fragments that may otherwise seem incompatible, but whose openness grounds meaning, and the wide space of re-searching becomes the meaning.

4. My ruby slippers, I have borrowed from *The Wizard of Oz*. I don't suspect that I fully understood the story as I was growing up, but today I see it as a cautionary tale of the journey that might be required to "heal old childhood and life wounds and to truly be able to be successful and adults in the world ... [ultimately a] path of healing and self-realisation that one must take alone to come of age in the world" (Boyd). The definitions of truth and fantasy are those pieced together from multiple Google searches, personal experience, and online dictionaries.

5. The pieces that follow the definitions of truth and fantasy were written as part of a workshop at the Iceland Writer's Retreat in 2015.

6. The glass slippers, of course, belonged to Cinderella. As I grew up, I came to understand them as illusion, increasingly aware that a prince does not make us whole... only we can do that.

7. I am grateful to live and write this chapter on the traditional territory of Nipissing First Nation and the Anishnabek, within sacred lands protected by the Robinson-Huron Treaty of 1850.

8. I love the word "nevertheless" for all it offers this generation: a strong invitation to speak up and be heard regardless of how hard others attempt to silence (see for example, https://www.washingtonpost.com/news/the-fix/wp/2017/02/08/nevertheless-she-persisted-becomes-new-battle-cry-after-mcconnell-silences-elizabeth-warren/ and https://time.com/5175901/elizabeth-warren-nevertheless-she -persisted-meaning/.

9. The place was Limberlost Forest (2018). The event was the Muskoka Yoga Festival. The invitation was to ask a question and listen to the

land's response. The result is this poem, which is also reminiscent of Shel Silverstein's *The Giving Tree*, and Plain White T's musical interpretation of the song which can be found at https://www.youtube.com/watch?v=8wGhqtWR4uo

10. In 2014, I attended a weeklong retreat with Dara Marks and Deb Norton entitled the Inside Story at Hedgebrook on Whidbey Island. As the story goes, the founder was searching for "home" but the land invited something different "a home for more than one woman, a place for women to come and be in solitude and community." See https://www.hedgebrook.org/about-us-overview. This was a real message in a real journal offered to women writers. I am so happy to be a Waterfall sister.

11. Survival and darkness sections were originally written early in 2007; they have since been revised and reframed. "Signs" is based on a real-life experience at Hedgebrook during 2014.

12. Long into my children's and graduate school, I encountered Nietzsche in the work of Viktor Frankl's *Man's Search for Meaning;* these words gave me strength as well as understanding. It is my understanding that this maxim originally appeared in Nietzsche's *Twilight of the Idols* (2).

13. I now find comfort in Lyanda Lynn Haupt's words: "Our new ways are disruptive. They will look weird. This is good. Let us not care, but enjoy that glimpse in another's eyes that we will find sometimes—the one that says, "You're not crazy. I feel it too" (28).

14. Watching Disney's *Frozen* for the very first time, I felt that I had truly found my life story in Disney. The fundamental message was that we need to love and accept self before we can extend love and acceptance to others. In my explorations of Chödron and others, I now recognize this as a practice of loving-kindness.

15. No word of a lie. This actually happened. Those who have been to Hedgebrook have walked along the shores of Useless Bay and will recall the sign.

16. "Good mothers," as described by Andrea O'Reilly, "are nurturing, altruistic, patient, devoted, loving, and selfless; they always put the needs of their children before their own and are available to them whenever needed" (22).

17. This concept of shadow is attributed to Carl Jung, as discussed by John Hollis, and is widely used.

18. Alas, this story is true as well. In 2016, my daughter and I travelled to Guatemala for a Storyteller Within yoga and writing retreat (see https://www.thestorytellerwithin.com/). In many ways, I was seeking to make the strange familiar, the unknowable knowable, the unspeakable heard, the invisible visible, the truth fantasy, and the fantasy truth. I found some of what I thought was missing in the deeply descriptive, connective, and transformational spaces of the Yoga Forest.

19. Arriving towards the end of this particular exploration and knowing it for the first time, I am better able to situate my experience within a broader time and space, seeing the threads that bind together my story, my mother's story, and that of my children, wondering if perhaps I was living out the wounds of my own childhood; this lack of realization may have left my children with wounds of their own. But in that time and space, there was little awareness as I was quite bluntly, growing up with my children. That story is best left for another day.

20. I describe the use of m/other as a concept that reminds us that, as m/others, we need to treat ourselves as we would others entering our home. Radical guest mentality that affords us the same dignity, respect, care, and kindness as we do others. A word far more expansive than mother. A creation of time, space, knowing, doing, failing, resisting, theory, and praxis. Deep knowing and reconciliation that often emerge long after children are grown and return as guest in your home. Way of being that is part of all we know and do from the first moment we arrive in this m/otherworld.

Works Cited

"About Us." *Hedgebrook*, https://www.hedgebrook.org/about-us-overview. Accessed 19 May 2024.

Absolon, Kathy. *Kaandossiwin: How We Come to Know*. Fernwood Publishing, 2022.

Belenky, Mary Field, et al. *Women's Ways of Knowing: The Development of Self, Voice, and Mind*. Basic Books, 1986.

Berlant, Lauren, and Kathleen Stewart. *The Hundreds*. Duke University Press, 2019.

Bochner, Arthur, and Carolyn Ellis. *Evocative Autoethnography: Writing Lives and Telling Stories.* Routledge, 2016.

Bonnaffons, Ann. "Bodies of Text: On the Lyric Essay." *The Essay Review,* 2016, http://theessayreview.org/bodies-of-text-on-the-lyric-essay/. Accessed 19 May 2024.

Boyd, Richard. "The Wizard of Oz—A Myth for Our Age." 2015, https://www.energeticsinstitute.com.au/articles/wizard-of-oz/. Accessed 19 May 2024.

Brown, Brené. *Dare to Lead: Brave Work. Tough Conversations. Whole Hearts.* Vermillion, 2018.

Callahan, Shannon. "The Female and the Fragment(ed)." *Body Studies,* vol. 2, no. 2, 2020, pp. 9–13.

Charlene. "I've Never Been to Me." *I've Never Been to Me.* iTunes app, Motown, 1976/1982.

Chödron, Pema. *When Things Fall Apart: Heart Advice for Difficult Times.* Shambhala Publications, 2016.

Dreamer, Oriah Mountain. "The Invitation." *The Invitation.* Harper One, 1999, pp. 1–2.

Elias, Camelia. "Clowns of Potentiality, Repetition, and Resolution." *Cercles,* no. 14, 2005, pp. 41–57.

Frankl, Viktor E. *Man's Search for Meaning: An Introduction to Logotherapy.* Translated by Ilse Lasch. 3rd ed., Simon & Schuster, 1984.

Goldberg, Natalie. *Old Friend from Far Away: The Practice of Writing Memoir.* Atria Books, 2009.

Haupt, Lyanda Lynn. *Rooted: Life at the Crossroads of Science, Nature, and Spirit.* Little Brown Spark, 2021.

Heilbrun, Carolyn G. *Writing a Woman's Life.* Norton, 1998.

Hollis, James. *Living and Examined Life: Wisdom for the Second Half of the Journey.* Sounds True, Inc., 2018.

hooks, bell. *Yearning: Race, Gender, and Cultural Politics (2nd Ed).* Routledge, 2014.

Indigo Girls. "Closer to Fine." *Indigo Girls,* iTunes app, Epic, 1989.

Janisch, Bev. *Awakening a Woman's Soul: The Power of Meditation and Mindfulness to Transform Your Life.* Bev Janisch Publishing, 2019.

Leary, Mark R. "Emotional Reactions to Threats to Acceptance and

Belonging: A Retrospective Look at the Big Picture." *Australian Journal of Psychology*, vol. 73, no. 1, Jan. 2021, pp. 4–11.

Marks, Dara, and Deb Norton. *The Inside Story—Seminar Notes*. Hedgebrook, 2014.

Marshall, Peter. *Now I Know Why Tigers Eat Their Young: Surviving a New Generation of Teenagers*. Whitecap Book, 2000.

Martin, BettyAnn, and Michelann Parr. *From Mourning to Greeting: The Predicament and Possibilities of Maternal Regret. Maternal Regret: Resistances, Renunciations, and Reflections*. Edited by Andrea O'Reilly. Demeter Press, 2022, pp. 201–219.

Mullins, Shawn. "Lullaby." *Soul's Core*. iTunes app, Columbia, 1998.

Murdock, Maureen. *The Heroine's Journey: Woman's Quest for Wholeness*. 1990. Shambhala, 2020.

O'Reilly, Andrea. *Matricentric Feminism: Theory, Activism, Practise, The Second Edition*. Demeter, 2021.

Palmer, Parker. *A Hidden Wholeness: The Journey Toward an Undivided Life*. Jossey-Bass, 2009.

Parr, Michelann. "The Possibility of Everything: A Mother's Story of Transformation." *Writing Mothers: Narrative Acts of Care, Redemption, and Solidarity*. Edited by BettyAnn Martin and Michelann Parr. Demeter Press, 2020, pp. 205–33.

Plain White T's. "The Giving Tree." *YouTube*, 1 Nov. 2013, https://www.youtube.com/watch?v=8wGhqtWR4uo. Accessed 19 May 2024.

Reilly, Katie. "Why 'Nevertheless, She Persisted' Is the Theme for This Year's Women's History Month." *Time*, 1 Mar. 2018, https://time.com/5175901/elizabeth-warren-nevertheless-she-persisted-meaning/. Accessed 19 May 2024.

Rich, Adrienne. *Of Woman Born: Motherhood as Experience and Institution*. 1976. Norton, 1986.

Rohner, Ronald P. "Introduction to Interpersonal Acceptance-Rejection Theory (IPARTheory) and Evidence." *Online Readings in Psychology and Culture*, vol. 6, no. 1, Aug. 2021, https://doi.org/10.9707/2307-0919.1055.

Ruddick, Sara. *Maternal Thinking: Toward a Politics of Peace*. 1989. Beacon Press, 1995.

Schmidt, Victoria Lynn. "Victoria Lynn Schmidt's Heroine's Journey Arc." *The Heroine's Journey Project,* https://heroinejourneys.com/heroine-journey-ii/. Accessed 19 May 2024.

Shields, Carmen. "Using Narrative Inquiry to Inform and Guide our (Re)Interpretations of Lived Experience." *McGill Journal of Education,* vol. 40, no. 1, 2005, pp. 179–188.

Toewes, Miriam. *The Life of a Writer.* Iceland Writers Retreat, 2014.

Vygotsky, Lev. *The Mind in Society: The Development of Higher Psychological Processes.* Harvard University Press, 1978.

Wang, Any. "'Nevertheless, She Persisted' Becomes New Battle Cry after McConnel Silences Elizabeth Warren." *Washington Post,* 8 Feb. 2017, https://www.washingtonpost.com/news/the-fix/wp/2017/02/08/nevertheless-she-persisted-becomes-new-battle-cry-after-mcconnell-silences-elizabeth-warren/. Accessed 19 May 2024.

15.

If You Are a Mother

Hannah Frostad

If you are a mother these days,
You stand in hope waiting for your village.
All the while deep down knowing the scarcity of this resource.
So you continue malnourished.

If you are a mother these days,
You hear the constant echoes of unsolicited narratives dictating *your*
identity. Narratives that have held for generations—like a parasite,
affectionately passed down as a family heirloom.

If you are a mother,
You know the weight of *her* words.
When a mother's desperation finally wells up and escapes
—breaking the barrier in a single word.
—help

Involuntarily *our* bodies have learned *and may even now* brace for
the inevitable.
Standing firm, she maintains the illusion of strength; engaging the
dams, besieging her tears—
A defence mechanism, an adaptation learned, callouses preserving her
soul.
You will not let them hurt you again.

If you are a mother,
You already know the outcome.
Her request will be trivialized; humoured with hollow empathy.
Our reality so often reduced to a season, a rite of passage, a badge to
be earned.
As if these words are sufficient rations for survival.

To be a mother,
Is to know the lonely journey to a forbidden territory.
A territory they say your thoughts can never enter *or even entertain.*
Terrain that you dare not speak of with your closest confidant.

So instead, you repress the secret
because even allies come with thresholds.

Secrets that scare even you.
Who knows what consequences will unfold—
If you dare express hope for *escape,*
To say *"what if"* or worse

—regret
A sin with no absolution.

If you are a mother,
You know the reincarnation that comes overnight.
A simultaneous feeling that part of you is forever lost,
yet an underwhelming sense that nothing has changed.

If you are a mother, you know the fear
that swells in you the first time you hold your child.
—your child
The words feel foreign, as this helpless stranger now clings to you for
survival.

If you are a mother, you are a suit of armour.
Like the shell of a tortoise, forever bound, tasked to defend and preserve.
Yet you still wait for your heart to embrace this urge.

With this armour, you now hold the tension of multiple loyalties.
Tensions that only emerge when the family challenges this new role
of protector.
How do you honour your heart?

If you are a mother these days,
You hold a range of emotions and weight of responsibilities.
Calculating endlessly—you are an organic algorithm, Engrained in
you to protect your offspring.

If you are a mother these days, you hold a voice within.
A voice that speaks only to you in a spiritual language, a dialect only
you hold.
A voice that leads you softly, but in the face of threat will rage
unapologetically.
It will not go ignored.

It is the fire that ignites your loyalty,
A flame that guides you through the fog of uncertainty that overrides
logic—it will not be betrayed.
Yet others reduce it to a 'gut'.

If you are a mother these days,
You know what it's like to have your body weaponized. As if you are a
subject to debate,
Your very presence risks offence.

But if you are a mother,
You know the power of *your body.*
While the world defines your value by an arbitrary number on your
waistband,
You, O mother—*are so much more.*
You are magic. Your body is magic.

O mother,
Carry your body with pride for the miracle she has performed.

Do not listen to the voices that demand you hide the evidence.
> *As if the aftermath is a shame to conceal.*

O mother,
Your scars are not a defect.
But a badge of honour,
Stripes earned as a warrior claiming your victory.

Embrace your body—
> *Love her,*
> *Be kind to her,*
> *Speak to her with words you would hold for your daughter.*

Do not withhold your grace from her.

If you are a mother,
You know this choice—*if you have that privilege*—is not binary.
You pour out your grief over a little stick revealing your fate,
Never fully knowing the journey each outcome holds.
While the gamble is binary—the future is painted in nuanced shades
of grey.

If you are a mother,
You understand there are no prerequisites.
Regardless of the boxes *or cages* they may build—
Telling you who you are or what you require.
> *Ovaries and wombs are not mothers.*

If you are a mother,
> You are an *embodiment.*

O mother,   you are *love*

you are *patience*

you are *compassion*

you are *generosity*

you are *grace*

you are *shelter*

you are *safe*

O mother,
You are the *embodiment of home*
        —and no one can ever take that from you.

Poet's Notes

My poem "If you are a mother" came from an English class prompt. Using Fadi Azzam's work *If You Are Syrian These Days*, we were encouraged to write a response reflecting on a personal lived experience or identity. Moved by the powerful metaphors describing the tension between the poet's grief and pride, I began to see how my experiences as a mother came with similar nuance. The poem "If you are a mother" is an outpouring of my thoughts and emotions as a mother.

16

Songs for My Daughters

Susan Picard

My mother once told me that the most terrifying time in her life was when I, her youngest of five daughters, was in a difficult relationship with a schizophrenic man. I replied, "But you lived through bombs dropping all around you during WWII." She responded, "Yes." I felt such shame for causing her so much pain, but in her eyes, I saw nothing but love. My daughters and I have been through some difficult times, and the biggest fear and source of pain have been that I might not be enough for them as they struggle with their challenges. So I write them love songs that I sing in my heart as we wander this treacherous territory, often as what appears to be adversaries.

This is my child
I prayed for her daily
When she was just a promise
In her father's eyes
I'll never forget
When I first heard her heartbeat
Or the joy that I felt
When she finally arrived...

I remember being in the grocery store, seeing pregnant women and young mothers with their babies, and wondering when my time would come. It wasn't such a long period that we tried to get pregnant, but it felt like an eternity once the decision had been made that, yes, we were ready. I was already in my mid-thirties and felt the pressures of biology, family, society, and expectation bearing down on me and my make-things-happen approach to life. After years of living in my head, trying to connect with my body and its reproductive properties was a bit of a challenge. It was one of those times when I felt what should be totally in my control was completely out of my control in many ways. Little did I know that in becoming a mother, I would become intimately aware of what it meant to feel out of control in ways I couldn't have imagined.

This is my child
I held her tightly
As a world awoke
To see two towers fall
This is my child
I watch her nightly
Searching for that breath of air
That makes her little belly
Rise and fall...

Despite the recognition that I had brought a vulnerable being into what sometimes felt like a world gone crazy, I was determined that I could keep her safe. Through those first months of worrying about whether everything was developing as it should, I learned mothering as most mothers do: hands-on and day-by-day. That said, one of the things I counted on was having a good relationship with my daughters. I had always had a close relationship with my mother. No matter where I went, children seemed to love me, and I loved them. One of my strengths as a teacher was the relationships I could establish with my students. I was meant to be a mother and would have a wonderful and close relationship with my daughters. I was confident of that. So we read and wrote stories together, went on long walks through the forest, made movies, and played in our garden.

This is my child
She grew up so quickly
Every new step she took
Drew her further away
I watched her embrace
A world that sometimes confused me
I had to let her go
Although I wished she would stay

I had been a straight-A student and late bloomer in the era of sex, drugs, and rock 'n roll, so social media—with its easy access to and quick sharing of information, both personal and otherwise—was a whole new world for both me and my daughters. That compounded with unexpected learning challenges, my husband taking on the role of stay-at-home parent, and my struggles in leading a misunderstood district-wide school program meant that when my daughters transitioned into puberty, several years apart, we were all in uncharted territory. Being the overthinker I was, I always found many possible paths to the heart of the matter—an exploration that likely only served to confuse the anger and frustration that began to be part of our lives. My idealism of "love them no matter what" became diluted with questions about tough love, boundaries, and responsibilities as I navigated this time with my husband, who had only brothers and knew less about issues facing girls.

> *This is my child*
> *I held her tightly*
> *When she came home weary*
> *Needing reprieve*
> *This is my child*
> *I pray for her nightly*
> *And ask for dreams to fill her soul*
> *And give her reasons to continue to believe*

I discovered poetry before I hit the double digits. At first, the rhymes were whimsical, but as I grew into adolescence, I became preoccupied with the problems of the world and my own inner reflections. I remember sharing some with my mother who asked me if everything was okay. If I needed to talk. I remember being surprised by her question. Why wouldn't I be? Hadn't I just transformed all my worries into the spectacular verses I had just shared with her? This is not to say that I wasn't affected by sadness and low times, but the act of creation was a pathway back to the light, and when the poetry became songs, the ability to express myself as a singer-songwriter was even more cathartic. There are very few times in my life that songs were not there to lift me above the turbulence I found myself in.

But my daughters were not me. I was forced to realize that my experiences of adolescence and dealing with emotions were not the same as theirs. This was a very tough lesson to learn, and it became the source of much drama in our lives as my daughters came into their own. When one, at the age of twelve, became intensely aware of the injustices in the world while becoming aware of her learning challenges, which her parents were only beginning to grasp, we entered an era of sadness. It would take us three more years to understand the depth of her learning disabilities and two more to find out the root causes.

She wears her worries like a wound she troubles every day
Never learned to leave it alone
And every gash she opens lets her bleed once again
Oh honey happy just wants to come back home
oh happy just wants to come back home

And she gathers tears from strangers and collects them in her heart
Imagining that their pain is her own
And she'll stand with them in battle without a shield or sword
Oh honey happy just wants to come back home
oh happy just wants to come back home

And you say
Your song
It's gotta be our song
We gotta be singing
those hurts out loud

And she walks the beaches daily waiting for the tide to turn
launching her bottles in the foam
and she's longing for some answers from that mystical beyond
but honey happy just wants to come back home
oh happy just wants to come back home

And you say
Your song
It's gotta be our song
We gotta be singing
That hope out loud

'cause honey, happy just wants to come back home
oh happy just wants to come back home

And then tragedy struck. A glioblastoma brain tumour stole my husband, partner in all things, and coparent, while an eighteen-year-old and fifteen -year-old lost their father. Within weeks, the curtain of COVID-19 cut us off from the world. I was determined to maintain the home we had built, the career to which I had dedicated much time, and keep our lives on track, but the determination that had served me so well started to falter as the challenges continued into the second year of saying good-bye to my husband without reprieve. Slowly, I came to understand that grief and loss have a way of mining your life for explanations, and over time, many distortions emerge rendering who you thought you were unrecognizable. As we struggled to find our way through, the distortions pulled us apart, serving us yet another loss. Finally, a psychologist friend made it clear to me that until I addressed my wellness and came to know myself again, it would be impossible to be the mother they needed. So began months of medication, meditation, writing, and long walks with friends. Over time, I was finally able to offer myself compassion. There was no perfect way to handle the challenges life placed in my path. I had to forgive myself for all the fumbling and missed steps. Wishing for impossible things was a prison only I could unlock. It was a daily practice of encountering the fear and regret to loosen their grip on me. Once I could do that, I could finally gain a powerful sense of my husband's deep love for us and ongoing presence in our lives. The distortions were gone.

As my daughters continued to struggle, each in their own way, I wondered if I could build them a lovemap that would help them understand what an important role they played in my life for so many years, even before they arrived.

Long before I knew your name
Or held you close or played these games
I remember how I prayed for you
When you were still a distant star
A dream still nestled in my heart
Every heartbeat was a prayer for you
I rarely bend my knee
To gods that I can't see

But for you, I had to reach outside myself
This was no accidental pairing
Or burden left for bearing
But an answer to a prayer that brought me you

Long before I knew myself
Long before you'd cast your spell
I remember how I prayed for you
When I was still a lump of clay
Partly formed and roughly shaped
Every pinch I made was a prayer for you
I rarely bend my knee
To gods that I can't see
But for you, I had to reach inside myself
This didn't come by chance
Fate had a helping hand
Through all the prayers that brought me you

When your world is in tatters
And you're wondering if you matter
Know you're the answer to a prayer I prayed for you
I never asked for perfection
An outcome or direction
My prayers were simply for you
I rarely bend my knee
To gods that I can't see
But for you, I had to reach beyond myself
But if in my search for truth
There lies a burden of proof
Then it's been borne out by the prayers that brought me you

Even now, I can remember how much I longed for my daughters, their father, and the family that we were and still are. I can remember what was in my heart then while acknowledging the naïveté of the woman who uttered those prayers. Guided by my own life experiences and one-sided view of the kind of child I was, I felt not only that I could handle what life was going to throw my way but also that my children would be special. I suppose every mother believes that to some degree, but as I interrogate that idea further, was it a belief that they were special in their own right or special because they were my children? Was I overidentifying with them, or did I think I would shape them? Even now there is a sense of shame that I might have failed to fully understand their uniqueness, both of who they are and their experience of the world. I felt shame that in their darkest hours, I had lost sight of who they were because of my preoccupation with how I saw them. Writing the song reminded me they had nothing to prove to me and that my biggest responsibility was to keep shining the light of love as they navigated the darkness even if they couldn't see it.

Calling on Dabrowski

In my early twenties, I came up with a theory similar to Kazimierz Dabrowski's theory of positive disintegration. It was after the experience with the schizophrenic man that caused my mother so much worry. It was a simple theory based on my experiences and heavily influenced by my work at a women's shelter. I called it my Lego block theory, and it described personality development as a structure you created out of values (and your interpretation of them) handed down from your parents and other authority figures in your life. As a child, you played with them a little like Lego blocks, building a structure that you hoped would keep you safe, not always knowing who had given them to you or what they might all mean. And then you let life test it. In my case, when I fell in love with a man with mental illness, the whole thing fell apart. This was not surprising, as nothing in my life experience had allowed me a view into the world that was his reality. I could have labeled him crazy or evil, shut the door on the experience and tried to fit back into the world I'd known before him, but that was not my nature. Instead, I took on the enormous task of examining each of the blocks, this time carefully considering which blocks had meaning and which didn't and how to put them back together in a better way so that I could handle what life had to dish out. I will admit that there were times I was angry with my parents for dumping inconsistent beliefs and values on me and not helping me put the whole thing together better, but I eventually realized that for it to have meaning and be liveable, it had to be my responsibility.

Dabrowski's theory goes into far more depth and detail. It speaks to the role of emotions in development and how our "overexcitabilities" (i.e., response to stimulus) influence how we experience the world. He speaks of a third factor, beyond nature and nurture, which allows us to recognize our agency in shaping who we wish to be—something far more difficult than most of us realize. In his theory, anxiety, depression and some forms of neurosis are signs of this third factor or developmental potential. Although I was unfamiliar with Dabrowski, I spent my twenties playing with my Lego blocks, testing life on many fronts and experiencing considerable disenchantment with the world, life, and most often, myself. While I experienced my share of anxiety and depression during this time, I also found points of exquisite freedom. In the end, I thanked my parents for the gift of resilience, having modeled it so beautifully in so many different ways because though sorely tempted, I refused to give up. In my difficult times, imagining things that could be or should be, I had endowed myself with a purpose.

> Human and social reality appears to be submitted to the law of positive disintegration. If progress is to be achieved, if new and valuable forms of life are to be developed, lower levels of mental functions have to be shaken and destroyed, and a sequence of processes of positive disintegrations and secondary integrations are necessary. Consequently, human development has to involve suffering, conflicts, inner struggle. Positive maladjustment, challenge and rebellion are as good a part of any culturally growing society as creativity and respect for the law. (Dabrowski et al. 16)

My twenties were punctuated with many songs of anger, disenchantment, and hopefulness in response to my Lego block explorations in love and life. I relied on the songs to navigate my way through the dark places; they gave me new perspectives on the situations and relationships I was finding myself in. I remember my dad suggesting that my fumblings through trying to find love were a way of gathering more song material. Those were prolific days! While initially many of the songs expressed anger and frustration with relationships—"Though I know you liked to screw me, I don't think you ever knew me"—eventually a more reflective voice evolved: "The way that I live life now, the way that I do the things that I do, all part of a tapestry with threads that lead to you." While, for me, composing and performing songs was just something that I did, Dabrowski describes the creative instinct, often a marker of developmental potential, as "an assembly of cohesively organized forces, often of great intensity, oriented toward a search for the new and the different, in the external and the internal reality" (Psychoneurosis, 293). Looking back at them now, I can see evidence of that third factor: "the dynamism of conscious choice (valuation) by which one affirms or rejects certain qualities in oneself and in one's environment" (Psychoneurosis, 306). I can't say where the need to write songs came from. It just showed up one day, and it has kept showing up ever since.

Knowing disintegration and suffering are necessities of life can make it feel less personal as you grow older. It doesn't mean you don't suffer; it just means that you know that life will go on, even though sometimes you wish it wouldn't. Even so, keeping that light burning while the girls raged at the dark and many around me suggested good parenting practices wasn't an easy task. This was all new to my daughters—the injustice of a world that would take someone you loved for no apparent reason. We navigated our way one day to the next on a precarious path at the edge of a deep abyss. I tried every rational argument I had to keep us on the path and moving, but I didn't always choose my words and timing as carefully as I could have, not always giving the internal turmoil its due. I didn't always consider what might be happening internally, when externally I saw rebellion and lack of productivity.

> The process of disintegration is also noticeable in the case of serious internal conflicts which lead to stupor and imobiliation, to the weakening and diminution of awareness, or its hyperactivity. Among such states of disintegration, we can also include states of existential anxiety, existential "spasms" in which we find ourselves estranged from others and undergo experiences of psychic or emotional depletion, emptiness and "nights of the soul." These types of disintegration are most common in psychoneuroses. (Dabrowski et al. 17–18)

In studying Dabrowski, I dug deeply into what he meant by disintegration, the process by which there is an actual loosening and dissolution of the structures and mental functions in the brain. Often brought on at puberty, menopause, and by critical experiences, the term itself covers a wide variety of states that "from temporary loosening of contact with reality observable in severe fatigue, boredom, depression, stress, mental conflicts, disequilibrium, neurosis or psychoneurosis to a split of personality in schizophrenia" (Dabrowski et al. 164). Having experienced my own disintegrations and constructed my own theory, I knew the challenges and importance of this developmental process. But to experience it with my daughters after losing my husband, exacerbated by some degree due to menopause and puberty, with very different manifestations, was not only difficult but also often unfamiliar. By putting on my oxygen mask first, I was able to become a better support to my daughters while inadvertently adding to the distress by not only moving forward with life but also restructuring how I now understood my life in light of my husband's death. Did they fear they would be left behind and abandoned in a world that no longer existed? Could they love the person I was becoming?

William Tillier explains how the first unilevel disintegration can come as such a shock: "The individual is often immobilized by the inability to decisively choose a course of action ... [and] if the individual is to move on to the higher levels in Dabrowski's theory, this critical shift to multi-levelness must occur" (63). Multilevelness in this case would be the ability to assess and order one's value system, given the world they had no longer existed as they knew it. Without this, the individual is in a state of ambivalence and ambitendencies where, Dabrowski tells us, things like love and hate, joy and sadness, excitement and depression "are experienced as pulls of equal value," and as a result, individuals "do not tend towards a solution but seek immediate palliatives like alcohol, drugs, or suicide" (306).

Whereas I had been able to engage developmental dynamisms to help me through the disintegration, it's difficult to know the extent to which others have discovered theirs and what dangers might lie before them. As a mother, you want nothing more than to protect your children, so you wonder if you can somehow do the work for them. Thankfully, I had those in my life who reminded me to trust in the true selves that my husband and I had nurtured in them when they were young and remember there is no schedule or map for this journey. As much as we shared the same living space, our internal worlds are places that we face alone until we are able to figure out who we want to be in that external milieu.

This transition is a difficult time, demanding a significant amount of energy. The developmental process sweeps one along, and as it does the person and their view of life change. It is a time of great uncertainty and ambiguity: "Where am I going?" "What should I do?" "I thought I understood life; now I don't understand anything." The inner self (inner psychic milieu) struggles to find its new voice in the old, and rigid status quo environment. New views lead to new values and, often, to a new sense of injustice. The birth of the multilevel experience of life creates a powerful new phenomenon, a new experience—the vertical conflicts that become so vital in directing growth. As the higher is seen and endorsed, the lower must give way—must be inhibited, overcome, or transformed and transcended. (Tillier 65–66)

As the months passed, it was difficult to understand how we were doing as individuals and as a family. It felt like things were going one step forward, two steps back. When we took those backwards steps, I had trouble remembering all the progress we had made. I am certain my impatience was part of the problem. But then we moved to two steps forward and one back. We eventually came to one step forward and then another one and then another. Through this transition, it became imperative for me to revisit and understand what it meant to allow them to find their true selves—something I believed was a combination of who they were at their core and who they had yet to become and the hierarchy of values they had yet to form. Dabrowski reminds me that the "capability of experiencing feelings of veneration and esteem are one of the fundamental criteria of the development of personality" (Personality Shaping, 26), which is a subtle process. My support needed to be "increasingly more imperceptible, ever more subtle, ever more 'helpful' so as not to interfere finally, injudiciously and too distinctly" (Personality Shaping, 151) in their individual development. What it meant was that my desire for things to get better was becoming problematic. Pushing was an attempt to control the process, giving them a message that signified a lack of trust in that true self. This was a difficult paradigm shift for me, not so much in understanding it from a Dabrowskian standpoint but rather from breaking old habits and moving away from what felt like mothering. It dawned on me that perhaps I was not allowing them to grow due to my fear of loss—knowing that in coming into their own, they would need me less, and in needing me less, I would experience another loss. It felt like such a paradox. But it became a daily reminder to remind them that I trusted their process. I wrote them a new song:

I'll walk beside you
When you're not sure you're ready
When your feet are unsteady
And the world's just too big
I've got your back
When life throws you off track
When there's no turning back
Just finding your way

And I'll give you shelter from the storm
A blanket to keep you warm
'Til you're ready to go...

There's no hiding from
The pain that will meet you
The fear that will greet you
As you make your way
But there's no denying
The strength that's in healing
The power in dealing with
The traps that were laid

And I'll give you shelter from the storm
A blanket to keep you warm
'Til you're ready to go...

But go you must like the bird on the wing
Who can't hold back that first call of spring
Go you must like the waves with the tide
There's no hiding from the moon's watchful eye

And I'll give you shelter from the storm
A blanket to keep you warm
'Til you're ready to go

Not long after writing this song, I got a call from my eldest daughter. She'd had a terrible week, and she needed me. I went to her. It felt like an affirmation: Despite my shortcomings and all the struggles we navigated, I had managed to create that port in the storm. With every ounce of energy I had, I endeavoured to make it safe by steering away from any interrupting, judging, or advising. To create a real shelter and not just another storm. It was hard work, but it cleared the way for me to feel such unbelievable love and gratitude for the gift of the amazing women in my life and the new trust we could share.

***

She lived her life in a fairytale
Grimm was probably her best friend
She lived her life thoughtlessly
Waiting only for each moment to end
She kept waiting for something, but it never came
Her disappointment would not subside
And the hardest thing she had to learn
Was that Hans Christian Anderson lied.

And the story of the little match girl
Was the only thing that could make her cry
She dreamt the girl lit a candle
Before she finally died
And her heart clutched that candle
Sheltered it to gain some heat
But she felt she didn't need to share its warmth
To make her life complete.

"The Match Girl" was one of the first songs I wrote. While writing it at the ripe old age of eighteen, I realized I was all grown up and still a duck. Where was that swan I had been promised? I have been recently humming it to remember what it feels like to feel the crush of adulthood in a time of uncertainty. Nothing prepares you for the death of a story even though you survived learning that there is no Santa Claus, Easter Bunny, or Tooth Fairy. And our story keeps getting it wrong. It's the mother who dies in fairy tales, not the father. I theorize about why that is necessary for a happily ever after. How are the dynamics different from when you lose a father?

My youngest daughter and I see a stage production of Stephen Sondheim's *Into the Woods*. The storyteller dies in the second act, and it's up to the characters to figure out their own story. We laugh at the princes who are so wrapped up in themselves that they move from fairytale to fairytale to rescue the princesses, trying to recapture the storyline. We feel the pain of the characters—sons and husbands, mothers and wives—as a giant they've all had a hand in releasing indiscriminately squashes things as it looks for a culprit. We leave, marveling at the ability of the young actors to memorize so many lines and songs and play their characters so convincingly. I suddenly feel hopeful that we will figure out a way to live our own story—one that allows us the space to grow lovingly together despite the unexpected twists and turns our story has taken. We might have done things differently, but there's no saying where those paths would have led us and even imagining them is counterproductive. Does it really matter what others might have seen and thought about how we handled things? Isn't that where the judgment comes from?

> The well integrated person is usually considered to be one who acts quietly and efficiently, who is capable of quick decisions and action, and who generally acts with "common sense." The integrated person is thus seen as one who "takes himself in his own grasp" in order to adjust to the problems which arise in and from the environment.

> Since the above descriptions of integrated behavior are also considered "normal" behavior, society has come to view disintegrated activity and, indeed, disintegration of any sort, as morbid or pathological. (Dabrowski, Authentic Education, 44)

We live inside many fairy tales, and mothers don't often fare well. But I tell myself that since we are off-script, we have a little more control over how we will create this story. I watch my fiercely courageous daughters dare to disintegrate even as I, like much of the world, fail to understand this process, despite my own experiences. As I learn to travel alongside them, I realize this is what I had hoped I could somehow save them, and perhaps myself, from—this terrifying process of experiencing what it means to be fully human. In the angry interchanges, it was easy to forget that "superficial knowledge of oneself is transferred to the interpretation of the attitudes and behaviors of others, which, in turn, is reflected back upon oneself" (Dabrowski, Authentic Education, 20). I didn't realize that action on my part would rob them of what it means to be inherently authentic: choosing your response to the world. This authenticity culminates in "an appreciation of personal dignity towards others with the same attitude towards ourselves which in turn transfers these attitudes to the group" (Dabrowski, Authentic Education, 2), something I see growing in them daily. I also didn't anticipate the time and energy it requires and how different this journey is for each of us. And I forgot that the world is rife with iterations of the same old stories that can take a lot of time to sort through.

She found a new companion
Some called it a harlequin
She lost herself in each fantasy
Oh when would her reality begin
She tried to live the beauty of each lie
Only to find that there was none
And as the dreams she held faded away
She found nothing had really been done

I can remember being touched by the story of the little match girl lighting the matches she couldn't sell one after another; each flame briefly ignites images of warmth that help her escape the reality of her situation. When she remembers the kindness of her grandmother, she lights the whole bundle, and because of this, she dies with a smile on her face, the cold winning her battle to stay warm. It was a different kind of story. One of suffering. One without a happily ever after. Although it's tempting, I won't try to analyze my younger self who wrote the song, still

I wonder how the young girl in the song came into possession of a candle. Could it be Dabrowski's elusive third factor? That developmental potential that makes itself known?

As I reflect on it now, I realize that I have had to reignite that candle many times; having a candle has allowed me to use my matches sparingly. I still have quite a few in my back pocket. And I will need them.

And the story of the little match girl
Was the only thing that could make her cry
She dreamt the girl lit a candle
Before she finally died
And that candle still burns brightly
There is so much in that flame
The tears and fears of the growing years
And a hope that won't be tamed.

Works Cited

Dabrowski, Kazimierz, et al. *Mental Growth through Positive Disintegration.* Gryf Publications, 1970.

Dabrowski, Kazimierz. *On Authentic Education.* Unpublished manuscript, no date.

Dabrowski, Kazimierz. *Personality-Shaping through Positive Disintegration.* Little, Brown and Company, 1967.

Dabrowski, Kazimierz. *Psychoneurosis Is Not an Illness.* Gryf Publications Ltd, 1972.

Tillier, William. *Personality Development through positive disintegration: The work of Kazimierz Dąbrowski.* Maurice Bassett, 2018.

17.

Quiet as Kept

Drisana McDaniel

Ceci says "It takes three generations. If you resolve your relationship with your mother, you'll both change, and your daughter will have it easier, but her daughter will be raised differently. In the third generation, the daughters are free."

—Aurora Levins Morales 56

Intuitive Knowing

Meeting Indigo

Dearest Time,

Somehow, we were duped into believing that you are a resource to be consumed. We were convinced to make the most of you. To bend you to our will. To save you. To partition you into slivers and formulas and apertures that correlate with finitude and tasks. We have been instructed to set you up to be objectified. Except Bayo Akomolafe unsettles those assumptions about you when he reminds us that "the past and the future touch" and how now is not marked by indifference, despite what we have been taught. Akomolafe attests: "My people, the Yoruba people, speak of circular time, slushy time, or time that collapses on itself. There are no arrows of time that fly forwards in Yoruba Indigenous imagination, none of the incessant tick-tocking that has fuelled progress, that has become the soundtrack of our busy, delimited lives" ("When You Meet").

This resonates. If my relationship with you, dear time, was only forward-facing, I would not know that gift of breaking to make generational medicine, of how it is that I could discover the panacea for peace and healing across timelines that hold mothers and daughters.

Before I read about circular time and how healing is nonlinear.

Before I experienced myself looping through portals and lopping along, licking recurring soul wounds.

Before I read Meredith Hall's revelation that "a mother's body incorporates into her own the cells of her children, as if they recognize each other, belong to each other" (176–77).

Before I (re)membered.

Before this, I heard her. It's more exacting to say that I sensed her, my eldest daughter who came to teach me about the love of generations. To save me for later.

I sensed my maternal grandmother in the same way, but later. Every night, I would lie awake and listen in the darkness, feeling the heat build on my skin as my partner's breathing filled the room.

Every night, in the darkness of our bedroom, with the background sound of my partner's deep breathing, I would lie still with the sheets sticking to my sweat and listen.

Indigo would come to my consciousness in the quiet, early hour just before the break of dawn. This was when I realized that words could disrupt the holy transmissions flowing through my heart and womb. It was as if she pulled gently on my heartstrings beckoning me to listen to the wisdom of my heart.

This, despite how I watched her father at night, captivated by him, even with the multitude of transgressions.

This, even as I revealed that I might be pregnant.

This, as he laughed it off.

We weren't trying to have a baby, yet we weren't taking any precautions either. We were in a domestic partnership: We shared bills, cars, and health insurance and mutually cared for my son Izaiah from a previous relationship. My partner's indifference was unexpected. I stopped by the drugstore and bought a pregnancy test on my way to work the next day. Pressed for time, I asked to use the restroom; minutes later, two pink lines showed up in the window—Indigo was here. When her father came home that evening, I shared the news. He looked at me for what felt like an eternity before silently leaving to take a shower.

That was the first night of many that I slept in the guest room.

Things quickly shifted between us. What had been cheerful and sweet suddenly became gloomy and sour. Our art became blue funk and green with envy and black lies. Our art became sorrow of little faith. I slept so much that I grew fearful of missing Indigo's messages. Given that she lived in my body and the wisdom of the Great Mystery, she was never far from me. In my dreams, she would life-coach me.

I noticed the early signs that he was leaving. From someone else, I found out about his new hopes and passions.

My nights were filled with early-term contractions and anxiety.

Indigo was silent during this time, but I could feel her growing within, and I loved her. I learned about my capacity to love and accept even in the most difficult situations. And I grew.

Silencing and Surviving

In the beginning, postpartum wasn't exactly hard. I was blessed with a healthy son and daughter, and I had the luxury of postpartum healthcare and extended maternity leave. I had a brief moment to recover until I realized my lease was about to expire, and Indigo's father warned me that my health insurance would soon be cancelled. My sweet reprieve with Indigo was cut short as I scrambled to find a new home, pack my apartment, and learn how to pay rent. No surprise that I had difficulty producing enough breast milk for Indigo.

I kept all of this to myself.

Not even my parents knew about the state of my life: the details surrounding the breakup of my relationship; the uncertainty of my living conditions; the depression that caused me so much self-loathing; the disabling anxiety that kept me up at night; or how incapable I felt of taking care of my little family.

After signing a lease for a tiny condominium in east Atlanta, I returned to Charleston to wait out the summer before returning to work; I intended to leave Izaiah with my mother while I searched for an appropriate school for him.

I thought this was the hardest year of my life, but it wasn't.

The years that followed would be the heaviest yet.

I didn't know this, of course. I didn't know what heaviness was, and I certainly didn't know I would one day be better for it.

Suffering in Silence

For me, suffering was part of not knowing. Constantly living in a state of fear kept me everywhere but inside my body.

This is before I knew what it meant to recalibrate a nervous system.

This is when I worked to forget how I felt robbed each time I handed my infant over to her father and his newly pregnant partner.

This was when I traded my dignity for the two hundred dollars of child support he paid each month.

I assumed that my pain was unwarranted despite how relentless it was.

I found new ways to avoid feeling anything at all.

When I returned to work, I was quickly promoted to a position in a luxury retail sector, one of just a few Black[1] women working at the intersection of race, gender, and quasi-leadership. I came face-to-face with the sociopolitical oppression, racism, limited resources, gender violence, multiple role strain, and "double-minority status" faced historically by Black women—all risk factors for emotional distress (Ward et al.; Woods-Giscombe). We must work harder to disprove false assumptions and stereotypes related to our identity and behaviour in settings where we are not just rare but also stand out.

We cope by appearing self-confident, becoming and being strong, self-silencing, taking care of others, and denying our own needs (Jones et al.; Woods-Giscombe).

We are more inclined to handle our challenges internally, internalize our struggles, and approach our problems independently (Thompkins).

We conceal our emotional distress by presenting a façade of control (Chanequa Walker-Barnes).

We suffer quietly.

I didn't tell them anything that had to do with being a terrified, resource-poor, Black, single, and working mother. And my employers didn't ask.

I spent years caught up this way. And I'm not the only one.

Descending into My Past

I grew up in a home where I was reminded that "what happens in our house, stays in our house." Somewhere along the line, I learned to take that literally. I'd never thought twice about the fact that I moved through a series of traumatic experiences without saying anything until a decade later when I finally saw a psychotherapist. Talking with her, I realized that my silence did more than hold secrets within; it led me to flatten the feelings that were a deep source of wisdom and my birthright. Silence had estranged me from the source of myself—my erotic knowledge. As Audre Lorde declares, "That self-connection shared is a measure of the joy which I know myself to be capable of feeling, a reminder of my capacity for feeling" (33). The capacity to resource our feelings as a way of tending to our deepest needs and to name them out loud is essential to healing a legacy of silence. Not to be confused: silence and stillness are a medicine of sorts, but the silence of our suffering—lingering unsaid that is inherited and passed on—is what I am concerned with. Silences are shaped by context, as Ashley Barnwell explains when writing about family secrets: "[A] secret is something willfully hidden. It is a silence constructed via a series of communicative practices—editing stories, leaving out details, concealing connections—that are used by one or more persons to shield information from an/others ... a suspected secret can generate its own emotional effects and structural consequences, even if it turns out not to exist" (1112).

That lingering unsaid is what I would sidestep, and it would also be the fount of healing and wisdom.

It takes me a while—this process of allowing myself to descend—to dissemble the source of my malconformation and to bear the tragedy until it lets up as a consequence of time to consent to surrender. My silence would feed my shame. Shame lives forward and endures among Black women as performances of invulnerability, the denial of needs, depression, and anxiety (Jones; Shorter-Gooden)—protective practices that are both inherited and learned through socialization (Walker-Barnes). Although we may endure pain, we often do so privately and quietly, which is how it shapeshifts into shame.

I've learned that silence is a place where shame thrives, where it is ossified and picked up as a conventional way of being in the world but deeply felt in the body as pain. That pain and shame are distant cousins. While suffering is an inevitable braid in each life—one that I have not only encountered but have learned to cultivate a sort of acceptance for—shame is a quiet shadow I'd never expected. Shame corners me when I am wobbly, distorting my humanity. Even now, when shame arises, I am surprised at how my wisdom fails to rescue me on the spot. Shame is a place and a vice grip. Like any trauma, shame is incited within me unexpectedly. Shame gives way to trauma, which isn't something that we remember intellectually but is instead how the body works to protect us. Trauma events are stored deep in the soma and are triggered by the sensing body.

Each time I pass my daughter off to her father and his partner. Each warm night on the patio with cigarettes and wine thinking myself into the sunken place. Each evening sitting in rush hour hoping to make it to daycare in time to avoid being charged a late fine triggered shame. Every morning drive to work. Every conference call that creates a lump in my throat which does not pass until the children are in bed.

With this work, this writing and telling, I archive how my personal and professional experiences with shame and silence threaten my capacity to thrive in motherhood. I reveal my ongoing healing process alongside the contemplation of my motherline. I call forward the past to contextualize and heal my maternal lineage not just for me but for my mother and my children, revealing how time collapses, melts, and conjoins without end.

I reach in and out, knowing that this work is much bigger than just me.

Seeking to Know More: A Historical and Contextual Perspective

In graduate school, I learn that silences tend to be generational. Silences often live forward as mother wounds, and without healing, they give birth to generations of daughters who may experience hurt and betrayal as the fault of their own. Naomi Ruth Lowinsky recognizes the maternal lineage of women as a resource for integrating the mysteries of the past with the present. Paula Owens Parker affirms that comprehending the transgenerational past is important for our wellness in the present:

A significant part of healing is knowing personal, family, and cultural history. It identifies the strengths and weaknesses in the family and culture. It creates a solid sense of self, a "density of being," a groundedness in knowing one's self and all that it encompasses. It fosters empathy, forgiveness, tolerance, and acceptance of others. Understanding transgenerational trauma and how it affects the lives of the living and future generations lightens the previously unknown emotional, physical, and spiritual burdens of the past. (12)

For Black women, many of us are only able to trace our family lineage back two generations before we encounter fractures of information in our family lineage, leaving us to wonder, "How then, might we begin to integrate the mysteries of the past with the present if the past is largely unknown?" The ancestral silence of motherlines is worthy of exploration, integration, and healing not just for my wellbeing but also for others. Not knowing about our familial past may lead us to think that something is wrong with us, as opposed to thinking how past experiences in our family lineages may affect our present-day life—leaving us to carry things that didn't begin or originate with us. Contemporary suffering is often viewed outside such legacies: "Because modern Western cultures focus so much on the individual, we tend to experience our suffering as purely personal and private rather than as also being familial, communal, and intergenerational. When we believe that our core struggles in life live only inside ourselves, we may feel shame about our pain and feel more disconnected from others as a result" (Foor 123).

Even after death, "biological and psychic links—whether painful or joyous—connect mothers and daughters" (Hull 68). Thus, the motherline of women, healthy or not, has a profound effect on our psychology: Those who are disconnected from their motherline experience a disconnection from themselves, often leaving them feeling "isolated, abandoned, and self-estranged" (Lowinsky 118).

As descendants of enslaved people, Black women often inherit and share a history complicated by a legacy of oppression and trauma, a familial past that has significant implications for their present-day experiences: "Black women live in a state of constant trauma without being able to articulate that this is so. Fear and anxiety are regular parts of existence. Chronic fear weakens the immune system, making survivors more susceptible to illnesses they should be able to ward off. It leads to accelerated aging and premature death" (Daise 17). This state of living with inherited and constant fear is a public health concern made private, as Black women are less likely to consult traditional medical institutions for professional help and more likely to cope with religion and spirituality (Ward et al.)

Seeking to understand and heal my motherline, I continue to reach for evidence-based healing in the literature; I came upon the work of Shelly Harrell, Ashley Coleman, and Tyonna Adams who ask the following: "What might an intervention look like that facilitates African American women becoming more conscious of their extended ways of knowing, spirited and inspired living, interconnected love, balance and flexibility, liberation and inclusion, and/or empowered authenticity?" (65) I recognize that possibilities for intervention may "move beyond spirituality as survival and coping with adversity, toward the illumination and magnification of culturally syntonic, psychospiritual strengths and gifts that propel us toward optimal well-being, wholeness, and the highest expressions of both our individual humanness and collective humanity" (Harrel et al. 65).

Relational Knowing

The further I descend, the more I realize that my work is inseparable from my scholarly work. I find myself thinking about my motherline—that regardless of the tumultuous nature of the relationship with my mother, I can never be apart from her. I recognize that despite my desire to parent my daughters differently than how my mother parented me, when I am tired, triggered, overwhelmed, or fearful, I take on a parenting style similar to that of my mother, which I experienced as emotionally harmful. In other words, my mother is in me, even in ways I do not want her to be. As I seek to heal, understand, and forgive myself, Meredith Hall's words resonate deep within again: "[T]he mother's cells are also carried in the child. During gestation, maternal cells slip through the barriers of defense and join her child's cells as they pulse through (his) veins. My children carry me in their own bodies, mother and child joined forever, both beings bumping against each other every day" (176–77). This is not me being terrified of turning into my mother. This is me wanting to find a way to travel light, with more light. I am seeking a way to carry less and make space for more of what I know I am here to do with my life, to love my motherline and to hold this inheritance with deep reverence.

Despite the many times that I refer to trauma, I am unsure about Carol

A. Kidon's views that long-term psychological effects of survivor trauma might be transmitted from generation to generation, so I turn to Daniel Foor for hopeful guidance: "When we reconcile with ancestors who experienced different types of persecution or who enacted violence and oppression, we make repairs in our personal psyches and family histories that, in turn, mend cracks in the larger spirit of humanity" (4). I do not deny Naomi Ruth Lowinsky's understanding of generational trauma looping:

> Looping is an associative process by which we pass through our own experience to understand that of another. Looping ties together life stages, roles, and generations. It disregards linear time. It involves a cyclic view of life; it finds meaning in patterns that repeat ... you reexperience your past in your children and anticipate your future in your parents, while at the same time your children constellate the future and your parents the past ... in this sense, one is cycling through time and standing still. (22)

I desire another way to be curious about what it means to carry the experiences of lineage in the sensual body. What is the texture of looping in contrast to trauma? Tender and pliable. Saturated with hope and possibility. An extended way of knowing what came first and what lops along, collapsed, circuitous, and innermost. The experiences of my lineage are entirely felt but not a burden. It would be profane to see it as such. Looping and what comes with it is birthright—my birthright not to reinter by swearing it to secrecy but to unearth and rename. This work is lovingly washing the bones of those who have gone before me, a practice of transmuting trauma into joy.

"Women break through everything and go on living" (Salami 114). What does it mean for me to consider this even as I recognize that survivor trauma may live forward? Can I grant that cultural and generational trauma has real effects? Yes. "Joy [is] the one 'weapon' that can truly, if unintentionally, disarm the power of the oppressive narrative" (Salami 78). If it is so that I am part of a family lineage that carries with it trauma, then I carried Indigo in my body as I experienced my trauma. Am I doomed to reckon with psychic pain that continues forward? That's not what Ceci said about daughters being free, and that's also not what Minna Salami offers:

By joy, I am not speaking of its close relative, happiness. I am referring to an inner quality that is itself political in nature. By *joy*, I mean the type of emotion that may emerge if you had a near-death experience but survived, because to thrive under a system of oppression requires such intentionality. I mean the presence of hope. I mean being yourself even if it clashes with the approved perceptions of how you should be. I mean ease and lightness of being. (78)

My way of knowing has something to do with holding all possibilities and temporalities *in a* relationship together. Yes, there is looping. Yes, there is joy. Yes, there is hope and audacity.

There is all this and healing, and then the children can be well.

Relational Silence

you had to have a last name. last is a function. and a descriptor.

but the types of names that last are the paternal names.

and if you give yours away to take on the name of another man

or if you keep the one your mother gave hers away for,

or if, like with my people, you steal the name

in some grab towards impossible accountability

it is still never the name of the mother.

which is just another evident example of what you already know.

they don't want you to remember me, they don't want you to remember free.

they do not want you to know my name. but you know it. don't you?

so then build your memory early in the morning out of secrets and intuition.

make your archive out of unauthorized claims.

craft your knowing out of water and heat.

wake up and write down my name.

—Alexis Pauline Gumbs

Both of my daughters have my last name.

Their first names are what they named themselves before they took their first breaths.

I listened to nonverbal cues to learn their names.

Relational silences can have positive elements.

Silence—its modalities—must be differentiated (Cheung). Silence can be articulated, as much as it can be prescribed, enforced, and insisted upon. Silence makes space for imagining futures and listening to the past, which may complicate the veracity of objective others. For those reading this who share my lineage and cannot hear beyond words that can be uttered or read.

Remember, words can disrupt the holy transmissions flowing through the heart and womb.

Ancestral Silences

> Just as we have learned to forget, we can learn to (re)member.
> —Cynthia Dillard xii

I wonder if shame floats in the DNA pool until we break the silence and turn towards the source of suffering with outstretched palms. Surrender. Breaking as taking to embrace shadowed spaces as refugia. Breaking as heeding the call to become with what is.

For a long time, I felt ashamed of my relationship with my mother, especially once I realized that some mothers and daughters enjoyed loving friendships with each other. I struggled to see my pain as valid, and I often questioned my sanity when my mother and I could not resolve our conflicts, which was often. I thought it was my fault for a few reasons. When I was a child, I was constantly silenced by my mother for talking back and did not have a resource to process my deepest feelings and concerns or to receive feedback. My mother told me I talked back a lot and constantly reprimanded me for being bossy. On the one hand, she celebrated my accomplishments; on the other, she consistently shamed me for not going along with her ideas, gossip, and will. Subsequently, I just felt wrong, as opposed to harmed.

While attending graduate school and attending therapy, I decided to get serious about my ancestry. Just as I sensed that the troubles that I experienced in my relationship with my mother had a deeper source, I also came to understand that any effort to comprehend experience is precipitated by the emotional and mental distress we experience and that dysfunction is the consequence of being disconnected from our ancestors, experienced as alienation (Some). Sickness, even. I found a way to consider how the unknown abuses of the past affect me in the present (Some). I am struck by the possibility that ancestral silences in the motherline may lead Black women to experience psychological pain, trauma, and feelings of disconnection, and I am relieved to know that shame, humiliation, anger, fear, and helplessness do indeed stifle mourning. For so long, I just sat with those inner reverberations, doing what I could to keep them down, so to speak—keeping the cycle ongoing.

In retrospect, I know that I was silencing myself, which is a deterrent to mourning: "When suffering is forced to go underground, it becomes suppressed, uncontrolled, and inherently unconscious" (Parker 64). Study, therapy, ritual, and spiritual practice might help to excavate the source of suffering that was more than mine alone.

While mining for resources on the effects of ancestral silences on Black women, transgenerational trauma, spirituality, and healing of family lineage, I find the data to be thin. While there is plenty of information about Black American women and religion, it is challenging to find academic analyses on the relationship between spirituality and healing ancestral lineage. Initially, I suspected that this disparity was an effect of Western religious colonization, whereby practices of ancestor veneration among enslaved Africans were discouraged or forbidden by white slaveholders and eventually disappeared over time. Likewise, Black women weren't necessarily writing about our multiple ways of knowing what we know. Some of us were, but mostly we knew what we knew, and we knew it together. It didn't matter who questioned the truth. We have a tremendous wealth of wisdom in the archives from our Black academic collective ancestors to cite, but how to cite those who left no diaries? As Foor reminds us: "Many contemporary communities (religious and otherwise) reject the existence or relevance of the ancestors, this lack of consideration functions as a kind of ancestral amnesia with respect to family, heritage, and culture" (30–31). While I agree, I also suspect we have been subsumed by those mores of dominator culture, making our experience of ancestral amnesia the result of ancestral survival actions that may have compromised an intact bloodline and its spiritual practices.

What I mean is this: While some of us may experience a particular type of amnesia regarding our motherline, others have inherited "wonder working power ... mystical gifts of healing, foreknowledge, and inter-dimensional communication" (Holmes 332). We are encouraged to host encounters with the numinous, where we may access ancestral wisdom and reclaim the mystical legacy of Africana and Indigenous people, thus accessing multiple cultural, religious, and spiritual resources that facilitate healing (Holmes 345).

More and more, those of us who had a hard disconnect from the African diaspora and religious consciousness via the traumatizing violence of slavery, Christian expansionism, and colonization by Europeans are making excavations, (re)membering as a promise to all of the ancestors: Touching our spirits is quite literally a covenant we have made with the ancestors who chose to survive so that we might have the awesome opportunity to thrive as Black people today" (Dillard xv). How we come to (re)member is multiple. The development of strength and resilience "as protective processes (getting stronger), psychospiritual strengths/gifts can facilitate the reduction of distress and disconnectedness and contribute to relieving the suffering of women of African descent" (Harrell et al. 49–70). Ultimately, how I choose to go about healing is determined through my process of contemplation, discernment, and intuition, where contemplation is conceptualized as an extended way of knowing—the "quest for the real beneath appearances; the dignity that makes meaning of our suffering fundamentally spiritual" (Lanzetta 42). Along with discernment and intuition, I engage the silences with the entirety of my being, listening with my feelings, bodily responses, and intellect (Franzmann). By adopting this approach, listening becomes a practice of actively engaging with my ancestral silences as significant phenomena. So I embark on a journey where I prioritize curiosity about the process rather than seeking "some definitive answer to its meaning" (Franzmann 18). Together with curiosity, there is also wonder—wonder as sensation; which is felt, encountered, and entered with. It is the sensation of "how a body is in contact with a world, then something becomes sensational when the contact becomes more intense. Perhaps, to feel is to feel this even more" (Ahmed 22). Wonder as sensation is power, and wonder is a necessary dimension of freedom (Holmes). The rituals and spiritual practices of Africana women enlarge their capacities to see and sense beyond the limits of the linear. Spiritual practices have the potential to heal, instruct, and connect us to the source of our being: "[W]hether contemplative practices emerged among family or church members did not really matter; our practices pointed beyond us towards ancestors and progeny" (Holmes xxxiii). In (re)membering, we may discover how to heal, sense, and be in the right relationship with our motherline.

Hope in Adversity

Healing is as unique as each woman, and no one path will work universally. Ultimately, what animates healing is hope:

> Where there is hope, there is difficulty. Feminist histories are histories of the difficulty of that we, a history of those who have had to fight to be part of a feminist collective, or even had to fight against a feminist collective in order to take up a feminist cause. Hope is not at the expense of struggle but animates a struggle; hope gives us a sense that there is a point to working things out, working things through. Hope does not only or always point toward the future, but carries us through when the terrain is difficult, when the path we follow makes it harder to proceed. Hope is behind us when we have to work for something to be possible. (Ahmed 2)

Many Black women have found the power to heal ancestral silences in their motherlines through prayer and ritual, engaging in descendant memory work, reimagining the ancestral past, finding reverence in the absence of an intact story, drawing on life principles and psychospiritual strengths/gifts (Harrell et al.), or integrating of all or any of these modalities.

This work calls for commitment. Patience, too. It has taken me years, and healing does not have an endpoint. It is, rather, an orientation.

Prayer and Ritual Practices

"Let us be the healing of the wound."

The Coyolxauhqui imperative—la sombra y el sueño

—Gloria Anzaldúa 303

"Don't send your prayers to distant corners of the sky,"
he said in a dreamy voice. "The deities are nearer than your breath.
It is love that binds them to us."

—Diane Skafte 67

Healing minister of prayer, Paula Owens Parker, developed a generational healing service for African-descended individuals and their families. This approach works to break generations of traumatized learned behaviour and attitudes, bringing about a restored, repaired, and renewed identity that provides a more stable and less stressful way of life for themselves and future generations. She uses Bible stories to illustrate how people are influenced by their ancestors so that her clients begin to recognize what patterns need healing. Ritual practice is common among women of colour; rituals may be learned or created. Luisah Teish believes that rituals result in attunement with ancestors: "By attunement, I mean sacred acts that will help you realize your kinship with [ancestors] (90)." Teish emphasizes that we should have reverence for our "ancestors [who] function as guides, warriors, and healers" (88). Nancy Thompson cocreates rituals to facilitate a collective healing experience and lead women "through the mysteries of death and renewal, taking us through the darkness to a place that goes beyond our fears, failures, and frustrations to connect with a deep source of transcendent understanding and creative inspiration" (325).

Leaving behind most immediate spiritual lineage of Christianity and any fears of a patriarchal God, I choose to ease in, slowly and intentionally, on my own. In *Ancestral Medicine: Ritual for Personal and Family Healing*, Foor reminds me to be patient and creative and to keep open a space to do the sacred work of (re)membering my motherline—specifically my maternal grandmother. I do not take on work that feels like it is not mine to do. So I ritually sit with my altar and photos, make simple offerings, and gather the information wanting to be known. Engaging

in this way is slow and humbling, and giving reverence is more important than imposing my will—or anyone else's—on the process that I am
called to do. I mean what I say when I emphasize that I was called. Prayer
and ritual are how I respond. Prayer and ritual are responsive practices,
keeping us safe from creating new wounds as a reaction to woundedness.

Engaging in Descendant Memory Work

> If you want to understand any woman you must first ask about her
> mother and then listen carefully. Stories about food show a strong
> connection. Wistful silences demonstrate unfinished business. The
> more a daughter knows about the details of her mother's life—
> without flinching or whining—the stronger the daughter."
>
> —Anita Diamant 2

There is no greater agony than bearing an untold story within you
(Hurston). Telling the stories of ancestors may bring peace to one's ancestors and, therefore, heal the motherline and reconcile ancestral legacies, particularly those of silence. Rosalyn Terborg-Penn maintains that
her work preserving the history of her family lineage was led by the spirit
of the ancestors whose stories she was seeking. She brought peace to her
ancestors by following their guidance and discovered her inheritance—a
spiritual gift of power from her ancestral lineage. In women's search for
the past and telling the untold story of ancestral silences, the intactness
or linearity is less important than the story itself. Bayo Akomolafe discusses the shape of time as spiralling, and Gayle Greene and Carol P.
Christ describe "women's quests [tend] to be vertical rather than horizontal: women dive, surface, fly ... divine, excavate, dig in, dig out, and
engage in various sorts of archeological projects" (197).

I have no idea why I am called to this ancestral archeology of now,
but it is now medicine, for remembering begets future transformation.

Reimagining the Ancestral Past

> Regardless of the violence that persists,
> I must continue to rewrite the past from the vantage point of the present;
> to envision and articulate the stories of our ancestors
> and our past selves with humanity, divinity, and compassion.
> In doing so, we see our presence as the future manifestations of
> their efforts.
> With these examples, we can confidently continue our legacy of building
> futures for our descendants, and livable presents for ourselves.
> This is the healing work.
> —Sarah Makeba Daise 36–37

What matters is our capacity to act with agency—bending ancestral silences in a way that brings healing. Written texts and storytelling by African American women are a revisionist means of responding to an "'ancestral imperative' ... [that] serve to intervene in 'historical amnesia'" (Patton 4) and may include "anything that might be material for study (e.g., written or spoken words, rituals, dance, song, art, etc.)" through counter-memory (Franzmann 17).

As we imagine how to heal from the past, we necessarily acknowledge that the future is present and that the past is present: "To move beyond [the] pessimism that can result from discovering an ancestral past characterized by unfortunate suffering, African Americans must be able to reimagine both their pasts and futures" (Patton 25). Venetta Patton's offering supports me in making peace with the unknown elements of the relationship between my maternal grandmother and my mother—but Greene's reassurance kept me response-able. Responding to Toni Morrison's *Beloved*, Greene asserts that "ambiguity suggests a difficult balance in relation to the past: the past must be remembered, but not entirely; it must be forgotten, but not entirely; it can kill though it can also heal, and it is most healing when remembered in response to another and when 'told'... in a way that emphasizes the remembering and telling as a means of reconstruction" (210). Freeing myself to remember and retell across timelines may lead to another retelling that brings what needs to be brought forward for integration at another time, or, maybe as Greene explains, "Remembering and telling are generative and re-storative acts that will endow the past with flesh, blood, and a heartbeat" (212).

Finding Reverence in the Absence of an Intact Story

In some cases, ancestors may seem to disappear (Terborg-Penn). And secrecy may, at times, be secretive:

> There were certain things in my experience as a child, certain events, that were never discussed. Some stories, some customs, were shared only as knowledge was necessary and then with an attitude of hesitation, reticence. I believed the reasons for con-cealment centered around two issues. Sometimes the information revealed was too painful—so tremendously and profoundly painful that the act of recognition risked the release of a haphazard power, an energy whose discharge required a careful, almost ritual attention. (Harding 60)

Just the same, ancestral silences might also exist because those an-cestors did not want to be found. This raises important questions regard-ing our willingness to question longstanding assumptions about how our family lineage should make us be; perhaps, there is power in the possi-bility of being unredeemed, in thinking about the ways that Western, colonizing notions of connection and genealogical evidence contribute to a type of pathologizing of uprootedness that is harmful to descendants without hard evidence of their lineage. As velez discusses it:

> I feel like I'm curious about our obsession with this intactness, and I kind of actually feel like in the gaps I'm being asked to kinda fill things in and that's a deeper way that I'm able to connect and recall my ancestors. And to play, and to trust that it's in me and I don't need to have—I'm always thinking that I don't need this ancestral tree and be able to name everyone in my line, and there is *something* about that, and even that doesn't offer me much. So yeah, I do believe there is something beautiful about passing down that wisdom and offering that wisdom and stories and folklore, if there are cultures that are permitted to do that. I just was like, damn what a gift that you are able to access that, but yeah, it's

kinda deromanticizing the idea of connecting with them in this material form. Who is it to say that it's not intact in our bodies? (qtd. in Moray)

Calling Forward My Mother Wound

This mother wound is alive and intact in my body; I awakened to it, some twelve years ago, as I was finding joy and deep connection in mothering Indigo, who was five at the time:

Mothering a daughter is no small feat. It requires endless flexibility, a whole heart, and a humble spirit. Eckhart Tolle says that parenting is the perfect place to reach enlightenment. Queen Afua says that motherhood will make you over if you let it. Yes. She says it will create spiritual, emotional, mental, and physical muscle, and teach you how to master your own life. Many women have suffered emotional neglect at the hands of the one they call mother. So many have swallowed that pain, which then shows up in the way they mother their own daughters. It shows its face as they grow, waking up like a bear after hibernation.

They show Mama their love, or they devour her; the pain implodes and ricochets within their own bodies as dis-ease.

Breaking any cycle calls for wakeful awareness. When you are truly close to your daughter, she can sense your intentions. She sniffs them out with insight more readily than vision. She can "see" your heart.

What you think, she knows. Do not trouble her: Sweep yourself daily of the dust of the past. Do not burden her heart with your regrets, guilt, or shame. She can feel your authenticity. You are a nurturer.

Feed her light, feed her high vibrations, feed her the stars. Hold her forever. Lay with her for restoration. Inhale the sweetness of her. Praise her name. Bless her. Give thanks for her daily. Tell her who she is. Remind her if she forgets. Honour her. Celebrate her power. Be beautiful with her. Forever.

Be love to her.

Do not betray her. Do not betray her. Do not betray her.

I am thankful that the experience of parenting my own two daughters has helped to relieve some of my grief and heal my motherline and my mother wound. My mother and I have found a shared experience of love and joy through the lives of my daughters, which has unpredictably but thankfully brought us closer. Both my mother and I benefit from the looping of intergenerational connections, where we can heal the present with each other and in relationship with my daughters (Lowinsky 22).

Still, though, I carry significant grief in my relationship with my mother; most of this work is mine to do, and I am called to it. In ways that only I know, it is necessary to heal what lies beneath this grief while we are both still here. I do not choose to wait, reimagine, or find reverence in some distant future. I do this work from a place of full presence and experience what emerges in my quest as "clean pain" (Menakem). I hold what I find with deep love and care as opposed to judgment and blame. This approach, in contrast to experiencing dirty pain, is what creates collective healing: "Experiencing clean pain enables us to engage our integrity and tap into our body's inherent resilience and coherence, in a way that dirty pain does not. Paradoxically, only by walking into our pain or discomfort—experiencing it, moving through it, and metabolizing it—can we grow. It's how the human body works" (Menakem 20).

This pain stored in the body will live on in other bodies if not metabolized. Resmaa Menakem assures, "When we heal, we may spread our emotional health and healthy genes to later generations" (55).

Reaching for a Collective, Interdependent, and Unitive Consciousness

> Your life's work is an intergenerational project,
> an ancestral conspiracy, a continuous meeting of bodies,
> a queering of temporality. Your life is not yours to resolve,
> yours to complete, or yours to contain.
> It is necessarily the life of the many.
> Be thankful for the threadbare places of your life,
> for it gives the many who are yet to come something to stitch theirs into.
> —Bayo Akomolafe, "Your Life's Work"

More than one intuitive reading has revealed that my role in my family lineage is to break intergenerational cycles and heal the past to improve the future lives of my descendants, most notably my children.

As I settle into this collective, interdependent, and unitive consciousness (Harrell et al.), I know that my daughters and their descendants will benefit from the work I do now to heal this intergenerational trauma. I struggle to claim the source of power and belonging in my motherline, instead finding that it is punctured with silences, abbreviated by intentional forgetfulness, and heavy with trauma. It is difficult to recover because my living family has forgotten much or will not share about the past. What is shared about the past is complicated by the person telling the past—and this has real consequences. At one time, I asked my mother and my auntie for their recollections of my grandmother's life. I was surprised to be offered two very different accounts of my grandmother. Taking what I learned from them into a process of contemplation, discernment, intuition, and ritual—even in the less than definitive storying, I discovered a knowing that gave me peace and understanding for my grandmother.

I now know that the experience of Black women's estrangement from their mothers is not an uncommon one, and I feel less isolated. My scholarly work is animated by my desire to understand better my psychospiritual struggle as a mother, worker, and adult college student. I found myself deeply relating to other women who say that they never saw their mothers cry when faced with trauma and life challenges and who adopted the behaviour that was modelled—all the while feeling like something was wrong with themselves for feeling sad, anxious, and overwhelmed. I hear an "Allelujia chorus" when we can affirm our shared realities (Estes 321), and I find a deeper level of self-awareness (Collins). As I give voice to my silences, I recognize that risk is imminent, as did Audre Lorde: "Of course I am afraid, because the transformation of silence into language and action is an act of self-revelation, and that always seems fraught with danger." Through coming to voice with others, I realize that I did learn how to be strong, but I am acutely aware that performing strength is not the same as being resilient, recovering from trauma, and healing from life challenges.

I seek to know more and more about the stories of my ancestral pasts. I resolve to ask my mother about food, speak with the silences of my motherline, and move towards wellness.

Acceptance and Surrender

This work is recursive and spiralling. Throughout my life, I have experienced more than half of the symptoms attributed to Post-traumatic stress disorder, and I have often felt ashamed, isolated, and crazy for suffering as I did. I now recognize that as a Black woman, my trauma, like many others, is layered, multigenerational and epigenetic and affects our ability to perceive new realities. Because trauma carries, finding a (somewhat) clear and true story about the past will help to heal the future and imagine new possibilities. Today, I recall my 2013 work; in the stories about motherlines, I find experiences of trauma. Trauma doesn't dissipate in the death of our foremothers; it has implications for how we perceive ourselves in relationship to our suffering. Those who believe that their suffering is their own may experience a secondary pain more harmful than the original wound—a deep suffering that may result from ancestral legacies (Foor). For some, our relationships with our foremothers are complicated; when researching our motherlines, a simple record of birth dates, death dates, and pictures will not suffice. To heal, we must take a nonlinear approach to reality, looking at how what is not known about the past affects us in the present: "My work and my healing shape the future. Remaining in a constant state of fear and stress does more than diminish my own mental and physical health. It reinforces chains my descendants will have to break free of. This knowing is in us. In Black women. In me. Our foremothers are counting on us to live free" (Daise 29). If my distress has implications for my future, then my future can also be healed by reaching into the motherline, where I know more about what the women in my maternal lineage experienced (Daise 4).

Transcending Loss and Recovering the Self

> The search for the Motherline requires a
> downward journey into the realm of the ancestors.
> Here one discovers lost meanings, forgotten lives,
> generations of grief; here one begins to feel the power of ghosts
> one has feared to acknowledge.
> —Naomi Ruth Lowinsky 142

When we lack access to the stories of our motherline, we become self-estranged, and this self-estrangement manifests in the multitude of ways that we act out our lives (Lowinsky 18). I recognize self-estrangement as a part of my suffering. Because I grew up in a military family where both of my parents left home to put dysfunction, violence, and poverty behind them, my relationship with my extended family is virtually nonexistent. What I know of my extended family, I learned from my parents, and there were a few positive stories, which gave me limited access to the wisdom of how my ancestors survived challenges. Like many other African Americans, I am well aware that my experience of self-estrangement colludes with my unfounded feelings of shame: "The subject of shame is particularly significant when it comes to African Americans. It is as though people live with a constant fear of being exposed. I am not completely sure what exactly we are afraid of exposing. I only know that this fear is something a number of us live with, a collective knowing of sorts, the details about which have been long forgotten" (DeGruy 141).

Meeting the feelings of shame and the fear of being exposed has been a part of this work. Recognizing the silences that were not my own has lifted a tremendous weight off my motherline. Writing this narrative returned me to that collective fear because I am not entirely unafraid of how those who held these silences consciously or unconsciously will respond to this unearthing, recovery, and paradoxical work. By recovering the stories of our ancestral past, we can learn which intergenerational patterns are unhelpful and begin to shift such patterns to heal the past and imagine new futures (Foor). Personally, intellectually, and spiritually, I am finding my way to the wisdom of my lineage: I read texts to satiate my curiosities. I follow hunches of intuition. I make peace with paradox via contemplation. And I reconcile what remains unknown with what can be known as pertains to my motherline. Transcending loss arises from the courage to pass it on rather than letting it disappear entirely "emphasizing the importance of remembering and storytelling as a means of reconstructing and healing" (Greene 211).

Taking Charge and Claiming My Motherline

Thelma Dixon. Say her name.

My grandmother Thelma was born in 1927 in Biloxi, Mississippi, and she transitioned in 1986. The birthdate on my grandmother's headstone says that she was born in 1935; when she married a much younger man in her second marriage, she changed her age accordingly. Her mother, my great-grandmother, died when my grandmother was nine, and it is said that my great-grandfather married the woman who cared for her while she was ill. That woman is the only great-grandmother I knew of. I have her name as my middle name. She raised my grandmother and my mother. My grandmother graduated from high school, worked in a jewelry store, and married my grandfather when she was twenty-one, pregnant with my auntie. My mother was born six years later, and my grandparents divorced shortly after. My grandmother moved with her daughters to my grandparents' home.

From this point, there are multiple different recollections because of my auntie's silences and my mother's forgetfulness of the past, which I attribute to dissociative amnesia—an adaptative approach to sifting details into isolated fragments (Fisher). My mother remembers moving across town with my grandmother and my auntie. There are different stories about why this happened. The first is that my mother's grandparents removed her from that home to stop the abuse she endured by my grandmother (my mother's mother). The second is that my grandmother left my grandfather because he regularly assaulted her; he later sued for custody of my mother and won. According to this story, my grandfather never took my mother into his home but gave her to my maternal grandparents to raise. When asked about my grandmother, my mother remembers very little, and what she remembers is terrible. She remembers her grandparents fondly: they were strict, loving, poor, and churchgoing. Most of all, she remembers being loved by them, as contrasted with feelings of abandonment left by her biological parents. Perhaps my mother was too young to understand her mother's choices; what she remembers is that her mother rarely visited.

My auntie's memories of my grandmother offer me insight into my grandmother's nuanced, interior life. She says that my grandmother was an amazing cook but rarely sat down to eat a meal with her daughters. She loved Ray Charles, but she didn't dance much. She always worked hard, serving food in a school cafeteria and cleaning houses. She went without winter coats so that her daughters could have them. She was not violent; the worst thing to experience was her disappointment or raising her voice. She didn't smile much. She was likely depressed. When I asked about my grandmother's emotional and mental health, I learned, "You just didn't ask those questions. You weren't supposed to."

I don't talk about these differing narratives to my family. I don't want to retraumatize them.

I am beginning to understand how things come to be remembered differently by people. It makes sense that I am only now, while mothering my children, making peace with the past, as Lowinsky confirms in her discussion of the role of spiritual maturity in adult daughters of mothers: "It is at this stage of maturation that we can feel our way into the suffering of our mothers' and children's lives. For she who cannot sink into the pain of her mother's experience, who cannot imagine her grief, love, bitterness, life's tragedy, life's joy, remains forever a daughter, frozen in her development" (Lowinsky 51).

I now appreciate that our healing is connected to our willingness to sit with the lives of our maternal lineage with empathy and compassion. Consciously facing the past has moved me beyond the ambivalence in the present. Making peace with the truth of my maternal lineage has helped me to understand my mother and our relationship. Akasha Gloria Hull argues that "Everything we do, every experience we have, from this large, metaphysical, spiritual perspective is redemptive" (175). I suppose then that I can choose to perceive the tensions between my mother and myself as an opportunity to grow and heal.

I recognize that my pursuit of healing results from my status as a seeker and the privilege of being a graduate student of women's spirituality. I appreciate this freedom of choice given how I was raised—as a third-culture kid of parents who grew up poor and subsequently exposed me to opportunities that helped me to grow competent and independent. I have mixed feelings about Hull's assertion that every experience we have is redemptive. Perhaps, redemption is generational.

My mother, who has yet to spend time healing the trauma of abandonment that she experienced as a child, hasn't yet found redemption.

Perhaps my job is to do the recovery work on my family's behalf.

Perhaps that is why Indigo was sent to me.

Perhaps healing from the traumatic experiences in our family lineage from a metaphysical, spiritual perspective will lead to our transformation.

Perhaps I was determined not to maintain a toxic relationship with Indigo's father, avoiding an adverse childhood experience for my children. In addressing the trauma head-on, healing, recovering, and growing, I can heal the motherlines for my children, for myself, and most importantly, for my mother from whom I have inherited the "strong black-woman" identity (Walker-Barnes 3).

Perhaps, I have moved beyond performing the identity through healing and reconciling the context of my mother's childhood with my lived experiences, which has opened the door to forgiveness and compassion.

I now understand that my mother necessarily forgot so much just to survive.

I now recognize that my mother did the best she could with the resources she had at the time. My love continues to grow for her.

I am because she is.

Interconnected Love

With Indigo's arrival, I began to sense my grandmother's presence. I cannot say how I knew it was her, but I did. There was warmth in her presence. This was later confirmed by an intuitive I once visited, who sensed the presence of a woman ancestor standing behind me. She told me that this ancestor's name began with the letter T. was later confirmed. She told me that this ancestor found joy in watching me parent my children. When our loved ones transition, they are no longer bound by how they lived when they were embodied (Foor 35).

Perhaps my grandmother came to me to avoid being stuck forever in that place of story (Foor). Perhaps my grandmother was deeply grieved that she couldn't take care of her two children on her own. Perhaps my grandmother did her best with the resources available to her at the time.

Knowing that she is with us brings me comfort; she came into my life when I most needed comfort and when I needed to be witnessed.

Perhaps, Indigo summoned her when I summoned Indigo.

Black women have always called on our ancestors; it is a prominent theme in the new spirituality of African American women in the 1980s. (Hull 54). Now familiar with ancestor reverence, I approach the work of connecting with my grandmother with patience and intentionality. I draw strength from Foor, who advises, "If you ever have a sense that a beloved grandparent or parent is looking out for you, there's a good chance they are" (31). My family altar is a place for peacefully connecting with my grandmother and healing my relationship with my mother. To my altar, I bring coffee from my French press sweetened with cream for my grandmother. I burn sage, work with my crystals, and pull goddess cards. My altar is growing. There is a picture of me with my newborn Indigo having survived my trauma. There is a picture of my mother holding me as a new baby. There are multiple images of my mother as a little girl when she was living through so much trauma. My altar is adorned with baby's breath, stitchwork by my youngest daughter, Inanna, and a sun pendant that I was gifted after birthing my son. I'm still figuring out what to heal and how to heal. I heed Foor's warnings to be still, slow, and patient. I am sensing intently how to proceed in a patient, steady, watchful, and intentional way, knowing that change can also occur in the private, personal space of an individual woman's consciousness. Equally fundamental, this type of change is also empowering. If a Black woman is forced to remain "motionless on the outside," she can always develop the inside of a changed consciousness as a sphere of freedom. Becoming empowered through self-knowledge, even within conditions that severely limit one's ability to act, is essential. (Collins 111)

I grow within, working on what I can, and exercise my psychospiritual muscle.

Accepting Life Principles and Psychospiritual Strengths and Gifts

This work is a process of discovery. More longing than it is impulse. More love than grievance. This is embodied listening and soul talk. We have a choice in how we respond to pain and suffering. We can keep on keeping on, hanging in there, and live through a cycle that continues forward. Or we can attune ourselves to that deeper wisdom that holds the mysteries that bind us to each other—in my case, my grandmother, mother, daughters, and myself. We can listen for the unsaid. We can collect fragments of the narrative for safekeeping and wait for guidance. And we can reconstruct—lovingly accepting the work that mends broken hearts. This way, we restore the psyche and soothe the soul as our psychospiritual gifts are brought into being. With the heaviness lifted, we experience a love born of resolve, a force of liberation.

While some tensions remain between my mother and me, watching her love my children differently than she did me brings fresh admiration for her. Parenting my children differently breaks generational cycles. Feeling and accepting my grandmother's presence in my home heals my mother. In our nonlinear looping, my grandmother is experiencing joy, peace, and reconciliation, as we are. I once felt resentful that my mother chose to remember her mother as she has, but now I am compelled to regard her memories as significant. To heal, I fold the recollections of my mother's childhood into what is: "[T]hrough years of listening to my mother's stories of her life, I have absorbed not only the stories themselves, but something of the urgency that involves the knowledge that her stories—like her life—must be recorded" (Collins 240). My mother's story provides insight into how she became who she is. In knowing my mother's past and being with her as I raise my daughters, we are in the ideal place to heal our relationship while we are both still here. Although it might appear I am doing the repair work (27), I know that my mother is a coinspirer, whether she knows it or not.

Life Giving and Renewing

It's October 2022, and I'm attending the Wise Women's Herbal Conference at Kanuga sanctuary, near Asheville, North Carolina. On my first night there, I attend a breathwork workshop held on the lake pavilion at dusk. For about an hour, I breathe in rhythm to carefully curated music, with one hundred women. During the third last song, I leave my body to travel to another realm. I join my mother and my daughters, who are sitting in a circle holding hands. As we all sit together, I weep as light approaches our circle. I am not weeping in the circle, but I am weeping in my body on the pavilion. Somehow, I am present in both places, as a witness of the circle and inside of the circle. The light approaching us is like an orb, or a firefly—as it comes closer, she shows herself to be my grandmother. She sits in the circle, taking my hand and the hand of my mother, and together, we turn into flickering light beings. It is so natural: "All of it is natural. I mean, speaking to spirits, whoever is around you, it's perfectly natural; there's nothing supernatural about it. I mean we are here on earth, we're on the planet. Nobody has ever gone anywhere. That's why they're still here." (Walker qtd. in Hull 82)

In that moment on the pavilion, I embody healing, and I am reminded of Alice Walker's poem "Reassurance":

I must love the questions
themselves
as Rilke said
like locked rooms
full of treasure
to which my blind

and groping key
does not yet fit
and await the answers
as unsealed
letters
mailed with dubious intent
and written in a very foreign
tongue.

And in the hourly making
of myself
no thought of Time
to force, to squeeze
the space
I grow into. (40–41)

Endnotes

1. I use the terms Black, Black American, and African descended.

Works Cited

Ahmed, Sara. *Living a Feminist Life.* Duke University Press, 2017.

Akomolafe, Bayo. "When You Meet the Monster, Anoint Its Feet." *Emergence Magazine*, 16 Oct. 2018, https://emergencemagazine.org/essay/when-you-meet-the-monster/. Accessed 20 May 2024.

Akomolafe, Bayo. "Your Life's Work Is an Intergenerational Project. That Is Because 'We' Are Produced by the Manifold, by the Collective, So." *Facebook*, 4 July 2023. https://www.facebook.com/bayoakomolafeampersand. Accessed 20 May 2024.

Anzaldúa, Gloria. "Let Us Be the Healing of the Wound: The Coyolxauhqui Imperative—la sombra y el sueño," *The Gloria Anzaldúa Reader*. Edited by AnaLouise Keating. Duke University Press, 2009, pp. 298–303.

Barnwell, Ashley. "Family Secrets and the Slow Violence of Social Stigma." *Sociology*, vol 53, no. 6, 2019, pp. 1111–1126.

Cheung, King-Kok. *Articulate Silences: Hisaye Yamamoto, Maxine Hong Kingston, Joy Kogawa*. Cornell University Press, 1993.

Collins, Patricia Hill. *Black Feminist Thought: Knowledge, Consciousness, and the Politics of Empowerment*. 2nd ed. Routledge, 2000.

Daise, Sara Makeba. "Come On In The Room: Afrofuturism as Path to Black Women's Retroactive Healing." 2018. Union University, master's thesis.

Diamant, Anita. *The Red Tent*. Picador USA, 1997.

Dillard, Cynthia B. *Learning to (Re)member the Things We've Learned to Forget: Endarkened Feminisms, Spirituality, & the Sacred Nature of Research and Teaching*. Peter Lang, 2012.

Estes, Clarissa P. *Women Who Run with the Wolves*. Ballantine Books, 1992.

Fisher, Janina. "Dissociative Phenomena in the Everyday Lives of Trauma Survivors." Conference Presentation, Boston University Medical School Psychological Trauma Conference, 2001.

Gumbs, Alexis Pauline. *Dub: Finding Ceremony*. Duke University Press, 2020.

Franzmann, Majella. *Women and Religion*. Oxford University Press, 2000.

Ferguson, Bria. "Queering Trauma Recovery." *What IFF?* 1 May 2023, https://blogs.cofc.edu/wgsconnect/2023/05/01/what-iff-queering-trauma-recovery/. Accessed 20 May 2024.

Harrell, Shelly, et al. "Toward a Positive Womanist Psychospirituality: Strengths, Gifts, and the Optimal Well-Being of Women of African Descent." *Religion and Spirituality for Diverse Women: Foundations of Strength and Resilience*. Edited by Thema Bryant-Davis. Praeger, 2014, pp. 49–70.

Holmes, Barbara A. *Joy Unspeakable; Contemplative Practices of the Black Church*. 2nd ed. Augsburg Fortress, 2017.

Holmes, Barbara A. "Wonder Working Power: Reclaiming Mystical and Cosmological Aspects of Africana Spiritual Practices." *Esotericism in African American Religious Experience: "There is a Mystery."* Edited by Stephen C. Finley et al., 2015. Brill, pp. 331–45.

Hull, Akasha Gloria. *Soul Talk: The New Spirituality of African American Women.* Inner Traditions International, 2001.

Hurston, Zora Neale. *Dust Tracks on a Road: Autobiography.* University of Illinois Press, 1942.

Kidron, Carol A. "Surviving a Distant Past: A Case Study of the Cultural Construction of Trauma Descendant Identity." *Ethos,* vol. 31, no. 4, 2003, pp. 513–44. www.jstor.org/stable/3651794.

Greene, Gayle. "Feminist Fiction and the Uses of Memory." *The Second Signs Reader: Feminist Scholarship 1983-1996.* Edited by Ruth-Ellen B. Joeres and Barbara Laslett. University of Chicago Press, 1996, pp. 184–215.

Lanzetta, Beverly. *Radical Wisdom: A Feminist Mystical Theology.* Fortress Press, 2005.

Morales, Aurora Levins. "...And Even Fidel Can't Change That!" *This Bridge Called My Back: Writings by Radical Women of Color.* Edited by Cherríe Moraga and Gloria Anzaldúa. Kitchen Table: Women of Color Press, 1981, pp. 53–56.

Lorde, Audre. *Sister Outsider: Essays and Speeches.* Crossing Press, 2007. Ebook.

Lowinsky, Naomi Ruth. *The Motherline: Every Woman's Journey to Find Her Female Roots.* Fisher King Press, 1992.

Menakem, Resmaa. *My Grandmother's Hands.* Central Recovery Press, 2017.

Moray, Pavini. "What Happens After You Are Buried Alive? Art, Ancestors, and Black Erotic Power." *Bespoken Bones.* episode 7, 20 Jan. 2020, https://bespokenbones.com/episode-63-what-happens-after-you-are-buried-alive-art-ancestors-and-black-erotic-power/. Accessed 20 May 2024.

Parker, Paula Owen. 2016. *Roots Matter: Healing History, Honoring Heritage, Renewing Hope.* Pickwick Publications.

Patton, Venetta K. *The Grasp that Reaches Beyond the Grave: The Ancestral Call in Black Women's Texts.* State University of New York Press, 2013.

Salami, Minna. *Sensuous Knowledge: A Black Feminist Approach for Everyone*. Amistad, 2020.

Skafte, Dianne. *Listening to the Oracle: The Ancient Art of Finding Guidance in the Signs and Symbols All Around Us*. Harper Collins, 1997.

Some, Malidome Patrice. *Of Water and Spirit: Ritual, Magic, and Initiation in the Life of an African Shaman*. Penguin Books, 1994.

Teish, Luisah. "Ancestor Reverence." *Weaving the Visions: New Patterns in Feminist Spirituality*. Edited by Judith Plaskow and Carol. P. Christ. Harper San Francisco, 1989, pp. 87–92.

Terborg-Penn, Rosalyn. "The Spirit Keeps the Memory of the Ancestors Alive." *My Soul Is a Witness: African-American Women's Spirituality*. Edited by Gloria Jean Wade Gayles. Beacon Press, 1995, pp. 65–70.

Thompkins, Toby. *The Real Lives of Strong Black Women: Transcending Myths, Reclaiming Joy*. Agate Publishing, 2004.

Walker-Barnes, Chanequa. *Too Heavy a Yoke: Black Women and the Burden of Strength*. Cascade Books, 2014.

Ward, Earlise C., et al. "African American Women's Beliefs, Coping Behaviors, and Barriers to Seeking Mental Health Services." *Qualitative Health Research*, vol.19, no. 11, 20 Oct. 2009, pp. 1589–1601.

Walker, Alice. *In Search of Our Mothers' Gardens: Womanist Prose*, Harvest/ HBJ, 1983.

18.

One Momma

Pamela Vickerson

To be a mother these days is to experience extremes. Love. Pain.
And the stuff in between.
Mother is the symbol of life and strength,
the comforter, the counsellor,

but as a mother you'll be
criticized when you fail to live up to someone else's idea of a mother,
when you think for yourself,
when you break out of old roles,
try new things,
don't know what to do

or how to get out.
Judged if you stay.
Judged if you go.

"Experts" may lean across the table and make dire warnings when you
question their advice,
you may be accused of interrupting those who freely and regularly
interrupt you,
you may be ignored and told not to worry your pretty little head about it,
asked, "Are you sure?" a hundred times,
invited, in a myriad of ways, to doubt yourself.

As a momma you may be labeled in categories specially designed for you:
"just" a housewife
single mother
MILF
trophy wife
bitch.

Having a baby in a *nice* country
where women have rights
where Health Care is for everyone
may mean you have more chance to enjoy motherhood
to relish the time
and experience a new perspective
with this tiny person.
A new kind of laughter,
the smell of baby skin
the touch of the downiest hair
So proud.

Some joy
some in-between stuff
some pain

To be a momma these days is to realize you can't do it as well as you
had hoped,
that you don't understand all that you wish to understand,
that you are not a pillar of fine character and wisdom,
that sometimes you lose your temper and say stupid things.
That overwhelm can sneak up and slap you down

that you can keep getting up every day
and marching forward nonetheless.

You learn to face challenges and grow with your kids.
To believe them when they
try to communicate without words,
"Something is wrong"

Even after numerous appointments
and the scads of experts that still can't see it.
Appointments paid for by healthcare,
(which you are grateful for, nonetheless)

You may still have to find your own way
as a momma in Canada:

To be present through all the moments,
educate yourself,
insist with those experts,
reassure those kids,
even after you've spent a half hour sobbing in the shower
so that they won't hear
and won't be afraid
and the evidence of your fear is washed down the drain.

You keep your bad dreams to yourself,
the ones where you see his five-year-old little body in a coffin.

You smile when he comes out of surgery with dried blood spots on his scalp,
where the clamps held his head still
so that experts could enter.
You smile at that little face
because you know that your expression will tell your five-year-old that he is
alright.
And you want him to believe he's alright
because you have not given up hope.
And you won't.

Although you're "privileged"
your mind is in shock,
and your vision is tunnelled;
you're numb,
searching for answers,
and someone who can help.

To be a privileged mother,
living in a safe country,
with universal healthcare
does not mean experts have answers.

And cures cannot be purchased! No matter how much you fundraise.

Your cries to God may be answered,
the prognosis of "two years left" turns into
twenty-two more birthday celebrations and Thanksgiving dinners.

Grateful. But
any momma these days wants more time than that.
A momma that has been around a while knows that the privileged life
is not about money or power. Or ease.
It has something to do with saying, "Yes"
when after a heart-felt visit,
your twenty-seven-year-old asks you
to hold his hand while
he lays on his death bed, says he's ready to go,
and drifts into a sedated sleep
on one of the last days that the two of you will ever talk.

To be a momma anywhere is to suffer alongside.
And to comfort.
When there is nothing else to be done.
When comfort seems impossible.

Did you know that a momma in Canada can choose 24/7 palliative
care support to help her son die in the comfort of her own home?
She may even be surprised to see the doctor sit humbly on her living
room floor
next to her son's bed
and ask if he can pray for your family.
Even the experts may be able to redeem themselves.

"Ask me all your hard questions," you say to the younger siblings.
"What if I'm at work when he dies, and I can't leave?"
"What if we're at school when it happens?"
You wonder: will it happen while I'm sleeping next to his bed
and I'll wake in the morning to find he is gone?

You may each write the word "TIMING"
on tiny pieces of paper
and give them to God.

Friday evening, December 7th at 6:30pm, when the moment approaches,
you may have a sense
that the family should stay close by him.
Together you sing.
You witness the last two breaths.
You hug and cry.

A creative momma these days may drag the young kids' mattresses
into the grown-up bedroom and have a dance party,
jumping on the mattresses
to celebrate his freedom
and to be comforted by sleeping near to each other in the same room
for as long as it takes.

The real privilege of a mother:
the first breath
the last breath
everything in between.
To remember his personhood
resist the erasure of death
and honor him in memorial.
Live

until you take your leave
and in turn, someone does the remembering of you.

Poet's Notes

As part of a university English course, we were invited to write a poem in response to another writing: "If You Are a Syrian These Days." Fadi Azam's poem is one of loss, lament, resistance, hope, and perseverance in crisis. Replacing "if you are Syrian" with "if you are a mother," I began to reflect on my own lived experience and knew I could not write from the general perspective of a Canadian mother, only one mother. Everything in the poem "One Momma" is personal experience, and day-to-day these memories are mostly hidden and unknown by others. It was easy to write, but surprisingly it was only after the compassionate feedback of the mother-professor that I could reread my poem and cry out some of the pain behind the memories. I spent that whole day "releasing" while my family was out of the house. Even within a family that is sharing the loss of a loved one, the pain of each individual (whether a mother, a sibling, or stepfather [in our case]) is unique and not fully understood by the other. It is to a degree quite isolating.

Works Cited

Azzam, F. (2021). If you are Syrian these days. (G. Alatrash, Trans.). *Gutter Magazine.* (The magazine of new Scottish and international writing), 24, pp. 13–17. https://www.youtube.com/watch?v=vpob MibtOzA

Notes on Contributors

Kate Antosik-Parsons is an artist and academic whose work is concerned with gender and sexuality, embodiment, memory and the maternal. A postdoctoral fellow at Trinity College Dublin on the Reproductive Citizenship Project, Kate is currently working on a cross-border comparative study of abortion in Ireland after its legalization in 2019. Kate is a coauthor of the ground-breaking *Unplanned Pregnancy and Abortion Care Study* (2021).

Maya Bhave's PhD focused on Ethiopian immigrant women (Loyola University, Chicago). After teaching sociology at North Park University for ten years, she moved to Vermont, where she explores gender identity for female players in soccer, motherhood, child loss, and mothers' struggle for work, life, and family balance. Her most recent book is *War and Cleats: Women in Soccer in the United States* (2019). Bhave is working on a book called *Liminal Space: Motherhood, Identity and College-Aged Children*. She has taught for many years as an adjunct professor at Saint Michael's College, and most recently was a visiting assistant professor of sociology at Middlebury College.

Mandy Fessenden Brauer, PhD, is a child psychologist who has lived and worked in California, Gaza, Egypt, Armenia, and Indonesia. She writes bibliotherapy books published in English, Arabic, Georgian, and Bahasa Indonesian to help children better understand themselves and their world. She taught at the American University in Cairo and the Cairo University Medical School on a Fulbright. She, her husband, and two cats live in Egypt and Indonesia, where they enjoy wonderful walks beside the Nile or through ever-changing rice paddies.

Alex Maeve Campbell is a multimedia artist, writer, curator, and arts administrator living in North Bay, Ontario. She is a former editor of *Descant*, a Toronto poetry quarterly, and is the founder of North Bay's Downtown Gallery Hop. She is currently the executive director of North Bay's White Water Gallery.

Terry Anne Campbell, PhD, is a professor of education at Nipissing University. A storyteller and an elementary school teacher before joining the Department of Teacher Education, Terry's interests are centred around the dynamics of storytelling and story writing. Terry is the mother of Alex Maeve Campbell, artist and daughter extraordinaire.

Leanne Charette (she/her) writes poetry grounded in her experience as a disabled adoptee and mother. Her work has been published by Vallum Magazine, the League of Canadian Poets, the Festival of Literary Diversity, and PRISM International. She lives in Kitchener, Ontario with her husband and twin sons, surrounded by many houseplants.

Júlia Campos Clímaco earned a bachelor's degree in psychology from the University of Brasília and a master's in social sciences and education from Facultad Latinoamericana de Ciencias Sociales, Argentina. Her journey continued with a PhD in developmental and school psychology from the University of Brasilia, which included conducting research at the University of British Columbia, Canada. Her research expertise encompasses cultural and developmental psychology, disability studies, and feminisms, focussing on disability, rare diseases, motherhood, and matricentric feminism. She is also an analyst in science and technology at CNPq, specializing in psychology and social work. She has been a visiting scholar at the University of Northern British Columbia (UNBC) since 2022.

Hannah Frostad is a graphic designer whose love for creative communication has naturally led to the genre of poetry. As a mother of two small boys, this medium has created space for her to explore the emotional range of motherhood. Passionate about authenticity, honesty, and vulnerability, she is currently exploring what it means to be 'the village.' Although a newcomer to this art form, she is quickly discovering her poetic voice.

Debra Guckenheimer is a sociologist, activist, writer, and disabled mom. Previously, she was a researcher at Stanford University and the Hadassah Brandeis Institute at Brandeis University. She taught at Bowdoin College; California State, East Bay; and the University of California, Santa Barbara. Her work has appeared in *Embrace Race*, *Women's Studies: An Interdisciplinary Journal*, *The Feminist Wire*, *Handbook of Positive Organizational Scholarship*, and *Doing Diversity in Higher Education*. She has been recognized by the American Sociological Association's Race, Class, and Gender section and the National Center for Institutional Diversity at the University of Michigan. She has a PhD in sociology from University of California Santa Barbara.

Claire Haddon is a visual artist working predominantly with the physical qualities of photography and film. A fine art graduate, she studied at Middlesex University and has been making and exhibiting art ever since. Art and photography are passions that run throughout her life, and she has taught at universities and has run workshops for galleries, families, and schools. Claire Haddon lives in London and has four children.

Libby Jeffrey is a writer and settler on Treaty 1 Territory (Winnipeg). Libby has been featured in the Writes of Spring (Winnipeg International Writers Festival), the Mum Poem Press, and *Emerge 22* (Simon Fraser University). In 2020, Libby self-published *Babybytes: Becoming a Mom as the World Locked Down* and then founded MomAlong.ca, a creative writing group for self-identifying moms with babies.

Gertrude Lyons, PhD, has dedicated her professional life to exploring the transformative capacity of all people, with a focus on mothers. Dr. Lyons received her EdD in 2017 and has lectured, appeared on television and podcasts, published many articles, and produced her own podcast, *Rewrite the Mother Code*.

Drisana McDaniel (she/her) is a mother-worker-activist and race equity and justice facilitator. Her teaching addresses social injustice, racialized dimensions of trauma, resilience, capacity, and connecting across differences to experience healing and integrity. Through her practice The Alchemy of Now, Drisana attends to the nitty-gritty of our individual and collective experiences from an embodied, historical, social, and psychospiritual perspective. She envisions transformational justice as the fruit of contemplation and action. She has a passion for curating events to facilitate radical interconnectedness and is most hopeful about what can happen when we explore our connection to each other and the earth. Drisana lives with her two daughters in Summerville, South Carolina, and she has an adult son who lives in Atlanta, Georgia.

Rachel O'Donnell is an assistant professor in the Writing, Speaking, and Argument Program and the Gender, Sexuality, and Women's Studies Program at the University of Rochester. She has written about the political economy of bioprospecting in the Americas and revolutionary forces during the Guatemalan Civil War. She has previously published creative works with Demeter Press in *Mothers Without Their Children* and *Interrogating Reproductive Loss*.

Andrea O'Reilly, PhD, is full professor in the School of Gender, Sexuality and Women's Studies at York University and publisher of Demeter Press. She is coeditor/editor of thirty-plus books, including *Maternal Theory, The 2nd Edition* (2021), *Normative Motherhood* (2023), and *Coming into Being: On Mothers Finding and Realizing* Feminism (2023). She is editor of the *Encyclopedia of Motherhood* (2010) and coeditor of the *Routledge Companion to Motherhood* (2019).

Michelann Parr, PhD, is a white, able-bodied, cisgender woman, mother, daughter, sister, and scholar. She is the proud mother of three (plus one) children who range in age from thirty-four to thirty-nine, one of whom would identify her as a radical feminist. She has two grandchildren who benefit from her later years wisdom. Michelann is a full professor in the Schulich School of Education at Nipissing University. Recent and upcoming edited collections include *Writing Mothers: Narrative Acts of Care, Redemption, and Solidarity* and *Mothering Outside the Lines: Tales of Boundary-Busting Mamas*.

Susan Picard is a proud mother to two amazing adult daughters. Her career path has led her in many directions including social worker, crisis counsellor, teacher, farmers' market manager, musician, and consultant. Her curiosity and natural propensity toward questioning the way things are have driven her to complete an MA in teaching, curriculum, and learning and a PhD in educational sustainability to gain a better understanding of what we mean as we strive for inclusion. A virtues project facilitator and appreciative inquiry practitioner, she believes in the importance of building on "what gives life," as we navigate possibilities for the future. It is through writing that she weaves together meaning from the fragments that accumulate as she challenges the structures that may be in need of a positive disintegration.

Teela Tomassetti recently completed her doctorate through California Southern University and is a registered provisional psychologist from Alberta, Canada, specializing in birth trauma. Before this, Teela was a therapist for two decades, supporting survivors of domestic violence, sexual assault, childhood sexual abuse, and tragic losses. After suffering her birth trauma through midwifery violence and an excessive hemorrhage almost taking her life in 2021, Teela decided to start the fast-growing Instagram account @theteaonbirthtrauma, where she breaks the silence and supports thousands of survivors in finding their voices. Her doctoral research focused on the fawn trauma response in birth trauma survivors, the intersectionality of race, gender, and systemic oppression, and how providers can begin to dismantle it.

Pamela Vickerson grew up with her younger sister and brother exploring their little part of Alberta: first in the prairies of Gleichen, then the forests and mountains of Banff, and finally (at twelve years old) city life in Calgary. As a mother of four and an insatiable reader and learner, Vickerson balanced her early passions by taking personal-interest night courses while her children were young. When her youngest child entered grade school Pamela, at forty-eight, enrolled at the Alberta University of the Arts (formerly Alberta College of Art and Design) to pursue her fine arts degree. She spent the next nine years slowly studying for her degree while balancing family life, the special needs of her oldest son, and the unique challenges of his life from a wheelchair. In 2018, Pamela took a semester off to help her family navigate four months of her son's palliative care at home, which was both painful and beautiful. This experience profoundly impacted friends and family alike. Her multidisciplinary visual arts and writing practice have become vehicles to remember, process, and embrace grief and healing. Vickerson gratefully creates and lives alongside her husband, their two youngest children, and their cheeky whippet in Moh-kins-tsis/Calgary.

Deepest appreciation to
Demeter's monthly Donors

DEMETER

Daughters
Brent & Heather Beal
Carole Trainor
Khin May Kyawt
Tatjana Takseva
Debbie Byrd
Tanya Cassidy
Myrel Chernick
Marcella Gemelli
Donna Lee, In Memory of Dee Stark, RN, LNHA,
Trailblazer for Women, Women's Rights Advocate
Catherine Cheleen-Mosqueda

Sisters
Fiona Green
Paul Chu
Amber Kinser
Nicole Willey

Mother
Mildred Bennett Walker (Trainor)

Grandmother
Tina Powell